Gypsies, Wars and Other Instances of the Wild

Gypsies, Wars and Other Instances of the Wild

Civilisation and its Discontents in a Serbian Town

Mattijs van de Port

AMSTERDAM UNIVERSITY PRESS

Cover illustration: Janko Brašić, *Panic* (1967), in: Nebojša Tomašević (1978), *Naïve Maler Jugoslaviens*, Stuttgart, Parkland Verlag.
Cover design: Joseph Plateau/Peter Kingma, Amsterdam
Lay-out: Brassica Producties/Wouter Kool, Leiden

ISBN 90 5356 311 3 (hardback)
ISBN 90 5356 315 6 (paperback)

© Amsterdam University Press, Amsterdam, 1998

for Jan Hooiveld

Contents

List of Illustrations

Acknowledgements

Many people have contributed in one way or another to the completion of this book. I would like to mention a few of them by name.

I am grateful to Bonno Thoden van Velzen for the support and inspiration he provided for the writing of this book. I would also like to thank the staff and colleagues of the Amsterdam School for Social Science Research: Anton Blok, Bram de Swaan, Jojada Verrips, Hans Sonneveld, and the secretarial staff. The department of Cultural Anthropology of the University of Utrecht was extremely generous in providing the financial support for this project; my special thanks to Ton Robben and Arie de Ruyter. I am grateful to the Dutch Organization for Scientific Research (NWO) for funding the English translation, and to Peter Mason for doing it.

But this book is above all based on the conversations that I have had over the last few years with Milena Veenis, Anne Gevers, Margot Morshuis, Ido de Haan, Pepijn van de Port, Florike Egmond, Birgit Meyer, Rada Drezgić, Steven Banfield, Ger Duijzings, David Bos and Dubravka Žarkov.

I shall not name friends, acquaintances and informants in Novi Sad and Beograd in order to preserve their anonymity, but that in no way alters my honest appreciation and respect for the trust, openness and inimitable hospitality they displayed at a time and period which must have been one of the most dramatic episodes in their lives.

My parents and my family – in its full, extended guise – were an invaluable source of support during the particularly trying periods of the research.

Finally, my thanks to Jan Hooiveld, who accompanied me more than anyone else on the muddy roads of Serbia. I couldn't have wished for a better friend.

Introduction

O Thebes, old nurse that cradled Semele,
Be ivy-garlanded, burst into flower
With wreaths of lush bright-berried bryony,
Bring sprays of fir, green branches torn from oaks,
Fill soul and flesh with Bacchus' mystic power;
Fringe and bedeck your dappled fawnskin cloaks
With woolly tufts and locks of purest white.
There's a brute wildness in the fennel-wands –
Reverence it well. Soon the whole land will dance
When the god with ecstatic shout
Leads his companies out
To the mountain's mounting height
Swarming with riotous bands
Of Theban women leaving
Their spinning and their weaving
Stung with the maddening trance
Of Dionysus![1]

– Euripides, *The Bacchae*.

The Grand Finale of my stay in Novi Sad – as Jasna, my informant and friend, had dubbed it – was to be a wild night with the Gypsies: grilled meat and raw onions, cigarettes, Gypsy music and lots of drink. Jasna had claimed this evening weeks earlier: 'The last evening's mine, and then we *must* go to the Gypsies!' She had asked known connoisseurs in her circle where it was still possible to hear real, authentic village Gypsies. Begečka Carda, she was told, a bar on the banks of the Danube, just outside the hamlet of Begeč. So that was where we headed for. Jasna, my Dutch friend Jan and I left town in a rattling Renault 4. The road was asphalted for a couple of kilometres, and then became little more than a cart track leading towards the pitch-black undergrowth along the banks of the river.

Disappointing news awaited us on arrival. The Gypsies had played that afternoon and evening, but they had been taken home drunk an hour before. Were these really the best Gypsy musicians in the Vojvodina? The woman manoeuvring her way between the stacked chairs to sweep the floor could not tell us much. Nor did she seem particularly interested. 'People who come here say they're pretty solid', she said with a bored expression, leaning on her broom.

Jasna's carefully planned Grand Finale was ruined. The Gypsy musicians we found in a roadside restaurant on our way back to Novi Sad did their best, but they could not dispel the mood of anticlimax at our table. For Jasna there was only one thing to be done. The next day we would try again. My protests – 'No, no, I deliberately kept the last day free, there's too much to do' – were swept aside. We would only go for an hour, around lunchtime. We would go to a different place. It was bound to be a success. We would have fish soup (after all, you have to eat anyway), we would not ask the Gypsy musicians to come to our table, and we would be back in an hour or two, so that my other plans – she could not help curling her lip a little as she said it – could easily be taken care of. As my hostess, as a connoisseur of the Vojvodina and its customs, and as a devotee of Gypsy bands, her sense of honour would be offended if she were not allowed to redeem the failed farewell evening.

And so it happened. The day after the debacle of Begečka Carda, we set off for *At the End of the World (Na Kraju Sveta)*. Jasna had mentioned this Gypsy bar before. Vague tales of glasses smashed on the floor, banknotes being scattered about, Gypsy music until the small hours, followed by befuddled ramblings across muddy, deserted fields.

At the End of the World was supposed to be 20 to 30 kilometres from Novi Sad, near the village of Kovilj, but when we got there an old peasant woman told us, chuckling beneath her black headscarf, to go 'further, much further, yes, you just go further that way'. She nodded archly towards the open road.

Desolation. The empty plains of the Vojvodina stretched out endlessly without any relief. A river, then a forest, dark and impenetrable. Then, further upstream, a shed, colourfully painted with pictures of the different kinds of freshwater fish that were served there.

Inside it was smoky, noisy and unbelievably packed. The light that penetrated the grubby windows was yellowish, and only a single naked bulb provided a little extra illumination. Cement floor. Assorted ramshackle tables and chairs. A Gypsy band of six musicians playing for a table in the corner. 'Have you reserved?', a sweaty boy in a creased shirt wanted to know. We hadn't. It struck me as an odd question, here at the end of the world. It didn't really matter, as we were able to join five middle-aged men in high spirits. We decided on fish, large dishes of deep-fried fish with sauerkraut salad and chunks of bread. The simple white wine was served in straight lemonade glasses filled to the brim. A glance around me revealed an almost all-male clientèle. Some of the men looked as if they had come straight from their office into the wilderness – wearing immaculate suits, with tie loosened and collar button undone – while others had the impressive moustaches and dented Serb *šajkača* berets that are more what one might expect in a setting like this.

'It's not what it seems', Jasna whispered to me, explaining that the owner deliberately kept the place in this poor and dilapidated condition. 'He earns money like water. Everyone who is anyone in Novi Sad comes here. They even come here all the way from Belgrade. Sometimes you can even see *corps diplomatique* licence plates outside.'

The importance of this question of authenticity seemed to dwindle with the increasing consumption of alcohol. This wasn't going to be a one or two-hour lunch, I realised uneasily. The Gypsies were beckoned to sing requests for us. The others at our table, who all worked in construction, tried to outdo each other in the money they offered. One man loudly reminded another of the money he owed him; the debt was immediately settled, and the considerable sum went straight to the Gypsies. Jan and I, already nicknamed 'the Vikings' by our five companions, had to get as drunk as they were, which was clearly supposed to break down the barriers between us. One bottle after another was served, and the glasses were invariably filled to the brim. The musicians had already sat down and seemed to be taking control; the old songs of the Vojvodina, with their sentimental texts and sugar-sweet tunes, were increasingly giving way to *bećarci*, obscene bachelor songs, and others with rabid nationalist lyrics, all to the frenetic accompaniment of the accordion. These Gypsies knew their audience.

At this point, eight heavily armed members of a volunteer militia brigade in camouflage had also arrived at *At the End of the World*, ceremoniously laying down their weapons on the table. At first the other drinkers seemed disturbed by the arrival of these volunteers, but then they just got down to drinking and making merry with the music. The gesture drunken Serbs always make when they listen to Gypsy musicians – stretching their hands high in the air – acquired a special significance now these soldiers had appeared on the scene: surrender. Two of the male volunteers and the only female member of their company now linked arms and circled around in the stamping rhythms of the kolo. The word 'Brueghel' forced its way into my mind. And then: 'Balkans'.

Jan, who speaks no Serbo-Croat, was sitting at some distance from me, jammed between two Serbs. He chose the line of least resistance and abandoned himself completely to the wine and the music. There was a small incident. All the money he saw flying around apparently went to his head; he dug into his pocket and brought out a wad of banknotes to pay the musicians for a song. The wad looked thick enough, but with the endless free fall of the Yugoslav dinar it was worth no more than the price of a beer – much too little for a song, as I knew from my research.

It was a terribly tasteless thing to do; it was offensive to the musicians, I believed, after having spent a whole year trying to fit in with the local customs. I tried to stop Jan from making this blunder – 'It's much too little. It's much too little' – I hissed across the table – but the musician cut me short. The man accepted the notes with a wide grin. Jasna too threw me an irritated look and asked what I was getting so worked up about.

While everyone around me was in an intoxicated haze, I remained disconcertingly lucid. If anything, the wine seemed to have sharpened my vision. I kept seeing the Gypsy's plump fingers dancing over the keys of his accordion. I saw how he was sweating, how wet, black strands of hair clung to his forehead, how fatigue set in and he responded increasingly sullenly to fresh requests for more new songs, and then still more. He nodded almost imperceptibly as he pocketed the money. I remained conscious of time passing, I registered that it was getting dark outside. The old landlord came over, emanating a pungent odour of fried fish. Foreign guests, well well, what an honour and a pleasure, and a perfect occasion to deliver the inevitable tirade on the terrible Croats and the world's complete inability to understand the Serbs. I nodded and listened abstractedly to his excited flood of words, thinking of the friends who were going to drop by on this final day of my stay in Novi Sad and who were perhaps standing in front of a closed door at that very moment. The cheerfulness surrounding me, the exuberance, the way in which everyone and everything seemed to be conspiring to create an atmosphere in which boundaries can be crossed acquired a stifling and ominous air – were the volunteers' frequent glances in our direction merely curious, or were they hostile? Regular newspaper reports of shooting incidents in the Gypsy bars suddenly seemed very plausible. I decided that the old Serbs with their impressive moustaches were hired actors. I wondered whether the five merry men at our table were really so well disposed towards us. I wanted to leave.

Jasna urged me to relax. How could I be fussing about appointments, travel schedules and plans in the middle of our Grand Finale? None of that mattered now...

Cultural refuges

I went to Novi Sad in March 1991, exactly one year before the expedition to *At the End of the World*, to study the traditions surrounding the Gypsy bands and the meaning of the Serb bacchanal. I had adopted a dictum of the anthropologist Victor Turner to guide my research plans:

> Cultural performances [are] the eye by which culture sees itself and the drawing board on which creative actors sketch out what they believe to be more apt or interesting 'designs for living'.[2]

Turner's observation has always intrigued me. I kept on coming back to it to keep my research on course, both during the fieldwork stage and later, when interrogating my material. If the events that take place in Serb Gypsy bars are construed as cultural performances, as free zones where the imagination is unfettered, as cultural refuges in which recreation literally becomes the re-creation of the worlds people experience, what sort of design for living is sketched in these venues? And to follow Turner's definition of events like those in the Gypsy bar still further: in what sense could this scenario of Gypsy music, obscene songs, drunkenness, surrender, extravagance and the comprehensive rejection of Novi Sad's renowned bourgeois respectability be called interesting or more apt?

Four months after my arrival in Novi Sad, war broke out. This not only completely changed the course of my research, it also essentially determined my answers to these questions. But let us begin at the beginning, and describe the plans I had when I left for Novi Sad.

Unusual advances

I had already become acquainted with Gypsy bands and their performances on previous field trips to Serbia, and had learnt to appreciate them.[3] These frequently noisy and vibrant gatherings of Serbs and Gypsies in remote bars fascinated me. Seen against the backdrop of customary relations between these two population groups, these events are highly exceptional. For if there is one thing that dominates their everyday relations and forms of behaviour, it is the distance between the two groups.[4]

In an urban society like Novi Sad, contacts between Serbs and Gypsies are largely confined to casual encounters in the street or exchanges in a professional context. Other modes of interaction are almost non-existent. A battery of unwritten rules and laws, prejudices and negative stereotypes preserve the social distance.[5] At the beginning of the twentieth century, Tihomir Djordjević gave the following definition of relations between Serbs and Gypsies:

> In general, Serbs regard Gypsies as lower beings, too filthy and inferior to live the same life as themselves, or to be entitled to the same rights. A Serb

will never eat bread that has been kneaded by a Gypsy woman or touch any other food that she has prepared. He will never drink water from a receptacle from which a Gypsy has drunk, as Gypsies are unclean; he would rather drink from a dog's bowl. Moreover, it is almost completely unknown for a Serb to marry a Gypsy woman or vice versa. The few exceptions are spoken of as acts against nature.[6]

Although equal rights and opportunities for everyone in Yugoslav society have been propagated for the last fifty years under the Titoist slogan of Brotherhood and Unity, Gypsies were and still are the stigmatised and marginalised elements of society. They live in the slums and rubbish dumps, out there (na kraju sela), at the end of the village. 'The Gypsies may have had something to complain about in the old days', I often heard people say when the Gypsies' living conditions came up for discussion, 'but now they have equal rights, and the fact that they are poor and backward is mostly their own fault. They simply won't adapt'. The fear of contamination reported by Djordjevic has not changed either: on several occasions, informants asked me how I intended to solve the thorny problem of refusing the food and drink offered by Gypsies without causing offence.

Everyday relations and social (non)-interaction between Serbs and Gypsies are in sharp contrast to life in the Gypsy bar. Not only do the Serbs go to the outermost edges of their society to hear the Gypsy musicians, but once they have befuddled their minds with wine and succumbed to the spell of the songs, the Serb customers place themselves completely in the musicians' hands. The efforts made in the bars to build up an atmosphere of intimacy would be inconceivable and unheard-of in everyday life. In their desire for more music, more songs and more exhilaration, the Serbs invite the Gypsies to their table as their 'great friends'. More often than not this is a noisy scene with slaps on the back, expansive gestures to make room, loud and ostentatious manoeuvres to bring over extra chairs, yells for more bottles and more glasses. They want the entire kafana to see and hear it: we have succeeded! We are on an intimate footing with the Gypsies! Then the musicians are offered drinks and cigarettes as they play softly into the women's ears. These scenes often culminate in drunken Serbs fêting the musicians with warm and wet embraces.

The visits of Serb townspeople to the Gypsy bars are a dramatic version of a motif found in virtually all European cultures: the Gypsy world as the refuge for all who wish to escape from the claustrophobic clutches of their regulated lives, a haven where people can quench their thirst for the wilder pleasures of life. 'Only she lay and wished she were a gipsy', wrote D.H. Lawrence in *The Virgin and the Gipsy* of the fantasies of Yvette, the daughter of the vicar of Papplewick:

> To live in a camp, in a caravan, and never set foot in a house, not know the existence of a parish, never look at a church. Her heart was hard with repugnance, against the rectory. She loathed these houses with their indoor sanitation and their bathrooms, and their extraordinary repulsiveness. She hated the rectory, and everything it implied. The whole stagnant, sewerage sort of life where sewerage is never mentioned, but where it seems to smell from the centre to every two-legged inmate, from Granny to the servants, was foul. If gipsies had no bathrooms, at least they had no sewerage. There was fresh air. In the rectory there was never fresh air. And in the souls of the people, the air was stale till it stank.[7]

Ever since Cervantes' *La Gitanilla* (1612), the motif of a stay in the wonderful world of the Gypsies has been a recurrent theme in European literature. In the nineteenth century in particular, the Gypsy domain was exploited on a large scale to satisfy the yearnings of the bourgeois public, encased as it was in the rules, conventions and standards of decency prescribed by the bourgeois ideals of civilisation. 'Everything that was forbidden, marginalised or taboo in bourgeois life was projected onto that way of life',[8] Roland Schopf commented on the Gypsy motif in nineteenth-century German literature, and this applies equally to other arts in which the bourgeois imagination was crystallised. In operas such as *Carmen* and *Il Trovatore*, and popular operettas such as *Zigeunerliebe*, *Der Zigeunerbaron*, *Der Zigeunerprimas* and *Die Czárdásfürstin*, the ordinary man or woman could bask in the warmth of the Gypsy camp scenes. Paintings in bourgeois living-rooms displayed scenes of Gypsies crossing rugged terrain in their covered wagons, a band of Gypsies resting at the edge of the forest, or a weeping Gypsy woman with bared shoulders: glimpses of a life that was wilder, freer and less constrained. Bohemians took these exotics as their models in life-style and appearance.[9] And an endless series of pulp novels presented the dark and handsome Gypsy whose sultry glance would bring a flush to pale ladies' cheeks. In short, within the imagination of the European bourgeoisie, the Gypsy world was for a long time an irresistible dreamland. The Gypsy camp was Europe's erogenous zone, the closest wildness, invested with the unfulfilled desires, impossible yearnings and unsatisfied passions of bourgeois civilization.[10]

That the Gypsy motif has lost much of this sensual allure since then is clear. Gypsy romance and what was once unfailingly dished up as the wild and free life of the Gypsies have become the merest platitudes. The Gypsy has been summoned onto the stage of the European bourgeoisie so often that he seems to have been drained of his vitality along the way. Occasionally the wild Gypsy is massaged to give him back a little colour. This might be done to accompany the release of a flamenco film, the appearance of a spicy new cocktail snack or a new type of goulash sauce, or to help create a suitably wild and animated décor for chic industrial designs.[11] In general, however, the present-day wild Gypsy has degenerated into a pastiche expressive not so much of yearnings as of their lack of fulfilment.

In Serbia things are otherwise. The ancient motif of the Gypsy world as a refuge for all who want to escape from the stifling clutches of regular life has lost none of its power. Film directors, writers, playwrights, painters, composers, poets and comedians explore the Gypsy world. To judge from the extraordinary popularity of Emir Kusturica's epic Gypsy film *Dom za Vešanje*, released in 1988, they still appeal to a large audience that is very happy to follow them on their voyages of discovery.

The vitality of the Gypsy motif is expressed most potently of all in the Gypsy bars. Novi Sad has over twenty Gypsy bands which attract sizeable audiences every evening. For a city that prides itself on being the cradle of European Serbia, and whose inhabitants extol the virtues of modern times and *kultura*, ranging themselves behind the banner of European civilisation, this substantial demand for wildness is striking. Even more striking is the eagerness with which the clientèle of the Gypsy bars tear down this spotless banner of bourgeois decency and drag it through the mud. 'Give me wine! Let it all collapse!' are the words of a drinking song that was very popular while I was doing my fieldwork. The customers in the Gypsy bar loudly sing out the words after him, to the accompaniment of the accordion.

Dajte vina!	Give me wine!
Hoću lom!	Let it all collapse!
Dajte cigani na sto!	Bring Gypsies to my table!
Nek sviraju!	Let them play!
Nek me razbole!	Let them torment me![12]

The events in the Gypsy bar are significantly referred to as raising hell (*lumpovanje*),[13] making a scene (*napraviti lom*), or *terati kera*, an expression which means literally 'to drive the dog away', and should perhaps be understood in the same sense as the German *die Sau raus lassen*, suggestive of an animal within that is temporarily let loose. With obvious pleasure, the bar clientèle launch their attack on etiquette and abandon themselves to an orgiastic violation of their everyday endeavours:

Davim se!	I can't breathe!
Zlo me!	I feel ill!
Sve samoče!	Such loneliness!
U kafanu ja ću poći!	I'll go to the bar!
Pokvariću obećanja,	There I'll break my promises!
Prevariću osećanja,	There I'll cheat my feelings!
Lumpovaću cjele noći!	and raise hell all night![14]

'There's no girl prettier than the Gypsy-girl Marika', begins another popular bar song, and it continues:

Kada peva tuguje!	When she sings she's grieving!
a kad igra lumpuje!	When she dances she goes mad!
I svako vece,	And every evening,
kad prodjem kraj čarde,	when I pass the *čarda*,
svi pevaju!	everyone is singing!
Lumpuju!	Everyone's raising hell!
Ladi ladi lom,	Ladi ladi lom,
Ona pravi lom!	She makes a mess of everything![15]

Not control but exaltation, not moderation but excess, not frugality but extravagance, not clarity but intoxication, not reason but emotion, not compliance with rules, prohibitions and taboos but their deliberate violation, not constantly deferred gratification in the name of an ever receding future but a direct celebration of the moment, of the here and now. This, in a nutshell, is the programme that can come true in the Gypsy bars. And then, after another swig, the evaluation, to the thumping beat of the song with these words:

Hej!	Hey!
Lagala sam tebi!	I lied to you!
I lagala svima!	I lied to everyone
Al' nisam mogla lagati	But this here, in my breast,
ovo u grudima!	About this I couldn't lie.[16]

The Gypsy bars in and around Novi Sad are anything but moribund anachronisms. They are enclaves of theatrical wildness, stages on which are acted out precisely those poses and scenes the urban Serbs turn up their noses at: 'That used to be the Balkan way of life, all that lies behind us now'. And because they fulfil this role, they are frequented, cherished and preserved, by young and old alike.

Why? Why do the people of Novi Sad deliberately set out in a mood of festive bliss to tear down the social, cultural and moral systems on which they have structured their everyday lives? On 26 June 1991, when war broke out, this question acquired an unexpected new dimension. Why indeed? What is it that drives people to overturn the rules that guide their everyday lives?

How is this *possible?*

An enormous literature has appeared by now on what has been called the Third Balkan War,[17] all of it focusing on the same question: how has *this* been possible in Europe at the end of the twentieth century?[18] *This* refers more or less explicitly to the scenes of horror that dominated this war in the middle of Europe, to the lust for destruction displayed by such a large number of ex-Yugoslavs, the murder and rape in that country where people spent their holidays, the violation of every conceivable taboo, the complete collapse of humanist ideology and the return of concentration camps, ethnic cleansing and genocide on European soil after some fifty years of the promise: 'never again'.

Once the horrors have been described and the feelings of profound dismay expressed, most of these authors proceed to examine the historical, political and socio-economic roots of the conflict. The standard repertoire includes the inauspicious birth of the Kingdom of Yugoslavia, with Slovenians, Croats and Serbs brought together as South Slavs in a new political configuration, each group with its own distinct political and cultural history and its own distinct expectations and aspirations in relation to the future shared state. Attention is drawn to the dominant role claimed by the Serbs in this kingdom whose government came increasingly to resemble a dictatorship, to the bitterness of other groups, and to the extremely bloody struggle in the Second World War, involving not only the repelling of a foreign occupying power but also fierce enmity between the different ethnic groups. The creation of Socialist Yugoslavia is described as the invention of a country that – under the proud slogan of 'Brotherhood and Unity' – retained the meticulous use of allocation formulas to ensure that not one of the national groups could justifiably argue that it was being disadvantaged. Then comes an account of the death of Tito and the collapse of the Titoist dictatorship (with all the in-herent weaknesses of his Yugoslavia becoming painfully manifest) and the centrifugal force of nationalism; latent for generations and now re-vived by a smoothly run propaganda machine, it proved capable of ef-fortlessly replacing the rhetoric of Titoism with a new, ultra-nationalist message. This quickly gained intensity and flourished on the seedbed of untreated war traumas, whipped-up fears among ethnic and national mi-norities, a slump in the economy, and social unrest.

It will be clear that this summary does not do justice to the surveys or their arguments, nor would I for a moment deny that the studies to which I have referred have expanded our knowledge and helped to in-crease our understanding of the recent conflict. But does this format suf-fice to make us understand how this is possible in Europe at the end of the twentieth century?

One thing is clear, at any rate. Even after this stream of publications, the irrational dimension of the tragic war in the Balkans – encapsulated in that endlessly repeated formula 'people who were once neighbours or friends are now beating each other's brains out' – continues, unabated, to exercise people's minds. Bogdan Bogdanović expresses his dismay at this unreason as follows:

> My thoughts circle around one of the numerous abnormalities of today's civil war. I am aware of no military doctrine that would recommend as one of the prime objectives [...] the destruction of the city. And there is anoth-er diabolical fact that we shall not forget! The cities concerned are beauti-ful, among the most beautiful of cities: Osijek, Vukovar, Zadar, now even Mostar and Sarajevo have been added to the list. The battle of Dubrovnik – I tremble to speak of it, but I have to – was a deliberate, calculated at-tack on an example of extraordinary, almost symbolic beauty. Those ag-gressors are like a lunatic who throws hydrochloric acid in the face of a beautiful woman.[19]

A surgeon in a Sarajevo hospital, after his confrontations with the war:

> The war is cruel. People's behaviour is impossible to explain. Incom-prehensible. I don't think that anyone can ever explain what goes on in-side a person's head. How does someone become capable of turning ar-tillery on a maternity clinic or a hospital? On people who are standing in a queue and who fall dead to the ground still clutching the bread they've just bought? What can change people to make them capable of doing such a thing? Nor do these things happen by accident. Not today and then

maybe a month later. It happens systematically. Cruelty is too mild a word for it.[20]

Reviewing three years of work in the Yugoslav war, a war correspondent formulates the issue as follows:

> The precise origins of the mental regression in which murdering one's neighbours becomes possible and a near-hysterical upsurge of nationalism can take place is certainly one of the main conundrums raised by the civil war in former Yugoslavia, and one that is as yet almost completely unexplored.[21]

These are just a few passages highlighting blind spots in the standard analyses and explanations. The motives of the people who order and carry out the deliberate devastation of cities like Dubrovnik, Vukovar, Mostar and Sarajevo can scarcely be explained, or only very partially, by an account of the failure of the Titoist experiment. The motives of snipers who take pleasure in felling complete strangers with their bullets cannot be satisfactorily explained with an exposé of the flaring up of East European nationalism or a sketch of the dramatic extent of the economic slump. Nor can age-old animosity between the different sectors of the population serve to explain the actions of the Serb White Eagle militiamen in Ciglane concentration camp near Prijedor, who were said to have thrown babies and small children into ovens.[22] Such explanations are apparently attempts to capture people's retrospective rationalisations, or modes of justification conveniently supplied by politicians. The dissatisfaction with the customary explanations is perhaps best conveyed by a publicist discussing yet more historical accounts in yet more publications concerning the drama in Yugoslavia:

> Ah yes, history. It is conventional wisdom that the war in former Yugoslavia is impossible to understand without history. And this is of course quite true: nothing at all that occurs in society can be understood without history, and this is certainly true of the historically charged conflicts in former Yugoslavia. And yet the undifferentiated dragging in of 'history' has little to offer. Because how do we know where to look for the explanations? [...] What a whore is history, after all. Always ready to oblige everyone and anyone.[23]

I share this sense of unease about the usual analyses and explanations. Not because I consider the accounts inaccurate or redundant. It would be pointless to maintain that Titoism and the destruction of Dubrovnik are unrelated, or that the snipers are not susceptible to nationalist rhetoric and sentiments. And even the White Eagle militiamen were only capable of perpetrating their atrocities because they had learned in the past to identify Muslims as the enemy. In other words, the excesses of the Yugoslav civil war could not take place before certain necessary conditions had been fulfilled. The collapse of Tito's Yugoslavia, the erosion of the state's authority, the ethnic divisions and age-old definitions of enemies (and the presence of large quantities of weapons and the military preparedness and know-how of a population that had undergone regular training for several decades, in order to be capable, like Tito's partisans, of repelling a foreign intruder) should therefore be studied, analysed and described in this light. Still, studies describing the enabling conditions cannot take away the tormenting sense of incomprehension concerning the scenes that took place in this war. The unease remains. Intelligible causal relationships remain elusive; the excesses are still irrational and out of all proportion.

The persisting sense of unease has only recently provoked some scholars to search for new approaches in the evaluation of the war in former Yugoslavia. Glenn Bowman acknowledges that an 'analysis of the current situation must not only look into the reasons why ethnic divisiveness served as a successful means of grasping power but also into why the call to arms against former neighbours was responded to *with such passion*'. He explores the role of fantasy in xenophobia and inter-ethnic violence. Building on the ideas of Freud and Lacan, he demonstrates how the rhetoric of antagonism of nationalist propaganda exploits primal fears and rages.[24] Ivan Čolović discussed the erotic motives of the Serbian warrior.[25] Slavoj Žižek's comments on the war – although equally informed by psychoanalytical theory – point in quite a different direction, as he attempts to boomerang Western questions about Balkan violence by questioning the hidden motives of the questioner. Pointing to the lustful sparkle with which the western world looks at Bosnia, he leaves us with the uncomfortable conclusion that our repulsion at the bloody drama goes hand in hand with fascination and *jouissance*, obscene enjoyment.[26] Although I do not share the views of these authors in all respects I sympathise with these attempts to go beyond the usual explanatory models in order to explain how *this* is possible, and would like to think that this study is part of that effort.

The inability to understand the irrational dimension of the events in former Yugoslavia at least makes it clear where the challenge lies. The following rough outline (it would be premature and pretentious to present a well-defined or closed diagram here; I have deliberately opted for a draft that could be annotated and altered) pinpoints the areas that seem to me to require closer scrutiny.

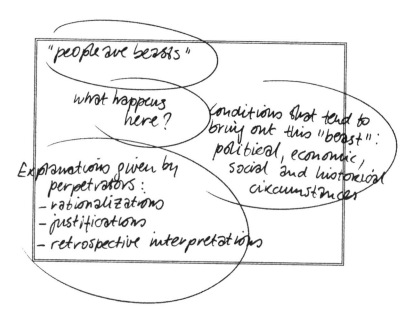

This rough outline identifies three clusters of information which we generally use in order to grasp events such as those in former Yugoslavia. To start with, we have the platitude 'in every human being lurks a beast'. This is a pronouncement with which it is hard to take issue, but one that scarcely has any explanatory value. We can say 'human beings are such animals' a hundred times without deriving the slightest sense of having understood things better than before. After this come the analyses and discussions of the social, political, economic and historical circumstances which create the conditions that bring out that beast. A definition of these enabling conditions will go a long way towards clarifying how things can have come to such a dire pass, but do not explain the actual occurrence of excesses, massacres and bestial acts (or indeed the absence of excesses in a situation in which the enabling conditions are operative). Finally, there are comments made by perpetrators themselves about their actions: their own explanations and rationalisations, the explicit motives they define. These too supply us with invaluable information, which we must certainly scrutinise in order to arrive at a better understanding, bearing in mind, however, that these are always reflections made before or after the fact. Moreover, such reflections are often disturbingly deadpan. The 25-year-old sniper Pipo from Sarajevo said he had killed 325 complete strangers. All he had to offer in explanation was that his mother's being arrested and beaten by the Muslims had enraged him. 'All I can do is kill', he says, 'I'm not sure if I'm normal any more. I don't even know what normal is. I can talk to people, but if someone pushes me, I kill him. It means nothing to me. That's not normal.'[27]

In between these three clusters of information, there seems to be an uncharted territory – a space in which the beastlike potential of human beings not only finds a fertile soil in which to grow, but also takes on cultural form, acquires connections, patterns, images and stories. Here, the beastlike potential becomes entangled, in an obscure way, with motives and drives that are embedded in social reality. This space where wildness and civilisation meet is still largely virgin territory. It is high time this omission was remedied, to endorse the words of Jojada Verrips, who has criticised the one-sided interest of social scientists in 'the precise degree of civilisation we have attained' and has underscored the need for serious studies of 'a long-neglected dimension of Western thought and activity – its wild, dark and uncivilised side'.[28] Anthropologists who have referred to this uncharted area and are engaged in exploring it include Michael Taussig, James Fernandez and Joseba Zulaika.[29] Taussig appears to be referring to it when he observes that the recurrent collective experiences of a group create a reservoir of images that are 'already formed, or half-formed, so to speak, latent in the world of the popular imagination, awaiting the fine touch of the [...] magician's wand'.[30] Fernandez alludes vaguely to 'that dark arena [...] where thought emerges from non-thought – where ideas arise out of that embedded condition in which we so often find them in anthropological work' and to 'an uncharted and imperfectly chartable hinterland to thought and feeling which nevertheless exerts its plenipotentiary attractions and repulsions upon us'.[31] Zulaika, asking 'how fixed is the category of "humanity"', notices that while playing, hunting or engaging in (terrorist) warfare, people 'may experience various degrees of slippage in and out of the human frame into animality'.[32] My own account of the Gypsy bars of Novi Sad likewise sets out to contribute to the tentative exploration of this twilight zone and to help answer the question of 'how this is possible'.

War and festivity: celebrations of unreason

'How is *this* possible in Europe at the end of the twentieth century?' was the question that played obsessively through my mind from the first time

I was confronted, during my fieldwork in Novi Sad, with the phenomenon of war. First, like so many other observers, I had to come to terms with the fact, reluctantly and in anger, that the promises invoked by terms like Europe and the end of the twentieth century were illusory. There is no getting away from it: this *is* possible, this *can* take place unchecked in Europe at the end of the twentieth century, just as it was possible in Europe at the beginning and in the middle of the twentieth century. This does not diminish the sense of outrage, but it does mean that the question needs reformulating.

I should like to begin this reformulation with the suggestion that my observations in the Gypsy bars may provide us with clues to gain a better understanding of the unreason that plays such a prominent role in the war in former Yugoslavia. War and festivity. The juxtaposition of these two phenomena – bearing in mind the reports of the suffering of the population in the war zones – appears ludicrous and in the poorest of taste. Yet the comparison has been made before, and a host of unexpected and hidden connections between the two worlds of experience have been laid bare. Georges Bataille and Roger Caillois, for instance, have both pointed out a large number of striking formal correspondences, such as the prominence of excess, the waste, the destruction, and the flagrant violation of rules, laws and taboos.[33]

The comparison between the two worlds is useful because it helps us find a way of reformulating the question 'how is *this* possible?' It may help us to find a way out of the impasse into which so many ideas about war, destruction and violence seem to lead: the idea that all these activities should be understood purely and simply as a means to an end. The comparison with festivity makes it possible to approach the subject differently. It allows us to keep an open mind about the possibility that war, destruction and violence may not be just a means to an end: they could, at least to some extent, be the very end that is being pursued.

When we are considering festive events such as those in the Gypsy bar, we have little trouble accepting the proposition that people enter this arena to raise hell, to set aside rational thought and reason in a celebration of unreason. The notion that this motive may play a role in the war in former Yugoslavia is a proposition that, on moral grounds, is considerably more unpalatable. Yet I think that this suggestion of a celebration of unreason is worth consideration and elaboration. Take the editorial comment that appeared in the *International Herald Tribune* of Monday, 17 July 1995:

> The outrages of the Bosnian Serbs are shocking for their substance and for their in-your-face quality. There is no attempt to conceal. There the sol-

diers are before our very eyes, herding civilians and refugees in front of the cameras, culling out the young men of military age on the 6 o'clock news. They are not being sneaky, they are taunting. It is as though the Bosnian Serbs, having measured the West's responses, were not simply flouting Western notions of justice and law but flaunting their defiance. They want us to witness their criminal behavior. This is the evident spirit in which the Bosnian Serb military chief hangs up and kills a pig in front of the Dutch United Nations commander, saying this is the way his people deal with their enemies.

What the war in former Yugoslavia forced us to digest is the fact that people proved willing to make a conscious and active choice to embrace regression, barbarity, a return to the wilderness. Take the Serb fighters who dream of a return to the Serbia of the epic poems 'when there was no electricity, no computers, when the Serbs were happy and had no cities, the breeding-grounds of all evil', and without Europe 'into which we will march as victors when the Serb people, in its struggle for survival, has changed Vienna into a new Hiroshima'.[34] Is this not confirmation that the struggle in former Yugoslavia was not determined by military and strategic considerations alone? These are the voices of people who, in festive mood, took on the role of barbarians.

The reports from the war zone contain numerous examples of violence for its own sake, a delight in fighting, cruelty and destruction, deliberate violations of international conventions and universally accepted standards of civilised behaviour. The young men who dropped an endless series of bombs on Dubrovnik have been described in several accounts as ignorant barbarians. But I am convinced, as is Bogdan Bogdanović, whose words I quoted earlier, that these young men knew perfectly well what city they were destroying, that they were quite aware of its historical significance and cultural value. Dubrovnik was the proud façade that Yugoslavia showed to the world, its credentials as a member of the old, civilised Europe. There was not a single Yugoslav, down to the most uneducated shepherd, who did not hear people singing the praises of this city of cosmopolitan culture, the pearl of the Adriatic, year in, year out. The point is precisely that many of the participants in this war were deliberately out to defy and overthrow this respect for ancient European culture. 'Well, we can simply build a new old Dubrovnik', remarked one of the young men when a journalist asked him what he was doing.

In former Yugoslavia, large groups of people elected to eradicate everything that we – and they – regard as valuable, civilised and humane. We may reassure ourselves with the notion that Yugoslavs are simply barbarous inhabitants of the Balkans, suggesting that if they had been a bit more civilised such excesses could never have taken place. But this is sheer self-deception. These people too grew up with the ideals of civilisation, with the humanist heritage, with hope and confidence in the Enlightenment. But they chose something different. This attack on civilisation and kultura, this rejection of reason and this flagrant contempt for reasonableness, is what I shall refer to in this study as the embrace of unreason. It is this decision to opt for unreason – a deliberate and fully conscious choice – that must be interrogated. And this is where this study may contribute to answering some of the questions that have been raised by the war in former Yugoslavia: after all, in their countless trips to the Gypsy bands, the Serbs of Novi Sad have elected time and time again to embrace regression, barbarity, the wilderness, the destruction of everything that we and they regard as valuable, civilised and humane.

However, before introducing Novi Sad and its inhabitants, I wish to comment briefly on the origins of this study, or rather, on the frequently alienating activity of capturing in an academic text the shifting, perplexing and chaotic world that I came to know in Novi Sad.

Research in wartime

Although the front line was some sixty kilometres from the city, and the townspeople were spared any direct confrontation with the violent conflict, the demise of Yugoslavia and the subsequent war completely governed the minds and feelings of myself and of everyone I spoke to.[35] I shall return to this point at length in the following chapters; here I shall merely include a passage from an interim report I wrote around mid-October 1991:

> I find the supermarket cashier in tears with a little transistor radio pressed to her ear. She does not see you, she does not hear you as robot-like she adds up your grocery bill. She is in the front lines somewhere. Wherever you go, a radio is broadcasting the news. 'What kind of life is this?' sighs the woman in the archives where I am working. 'For months now we have lived from one news bulletin to the next'. Some of the people I speak to try to avoid the subject – 'let's not talk about it' – but it proves virtually impossible: five minutes later the discussion always veers back to it again.

I was in a constant state of insecurity and tension too, uncertain whether I would be able to continue my research, and if so for how long and in what way. Questions that related not only to my safety, but also to the principle that anthropologists in the field are required to suppress their personal views and moral judgments and instead should listen, understand, empathise. Amid people who simply could not help rehashing minutely and at great length the message of the Serb radio, television and newspapers (which consistently located all evil, and laid all blame and responsibility for the dramatic events, beyond the boundaries of the Serb community), adhering to this principle was an arduous task. I constantly found myself having to repress sentiments along the lines of 'I have no desire to understand anything about this, I just want to condemn it' or 'just go ahead and kill yourselves in your poisoned complacency'. This culminated at some point in November 1991, when I found myself sitting in a chair in front of the television in my Novi Sad apartment, dazed, and realised that I had just used the plexiglass prism I had been toying with – the kind you use as a ruler – to mow down the newsreader who had reported the joyous liberation of Serb Vukovar. I don't think I ever came this close to committing murder. The next day I booked a flight to the Netherlands to distance myself from the situation.

This was not a course of action that was available to most of the people of Novi Sad. However loudly they proclaimed the Serbs had right on their side, and insisted on the need to understand the real truth about Serbia, most of the people I met were nervous, anxious and confused. Many were suspicious about my true objectives. During previous fieldwork in Serbia, in 1988, I had already encountered an evasive and uncooperative attitude towards people wielding questionnaires and displaying undue curiosity in certain kinds of information. This was particularly true of my research on Gypsies. Some people dismissed it as a waste of money that was typical of Westerners. In these uncertain times of war and disintegration, the mood of suspicion was understandably many times greater. Direct questions about the Gypsy bars and the goings-on there, which were broadly classified under the heading of cheerful and frivolous entertainment ('and now I should like to bring up an entirely different subject: how often do you visit Gypsy bars, with whom, how much do you drink there, how much do you spend there on average?') would have been insensitive under such circumstances. This forced me to adopt a passive research attitude.

Even so, this enforced passivity was a relatively minor difficulty. 'Everyone should just get on with their work' was an expression I frequently heard. It encapsulated the attempts on the part of the citizens of

Novi Sad to assuage their own feelings of panic and unease, but I soon acquired the habit of invoking it myself, and once I had become immune to the jokes about the cassette recorder I was bound to be concealing about my person, I too could get on with my work.

The biggest stumbling block to my research was of a more substantive nature. The collapse of the economy, the political disorder, and the rapid escalation of the war had transformed Novi Sad into a grimy, chaotic and squalid mutation of its own ideals and aspirations. The city was not itself. The dramatic events succeeded each other so fast that the stories people related about one another and their world sounded increasingly hollow. As we shall see, the *Novisadjani* had been telling each other for decades that they were true Europeans, and that they belonged to a modern society in which civilised people lived together according to the principles of reason and harmony. As the city had for a long period been part of the Habsburg empire, there were historical arguments in support of this proposition, and geographically speaking too there was every reason to say 'this is Europe'. Moreover, they were fiercely protective of this reading of their identity and the kind of world they inhabited, shielding it from anything or anyone that called it into question.

But the war had broken this story wide open. As yet only partly aware of what was happening to them, the people I met were finding all their certainties about who they were and the kind of world they inhabited pulled out from under their feet; the life they had lived, it turned out, was not a natural given but a story, and one that seemed to be slipping out of reach into a different time, a different phase of existence.

The people I spent my time with were understandably reluctant to relinquish the stories in which they had felt at home for most of their lives. Certainly not in front of someone like me. 'Why are you still here, actually? Why are you staying? To see all *this*?' asked a good friend from Novi Sad one freezing evening on the way to the cinema in January 1992, when I was loudly expressing my dismay at the horrors of the war. And although the questions were rhetorical and not intended to be unfriendly, a note of reproach sounded in them. And shame too (at least, this is what my notes of that evening record: 'it was "get lost!" from someone who is ashamed of something and doesn't want it to be exposed to the gaze of others'). But it was very rare for anyone to make a comment as direct as that. While the papers, the news broadcasts and the flood of rumours kept up the information about the terrible slaughter and bloody acts of cruelty taking place in the eerily close war zones, I was regaled with stories depicting Novi Sad as the Athens of Serbia, in which the enlightened and civilised nature of the inhabitants of this city was accorded a central role. 'Don't you worry now', said one acquaintance in an attempt to reassure both me and himself, 'this city is much too bourgeois to wage war'.

Needless to say, the world that my Serb interlocutors described to me increasingly took on the aspect of an ethereal fantasy world, a place constructed exclusively of stories. I realised that if I had been doing research in this society some five years earlier, I might have been entirely convinced by the fictions that the *Novisadjani* allowed to determine their lives. Then I would have come upon a bourgeois society here, and I would have been sure to find some way of explaining the significance of the anomalous Gypsy bands in such a society. But now, with everything in the process of disintegration, the fictions no longer carried any conviction. Not to me, and more importantly, not to the city's inhabitants.

This was clear from the other reactions I noted; not everyone was determined to deny the reality of war, struggle and destruction in order to prop up the fiction of a civilised, bourgeois society. Under the pressure of circumstances, some people took refuge in different stories about themselves and their world of a kind that could accommodate the outbreak of savage war. And such stories were certainly available. Some were supplied by the channels of war propaganda. These depicted Serbs as the eternal victims, struggling for survival, warding off the threat of complete extinction in the face of the hostile forces conspiring against them. But outside the propaganda, other stories circulated which, judging by the ease with which they were adopted and repeated, had slumbered just below the surface of public life, and which, given a little space, were now flourishing. 'We are not inhabitants of Europe at all' was the gist of these rival tales; 'we are inhabitants of the Balkans, and reason and harmony are simply alien to our nature'.

The chaos and confusion were aptly captured in a word some people used to describe the world I had come to study: *cirkus*. And on more than one occasion I was asked 'How can you do research here, now, to try to understand our culture? We don't even understand ourselves!'

'We don't even understand ourselves!' A remark like that warns of the need to exercise restraint in making pronouncements. So I shall not be drawing any conclusions in this study about the culture of Serbia or of Novi Sad. And I shall certainly not be making any pronouncements about 'what kind of people they are, those Serbs'. The society I was expected to describe and to chart confronted me inescapably with the lack of concepts such as culture, world view or cosmology. These concepts carry a strong implication that the members of a particular group or society imbue their existence with meaning in accordance with the principles of a homogeneous, monolithic interpretive system. That this is not the case – that instead, the file under each such heading would be found to contain endless layers of clustered stories, a bewildering miscellany of interwoven, diverse or even opposing accounts – was something I knew before I left for Novi Sad. Clifford Geertz said several decades ago that 'the culture of a people is an ensemble of texts, themselves ensembles, which the anthropologist strains to read over the shoulders of those to whom they properly belong',[36] and the theoretical shortcoming of 'anthropology's tendency to fix a unitary symbolic system at a distance'[37] has been widely recognised ever since. My plans to do research in Novi Sad on collective fantasies about Gypsies and the events in the Gypsy bar were hence partly inspired by a desire to do justice to this basic fact that in determining their point of view, people start from different – and often contradictory – interpretive frameworks.

But all my theoretical preparations and programmatic intentions could not prepare me for the *cirkus* of Novi Sad. Perhaps my dismay at the cacophony of divergent stories the people I encountered appeared to be drawing on is an indication of the fact that the insight that there is no such thing as a unitary Serb culture – or even a culture of Vojvodina or Novi Sad – remains very much an academic one. It is one thing to state in the introduction to a study that during ethnographic observation it is the dissimilarities rather than the correspondences among people that stand out most clearly, but to allow this realisation to be fully and consistently incorporated into the rest of the book is another matter altogether.

My stay in Novi Sad left me with little choice in this respect. The city was a research arena that compelled me to take seriously the multiplicity of stories and the fragmented consciousness of the people I met. But my visit also confronted me with the fact that as a researcher I was poorly equipped to study and describe the fragmented, disintegrating world around me. Or rather, my work there showed up the painful gap between our rejection of the concept of the homogeneity of culture as a viable theoretical concept and the actual business of research. For anthropologists in the field who are overwhelmed by the chaos of a reality which is strange to them, but about which they are nevertheless expected to produce a coherent account, derive precious little assistance from pronouncements about the absence of a system in the madness. In the absence of alternative well-defined concepts enabling them to comment usefully on this reality, a notion of culture as 'a system of shared meaning' or 'shared understanding' is something they can ill afford to dispense with.

Making a virtue of necessity in Novi Sad, I took advantage of what was in any case a thoroughly experimental research situation to go in search of other concepts, other approaches, other types of anthropological writing which would make it more feasible to do justice to the shifts and turns of reality.[38] The first step was to clear certain obstacles out of the way.

Chaos and the academic passion for tidying up

Faced with chaotic situations, the social scientist would appear to have only one answer: to arrange, to order. The plan printed below of a Gypsy dwelling in Belgrade, taken from a study by Vladimir Macura,[39] provides us with a good example of the academic passion for tidying up.

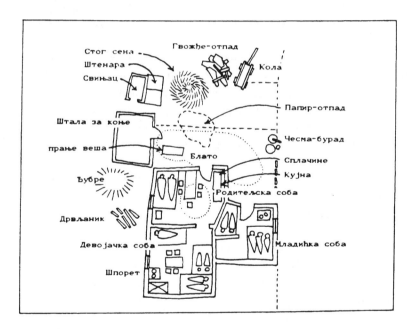

The scraps (*gvožde otpad*) at the top centre stand for scrap metal, the horizontal dotted line is waste paper (*papir otpad*), the longer, vertical dotted line is labelled mud (*blato*) and the sun-shaped dashes to the left of the house represent unspecified refuse (*djubre*). It further appears that the washing tub (*pranje veša*) is in the mud, that twelve people sleep in the hut, and that there is both a stable and a pigsty. On the same page as this floor plan, Macura has included two photographs of old barrels, planks and other rubbish, which he describes in a caption as coming from a yard shared by two Gypsy families. In this way, a space that this society regards as constituting the epitome of chaos and filth – the Gypsy hut – is reduced to a clean, neat and surveyable plan.

There is little to object to in this representation of a Gypsy hut: everything has been included, it is all accurate, and it has been presented in an aesthetically pleasing fashion. But what does it teach us? What kind of knowledge is produced by this little plan? And most importantly, what does it leave out?

Macura's drawing may not be entirely representative of the practice of the social sciences, but it is indicative of a certain tendency. 'Social scientists, from econometricians to ethnomethodologists, are obsessed with the postulation of pattern, of rules which purportedly govern behaviour, or some contrived regularity, or with testing their unfalsifiable metaphysics of regularities', comments Anthony Cohen.[40] More grimly, Hans Peter Duerr describes the scientist as an obsessive eradicator of weeds:

> He has no reverence for anything, neither does he love anything. He throws a net over the objects of reality, he divides and classifies them. They are organised, controlled and purified; everything that might grow profusely through the mesh is trimmed away. The objects weep, but the researcher sees no tears. He clears the forest and plants a garden free of weeds, growing only vegetables that can be consumed.[41]

Judith Okely too reflects on the obsessive need of academics to create order, blaming it on the unrelenting efforts within the social sciences, including anthropology, to practice so-called hard science:

> Let us examine the tradition that too often gives us the exact and natural sciences to mimic. Granted we are still unflustered by any quantification ideal, however, the metaphor of precise measurement leaks into our fictive hypotheses. Again, the practitioners whom we are supposed to imitate do not act in the way we imagine. A leading mathematician was asked how he went about solving difficult problems. His answer? *Think vaguely*. Would we dare to write that in a research proposal?

Positivism may have been discredited in principle, but it operates in practice, she rightly observes. What actually goes on in the arena of academic debate, in university courses, examinations and grant applications, revolves around the testing of hypotheses, the designing of courses in which budding researchers are taught fieldwork techniques, and the ideal of precise measurement – if not in the strictly quantitative sense, then in any case metaphorically – permeates everything.[42]

Of course, there is in itself nothing wrong with elucidating a subject by ordering material. Naming, classifying and structuring are mechanisms indispensable to all language users, and any textualised representation of reality, like Macura's drawing of the Gypsy hut, necessarily leaves things out. So it should be stressed here that my criticism of the academic passion for tidying up is aimed more at types and degrees of ordering than at structuring as a valid procedure.

What I take issue with is that for the description of the matters that were central to my study – the celebrations of unreason in the Gypsy bars, the circus-like appearance of a society in which old frameworks of reference had become obsolete and new ones were still inchoate, the unspeakable vileness of the war zones – in short, things dominated not by order but by a complete lack of it – the academic will to order mainly gives rise to feelings of alienation. It would not be impossible to reduce the Novi Sad that I came to know to a neat schematic diagram like Macura's little drawing. It would certainly be impossible to do so, however, without having the highly unsatisfying feeling of having left out of the picture the very core of what was happening in Novi Sad.

So what is the alternative? Michael Taussig, another vehement critic of the social sciences' heavy reliance on the concept of order, encountered a similar problem when he faced the task of trying to say something in academic prose about the *yagé* drinking bouts he shared with Indian shamans. *Yagé*, a substance that causes not only hallucinations but also nausea, vomiting and diarrhoea, is taken by shamans to enable them to focus on the power of disorder, the flashes of insight that emerge from chaos. To define the sudden insights generated by such sessions in accordance with the customary conventions of conventional anthropology proved virtually impossible. As Taussig notes, '*Yagé* nights challenge this ritual of explanation of ritual. They make us wonder at the unstated rites of academic text-making, at the means of creating intellectual authority, and, above all, at the conventions of "ordering" the chaos of that which has to be explained.'[43]

Taussig mentions Joseph Conrad's *Heart of Darkness* as an example of an alternative path to insight. He discusses the way in which Conrad succeeds in leaving intact the omnipresent ambiguity of the wilderness. Conrad penetrates the veil while retaining its hallucinatory quality. He describes a world in which horror can possess a certain majesty; in which terror manifests itself in all its misty intangibility; in which violence, however repugnant, also has an element of beauty; and where the primitive arouses desire as well as revulsion. 'Here the myth is not "explained" so that it can be "explained away", as in the forlorn attempts of social science', Taussig writes. 'Instead it is held out as something you have to try out for yourself, feeling your way deeper and deeper into the heart of darkness until you do *feel* what is at stake, the madness of the passion'.[44]

In order to diminish the alienation wrought by the translation of raw reality into the tameness of an academic text, I adopt an approach that is more akin to that of anthropologists who have been described as favouring a 'literary turn' in their reports from the field.[45] James Clifford comments on the false premises behind such a label: 'But the literary or rhetorical dimensions of ethnography can no longer be so easily compartmentalised. They are active at every level of cultural science. Indeed, the very notion of a "literary" approach to a discipline, "anthropology", is seriously misleading.'[46] Whatever label one would wish to attach, what I am referring to here is an expansion of the limited stylistic resources that are available to the writer of an academic text. To eschew effective rhetorical devices because they are held to be detrimental to the pursuit of objectivity is foolish. Granting ethnographies to be fictions – in the sense of constructed rather than untrue – could at least liberate the anthropologist from the academic shackles of schematic realism, which generates texts over which a precise and systematic style and clarity of structure have sole dominion. And granting that the writing of a piece of ethnography is partly, perhaps primarily, a literary endeavour could remove certain other constraints as well: the imperative of naming, the unrelenting insistence on explicitness and unambiguity, an unswerving confidence in the visibility and explicability of things. Postulate! Show! Define! Enumerate! Establish! Conclude! This would also release the anthropologist from the academic obligation to iron out everything alien, disturbing, alarming – everything evocative of the other – until they resemble the world with which we are reassuringly familiar. It could perhaps dispense with the clarification that somehow always exudes the dusty blackboard smell of the classroom. It might dispense with the idea that the informants cannot be understood until they have been admitted to the bleak landscape of the university building, with its insipid *ficae benjaminae* stuck in PVC plant-pots with clay grains and self-regulating moisturisers. It might even enable us to read about elsewhere without hearing the incessant hum of computers and the comforting ker-chunk-ker-chunk of photocopying machines.

The world is not, as the academic style would have us believe, a wide open and neatly trimmed English country garden. There are dark and murky regions which, if the glare of Enlightenment is turned on them, are changed beyond recognition. I intend to keep these regions within the scope of my enquiry, along with all the crazy people who inhabit them and the dark, irrational wishes and desires that ordinary people have banished there. This calls for what Clifford Geertz has referred to, simply, as 'authorship'.[47] Why should we limit ourselves, in our accumulation of knowledge and understanding of the societies we are studying, to the vacuum cleaner, the measuring stick, the abacus and the floodlight? Why should we deny ourselves means of expression that have long been valued in literature – tropes and metaphors, the lyrical outpouring, the suggestion, the impression, the evocation, the appeal to emotion and all those other possibilities that have been expunged from the schematic realist style of the academy? I wish to avail myself of all the resources of language instead of the crippled vehicle of academism; that is the strategy I have adopted to counter the alienation that comes with translating the-world-over-there to here.

Another strategy I would advocate to avoid the alienating effect of Macura's drawing is a constant messing up of my own claims. No watertight arguments, no fortress of self-proclaiming truth for the opponent to shell. No conclusion to round off the argument. Instead, I favour stories with cracks and draughts, texts where you can still find the remains, the greasy edges and crumbs of other, untold stories, other possible kinds of arrangement, other possible claims. The anecdote lends itself for this. So do unadulterated fragments of diary entries and interviews. But what this strategy requires most of all is close attention to the asides in conversations, to the lapses, the slips of the tongue, the contradictions and inconsistencies in the stories that our informants tell us.[48]

I have other doubts, however, about whether it is possible to translate the motives of people in former Yugoslavia to the knowledge system of academe in a less alienating fashion; doubts that cannot be assuaged by expanding the academic text to include literary modes of expression. These doubts basically come down to one simple question: Isn't it utter nonsense to suppose that you may bridge the gap between the worlds of the academy and war, between human experience in former Yugoslavia and in the serene university library? Isn't the distance simply too great to allow the creation of any basis for understanding?

I have not been able to answer that question. Certain aspects of the culture of the academic community (and, more broadly, of the culture of the prosperous middle classes of Western Europe) fill me with misgivings about this possibility. Is it possible for knowledge to be produced about the significance of senseless violence in surroundings in which (as I re-

cently experienced) merely calling for a meaty discussion is felt to be going too far, and where the least tendency to raise one's voice immediately
provokes general condemnation of a lack of self-control? And if authors
are required to vanish into impersonality for the greater good of schol-
arship – 'if [anthropology] is in the end merely a means of "finding ourselves" then it is pure self-indulgence and not worth doing'[49] – can we arrive at a better understanding of the wild celebrations of the Ego running
riot like those I encountered in the Gypsy bars of Novi Sad? I don't
know. When I note the determination with which people all around me
(out of an entirely understandable desire for self-preservation, of course)
had shielded themselves from a full awareness of the events in Croatia
and Bosnia, I am forced to wonder whether we truly want to know what
Macura's Gypsy hut leaves out, whether we *want* to understand how 'the
beast in man' is mysteriously connected with urges and motives that derive from social reality, whether such research does not run up against
strongest inhibitions in its path. Are we prepared to give up our neat picture of the world? (I am only too aware of my own reluctance to do so.)
Do we really want to read an academic text that is disturbing? (I have
read very few myself.[50]) Or are all our words, all our attempts to create
order, all our reassuring messages about well-defined, clearly charted societies like the incantations of shamans, intended to ward off the peril?
Fear not! There is no danger! Everything is under control![51]

As I have said, I have not resolved this question, and I present this
study in the full light of these doubts. Three factors – the passion for tidying up and neatly arranging, both within and outside the academic community; my personal experience of how painful it can be to have to give
up one's cherished images of people and the world; and the ensuing
doubts as to whether people are prepared to allow themselves to be
turned out of their stories – are the point of departure in seeking to arrive at a deeper understanding of the embracing of unreason in the
Gypsy bars of Novi Sad.

The world in stories

The terms 'the world in stories', or 'fictional reality', became crucial to
my approach in this book. Although their precise significance and value
must emerge in the course of the study itself, I should like to make a few
preliminary remarks about them at this stage.

The term 'story' is not intended to convey a disparity between falsity
and truth, between appearance and reality. By way of illustration, let us

take a woman in Vukovar who had survived three months of heavy shelling. She had moved back into the blackened ruins of her home, and as the television cameras zoomed in to capture her standing there amid the rubble, she lamented the loss of an indoor plant she had had before the bombing began. 'Such enormous leaves it had', she added. And the way she said it evoked an image of her watering that plant every day, from one year to the next, watching it grow and become fuller, and the growth of that plant strengthening her faith in the new era, an era of homes with indoor plants that could grow to maturity. Obviously those days with the plant were not a fiction but her life, in the sense of lived and experienced reality; yet amid the ruins she was forced to see that that life had also turned out to be a story.[52]

If there is one thing that Novi Sad taught me, it was everyone's complete reliance on a story, a story than can give meaning, direction and purpose to (certain aspects of) life. Clifford Geertz commented on this need for stories in his well-known 1973 essay on religion. Systems of religious faith become operational particularly when our analytical powers desert us, when our endurance is stretched too far, and when our moral instincts cease to function. It is when we are faced with the vanishing of certainties and the resulting threat of chaos, the experience of unbearable pain, and the visitation of evil – in short, what Geertz describes as 'events which lack not just interpretations but *interpretability*',[53] that religion provides 'the formulation, by means of symbols, of an image of such a genuine order of the world which will account for, and even celebrate, the perceived ambiguities, puzzles, and paradoxes in human experience. The effort is not to deny the undeniable – that there are unexplained events, that life hurts, or that rain falls upon the just – but to deny that there are inexplicable events, that life is unendurable, and that justice is a mirage'.[54] Salman Rushdie uses the term 'picture-making' for what is essentially the same concept: 'Waking as well as sleeping, our response to the world is essentially *imaginative*; that is, picture-making. We live in our pictures, our ideas. I mean this literally. We first construct pictures of the world *and then we step inside the frames*. We come to equate the picture with the world.'[55]

The dream of an orderly and well-signposted world, a story about the world that gives us the feeling that we have some grip on our experiences, a story that enables us to find our way through life, is obviously not a goal pursued by academics alone. The dream of a story that is 'true', that is shorn of all ambivalences and obscurities that can prompt scepticism, a story that supplies unambiguous meaning, that can *be*, unquestioned and undoubted, that is as strong as houses, a story, in sum, that does not have to be regarded as such, is cherished by most people, if not everyone. And once installed in a story, no one wants to be evicted from it.

My stay in Novi Sad (and the resulting engagement with the war in former Yugoslavia after my return to the Netherlands too) taught me, however, the extent to which the social and psychological need to render the world in stories that give it meaning conflicts with the chaotic and unpredictable dynamism of reality itself, a reality that has a force of its own and that often displays its refusal to conform to whatever individual or collective stories have been made to accommodate it. The images that the media have been bringing us from former Yugoslavia provide countless examples of stories being dismantled by reality. One of the most poignant examples was a newspaper photo, taken in Sarajevo, of a woman with a short, modern hairstyle and a large red shopping bag bearing the legend 'Glory'. She lay dead in what became known as Snipers' Alley, still clutching her bag, her face in the dirt. The sniper who had shot her was perhaps a boy wearing Levis, with a walkman playing tapes of U2, Madonna or Whitney Houston.[56] The enthusiastic participation in the modern world, the world of large red shopping bags sporting slogans in English designed to convey a sense of triumphalist consumerism – Glory! – the world of walkmans, Madonna and designer jeans, did not furnish any guarantees after all. Of anything at all. The war shuffles stories, so that everything ends up in the wrong place. Playing fields become cemeteries, city parks turn into the municipal firewood service. Hospitals become targets for shelling, prams are carts for carrying water, and when surgery has to be performed without an anaesthetic, plum brandy is found to possess unsuspected qualities.

The war tells us: nothing is what it seems. But the war also says: I am the reality, I am the ground under your feet, the certainty that lies beneath all uncertainties.

> That is the most crucial experience of my life, coming outside and seeing the blood in the snow, the brains still spattered against the wall. So I know what that is, ethnic frenzy, I know what imbeciles people can become.

These are the words of Aleksandar Tišma,[57] the writer who, more than anyone else, has recorded Novi Sad and its people. A thoughtful man, Tišma, who does not lightly refer to 'the most crucial experience of my life'. He is referring here to the Novi Sad razzias of 23 January 1942. All the city's inhabitants had to stay inside for three days, with the windows shut and curtains drawn, so that the Hungarian police could carry out their murderous mission. Thousands of Serbs, Jews and Gypsies were dragged out of their homes and murdered. In his history of the Jewish community of Novi Sad, Pavle Šosberger writes of these events:

> For three days lawlessness held sway in the city, and every person's life depended mainly on drunk, primitive policemen and soldiers who visibly enjoyed killing [...] On the orders of the commanding officer in charge of the razzia, units were despatched to clear the bodies off the streets and to take them in army trucks or trucks belonging to the city to the Danube, where they were pushed under the ice. It has been established that the soldiers and policemen robbed the bodies, pulling rings off fingers or even cutting fingers off to gain possession of the jewels. They also took money and valuable clothing for themselves.[58]

In the war that ravaged former Yugoslavia fifty years later, stories were put to flight once again by the derisive laughter of experience. In an impressive essay entitled 'Overwhelmed by national consciousness', Slavenka Drakulić writes that only now is she conscious of being a Croat – not by choice or desire, in fact, worse still, in the full awareness of the fact that 'the war has robbed me of the sole possession I had acquired during my life, my existence as an individual' – and finds herself compelled to accept this new, reduced identity as a Croat. Drakulić compares this Croat-ness with a piece of clothing. She would never have chosen it herself. She dislikes the colour, it is far too tight, the sleeves are too short, the collar is too stiff and the material is itchy. 'But it can't be helped, because there is nothing else to wear.'

> As it stands, no one in Croatia is permitted to feel non-Croat. And even if people actually experience this as a constraint on their liberty, it would still, perhaps, be morally wrong to tear this shirt off the distressed state, with all those thousands of people who are being shot, slaughtered and burnt, simply because of their nationality. It would not be right because of Vukovar, the town that has been wiped off the face of the earth. And because of the shelling of Dubrovnik.[59]

Whatever else may be thought and said about it, ethnic frenzy is ultimately blood in the snow, brains spattered against the wall. However else one may wish to define it, Croat-ness comes down to people who have been shot, slaughtered and burnt, the extinction of Vukovar, the scarred face of Dubrovnik. These are the banal, vulgar but unavoidable truths that war deals in.

It is my firm belief that the embrace of unreason that is the central subject of this book is directly related to the constant crises in the Yugoslavs' fictional reality, their recurrent confrontations with what might be described as the reality of *Die Dinge an sich*.

I also believe that if we wish to understand something of what happened to the people of former Yugoslavia, of their motives, of why they chose to embrace unreason, this concept of fictional reality, the world in stories, should be adopted as the point of departure. However different our worlds may be, and however narrow a basis they offer for mutual understanding, this particular area of tension, between fictional reality and reality itself, in any case, is an important area of common ground between our world and theirs. Everyone's autobiography contains turning-points (separations, illnesses, the death of beloved ones) when a story that remained unquestioned and unassailed as a given has been contradicted by reality.[60] And everyone knows those moments between stories when, through a temporary opening that soon closes up again, one catches a glimpse of non-fictional reality, reality *an sich*.

This posited correspondence constitutes the basis for my understanding of the cries of Serb nationalists, the references to idle stories (*prazne priče*), and the embrace of unreason. The tripartite structure of the book is a reflection of this.

The first part, Fictional Reality, comprises two chapters. *Fini ljudi. A Balkan Bourgeoisie* (Chapter I), introduces Novi Sad and the people I met there, and discusses the way in which the people of this city sought to position themselves in urban society using two clusters of stories about themselves, others and the world in which they lived. In one of these story clusters, Novi Sad represents the Serbia that has for centuries been part of civilised Europe. In the other, which leads a more underground existence, Novi Sad is no different from other parts of Serbia, and belongs to the eternally wild Balkans. *Borderland, Warzone* (Chapter II) offers a brief sociogenesis of this civilisation debate. It will become clear that in the development of Serb nationalism, notions of Serb identity are inextricably interwoven with a pose of wildness.

The second part, Beyond the World in Stories, consists of a single chapter, *Lessons from the Reform School of War* (Chapter III). This focuses on recurrent war and violent conflict as a continuous backdrop to experience. In the light of reports on the scenes that dominated the recent war in Croatia and Bosnia-Herzegovina, I discuss the damage which the experience of war does in stories that confer meaning. The reform school of war teaches people the need to have a fictional reality, while at the same time it impresses upon them the impossibility of unfaltering commitment to any story whatsoever.

The third and last part of the book, Imaginary Worlds, consists of the chapters *On Mud, on Gypsies, or, On People and the World as They Simply Are* (Chapter IV) and *Kafana* (Chapter V). It emerges that collective fantasies about Gypsies, and celebrations of unreason such as those connected with the Gypsy bands, serve as attempts to resolve the dilemma of the indispensable but unreliable story. Finally, in an epilogue entitled *The Embrace of Unreason*, I discuss ways in which the findings of this study may help us achieve a better understanding of the unreason of this war.

PART I

Reality as it is told

1 *Fini Ljudi*: A Balkan Bourgeoisie

> At first we were confused. The East thought that we were West, while the West considered us to be East. Some of us misunderstood our place in this clash of currents, so they cried that we belong to neither side, and others that we belong exclusively to one side or the other. But I tell you, Irinej, we are doomed by fate to be the East on the West, and the West on the East, to acknowledge only heavenly Jerusalem beyond us, and here on earth – no one.
>
> – St. Sava to Irinej, 13th century[1]

> I didn't tell her that in Zagreb the name of the Balkan cinema, where I had last seen her with her friends, has since changed to Europe, and that that change of name symbolises the whole idea behind the war.
>
> – Slavenka Drakulić, *Balkan Express*

If you arrive in Novi Sad from the north, from Budapest or Vienna, you know you're in a provincial town. The pastel colour of every town and village in the territory of the former dual monarchy is here faded and dirty. Only a hundred kilometres to the north, in Subotica on the Hungarian border, you can still find the unbridled thirst for decoration that makes cities like Budapest and Vienna what they are. 'The houses there have glaring yellow and blue colours', Claudio Magris remarked on Subotica in astonishment, '[...] they sometimes look like shells and they are adorned with curious decorations and ornaments, crowns like pineapples, cherubs with enormous breasts, gigantic bearded caryatids whose lower bodies turn into lions, that in turn are dissolved in shapeless waves'.[2] By comparison with the wild façades of Subotica, those of Novi Sad are subdued. Just below the eaves, beneath thick layers of paint, you can pick out ornaments here and there. Girls' heads, bearded men. But the reason you see them is mainly because the dirt – which always seems to blow from the same direction – adds relief to the slight protuberances. Not a flower-box in sight. Here and there the woven garlands of twigs with ears of corn, pine leaves, small apples, flowers and ribbons that can be seen hanging on houses and doors all over Central Europe. Most of them in Novi Sad look dull, dry, and neglected. Not because everything looks a bit dull and neglected here, but because of the tradition that you only replace a garland, hung on the occasion of the *slava*, the anniversary of the patron saint of the family, by the time next year's *slava* has come around. If it does.

But if you arrive in Novi Sad from the south, from the chaotic bustle of the big city Belgrade or from even further south in the Balkans, you feel positively back in Europe. The first impression is one of space and openness. The streets are wide, the squares are spacious, there is a system to the street plan. Women in blue dust-coats keep it tidy with brooms. The pigeons circle in slow formation above the squares, the residents move about calmly, and the majestic Danube flows imperturbably past. On sultry summer days people come to the river bank to sit in the shade of the willows and poplars, to play a game of cards, to chat with old friends, or just to gaze idly around them.

I love this Novi Sad. After a stint of research in the South of Serbia, in Vranje, I had sworn 'never again', but Novi Sad was different, more familiar, more friendly, and more aloof too. A place where people don't call you their best friend after five minutes. What is more, when I asked the first taxi driver I met whether there were bars with Gypsy orchestras and he replied: 'Which one are you looking for? Fine young Gypsies (*fini mladi cigani*) or real Gypsies (*pravi cigani*)?' my mind was made up. This was where I wanted to stay.

I rented a flat in one of the postwar neighbourhoods, number four in a row of sublets. Veljko Petrović street, number 73, on the ninth floor. Noisy mating rituals of pigeons on the window-sill. In the distance, between two blocks of flats, a glimpse of the Danube, and towering above it the castle with the mellifluous name of Petrovaradinska Tvrdjava. Boomtown Novi Sad. No pastel tints here, no woven garlands on the doors and walls, just grey concrete. Flat after flat rears up from the drained swamps, making way here and there for the remains of what must once have been outlying districts or hamlets. A city whose population more than quadrupled after the war as farmers' sons and daughters flocked from far and wide to find jobs in the new industries and government bodies, to find accommodation, and to feel that, despite being plagued by persistent mosquitoes, they had become cosmopolitan city folk.

The flat in itself where I found myself seemed the ideal location to collect stories about postwar Novi Sad. Slovak and Serb neighbours, names from Serbia, Hungary, Montenegro, Germany and Russia on the letterboxes downstairs, the whole mosaic of ethnic groups in the Vojvodina: Király, Mitrović, Šulc, Bodor, Kuzmanov, Mihaljović. A trembling old woman on the eighth floor. 'She's already in her nineties, but going strong', they told me. On the floor below a family that had turned its balcony into an enormous rubbish heap with nondescript refuse and half-rotten rags. The head of the family smoked cigarettes all day in his vest. His wife, a short, plump woman with fishy eyes and a terrifying but intriguing moustache, wore those boots that all Slav women seem to like: leather boots ending below the knee, underneath a skirt. (Those terrible boots. I once saw the sturdily built girl in the local supermarket kick a huge pile of boxes of soap powder from one side of the shop to the other with boots like that. She didn't pick them up, she didn't even look for a trolley, she just kicked them slowly over the tiled floor. With those clumsy boots. Baf. Baf. Baf. I'll never forget the blank look on her face as the ultimate picture of Novi Sad moroseness.) Opposite me a Bosnian Serb with his family, a businessman, afraid he'll be mobilized. Every time I met him in the lift, he never failed to congratulate me on being a foreigner. 'You can at least clear out.' A hopelessly chain-smoking Hungarian woman upstairs, with a son who came to ask whether there was any trade in pottery in the Netherlands. And Gypsies regularly begged at the door. A small, unsightly and completely wrinkled man who held out his hand without saying a word, and two young women with a child in rags who asked for old shoes every week without fail.

But it soon transpired that my initial fantasies about a diary that would easily be filled with stories and anecdotes taken from the rich social life that I would be able to build up in this flat were groundless. My neighbours were suspicious about the latest tenant at number 73, a foreigner to boot. Apart from a few exceptions, the contacts remained confined to the kind of awkward and brief conversation people have in a lift: about who stole the light bulb from the lift this time, about the ongoing devaluation and price increases, about the good old days and the bad new ones, about how in Tito's day there was at least order, and everyone had a weekend cottage. And about the war – 'what could *we* do', 'the people are paying the price', 'how can *we* do anything', '*what* can we do', 'the people just want peace', 'the people are suffering', 'we don't want this'. Tired faces, tired complaints, couched in the most general terms, without causes, without responsibility, without culprits. Questions about why I was there and when I would go. Had the Dutch embassy tipped me off about an imminent evacuation of foreigners? Some of them gradually came to see me as a sort of barometer to gauge the war pressure; as long as I was there, it would not escalate.

I got to know the residents of the city through different channels. First, through a number of people I had already met during previous fieldwork in Serbia. I had become one of their friends and acquaintances. Second, colleagues from the ethnological museum and a few students and members of staff from the city university provided me with access to other circles and networks. I consorted with *fini ljudi*,[3] as they were called in Novi Sad, decent people.

Fini ljudi. A good name for my discussion partners, whose preoccupation with their own degree of civilisation had surprised me from the very first day of my fieldwork. I remember how during the first months of my fieldwork I was in a state of mild panic about my failure to meet or make contact with authentic Serbs. Not that I had a clear picture of an authentic Serb – though lust had secretly informed me what they would be like: men with sharply chiselled features, moustaches, broad, hairy chests and big hands that rearranged the contents of their crotches once too often. It was rather that what I saw around me was nothing but a thoroughly bourgeois society. It did not seem to have the slightest connection with the sombre turn events had already taken. In a letter I sent home during my first weeks there, I commented in connection with my activities with a Gypsy orchestra:

> The restaurant where they play is top class and, to tell the truth, it's pretty formal. The musicians complain about it as well, because the audience won't loosen up, which means they earn less. During the last few days I've started to wonder whether I'm in the right place here in Novi Sad; perhaps the phenomenon of bacchantic excess does not exist here at all, and – as they keep on telling me – they really are more civilised than their southern neighbours in the Balkans. Those doubts were strengthened by an article I recently discovered in the library which describes exactly what I'm looking for, but concludes with the comment that '[...] the days of the great bećari (the name of fervent barflies here) are unfortunately no more'. Last night in the Old Coach restaurant I discovered that it's not as bad as that. A Gypsy musician had taken me to a spot where he said I could pick something up. And it really was a wild spot. It's pretty strange to feel relieved when you notice that Gypsies are still pushed around in a rough way, to put it mildly, by a bunch of overgrown thirty-year-olds.

Knowing what the war would bring, it is difficult to relive those dominant impressions of a bourgeois society I talk about in the notes on my first months in Novi Sad. So allow me to reproduce some of my jottings (slightly brushed up):

> Everyone here seems to be active in drawing boundaries to ensure that Novi Sad ends up in what people here regard as the civilised half of the

world. It seems to be about the boundary between Novi Sad and the countryside around it, between Novi Sad and Belgrade, between the Vojvodina
and the Balkans, between the former Austro-Hungarian territories and the
former Turkish Ottoman territories, between Central Europe and Eastern
Europe, between Tito's Yugoslavia and the Communist Eastern bloc
countries, between a 'Western' and an 'Oriental' sphere of influence.
People loudly claim allegiance to the city, to Europe, to the former Austro-
Hungarian territories, and are just as vociferous in denouncing the respec-
tive opposites: the village, the Balkans, the Orient.

Everything that is at hand and that refers in some way or other to the
West is deployed to close those boundaries with the Balkans. Those who
could afford it have literally barricaded themselves in during the last few
decennia with Western commodities, furniture and domestic equipment,
Hammond organs and cars, video recorders and lady shaves. They dress
in Western labels, envelop themselves in statements by authoritative
Western intellectuals and impenetrable clouds of Western cigarette smoke
and Western face powders, creams and perfumes. They prefer to drive
European cars, go to galleries, classical concerts, cocktail parties, coffee
shops with wood and shiny brass interiors (where cappuccino has replaced
Turkish coffee), the Chinese restaurant or other stylish restaurants.

If something comes from the West, it is virtually by definition better, even
at the present time of exaggerated self-importance and nationalism. After
hours of pure nationalistic propaganda on the radio, in which historians
tell how meals were eaten with golden forks in the court of the medieval
Serb prince Milutin while the English royalty still ate with their fingers;
and in which political commentators talk about the Serbs as a heavenly
people (*nebeski narod*), you suddenly hear a jingle on the same channel ad-
vertising the opening of a new bar with the slogan '*viski, vino, konjak, ništa od
naše sem čaše i flaše*', whisky, wine, cognac, we don't sell anything made by
ourselves except the bottles and the glasses.

Life is governed by conventions that we would call bourgeois in the
Netherlands. Hierarchical relations apply at work, people obey their
superiors, and accept low wages or even none at all. They never stop mut-
tering and complaining, but they do so furtively to themselves. The top pri-
orities are the home and the family. The men never stop doing jobs to the
house. The women do the decorating with Biedermeier bouquets, crochet
work, framed pierrot reproductions, hand-blown glass and other knick-
knacks. They watch European and North American films on the video.
They learn foreign languages and save up for a holiday on the coast (of
Montenegro) or a shopping arrangement (a short trip abroad to Trieste,

Vienna, Paris, Istanbul or Singapore with plenty of time to go shopping). Apart from these frivolities, they live sober and spartan lives. They eat wholesome food. Their views on hygiene verge on a dirt phobia. They keep themselves to themselves.

The people of Novi Sad are proud of the European, bourgeois and urban character of their city and life-style. When during a conversation with somebody we turned out to have a mutual acquaintance, he was described as dobar *čovek, pravi Evropljanin*, a good person, a real European. While the label 'decent folk' is not entirely positive in the Netherlands – they may be irreproachable, but their strict and uncritical compliance with conventions and rules of correct behaviour are soon felt to be narrow-minded, timid and insipid, *fin čovek* is primarily a compliment in Novi Sad. The people of Novi Sad pride themselves on the reputation that they have elsewhere in Serbia: a bit slow, a bit reserved, a bit cold.

And if it doesn't come naturally, just pretend...

A couple of Yugoslavian publications from the early Nineties on the rules of proper behaviour illustrate the programme, albeit in a rather grotesque exaggeration, by which the people of Novi Sad give shape to their lives as *fini ljudi.*[4]

The cover of the etiquette manual called *BonTon* (1991, 9th impression) shows a modern young woman in evening dress hand in hand with a chimpanzee wearing a coat and tails. It is hard to interpret this in any other way except to mean that even a chimpanzee can be turned into a gentleman. But the tone of the preface is not so light-hearted. The authors assume that *lepo ponašanje* (proper behaviour) has a regulatory effect that eases social intercourse. 'These rules of behaviour', they write, 'protect the weak and powerless', they offer 'a rapid and simple solution for problems that would unnecessarily delay the pace of modern life', and they 'make it easier for everyone to move in society with more ease, security and self-confidence'.[5] The city, modern society, we seem to be able to conclude from these words, is a world that feels awkward, makes people insecure and robs them of self-confidence. That the authors target a public to whom the world appears 'strange and incomprehensible' can be seen from the 15-page (!) glossary at the end of the book which explains important borrowings like *korektan, nivo, vulgaran* and *civilizacija*.

Although the authors must be well aware of the fact that people can be turned into *fini ljudi* – at any rate, that is the premise of the book –

they constantly emphasise in the text that it is really impossible. People who have learned the rules from the cradle have a headstart and will always be out in front. They embody the rules, and they have a natural sense of tact. On the other hand, people who 'did not have the opportunity or did not live in a situation in which they learned to master the basic rules of decent behaviour in their childhood' (I cannot refrain from anticipating and emphasising that a sentence like this entails a whole world view!) can catch up to some extent, according to the authors, as long as they apply patience and dedication. However, the authors drive the point home that it is not just a question of rules, empty forms or patterns, but that 'the individual's entire personality must be connected with the rules'. The ideal, no matter how difficult it may be, is:

> [...] that by constant practice and paying attention we learn to master the rules of behaviour so well that they come to form a part of us. Then our behaviour will be proper, not because we have learned the rules of behaviour, but because they *come over naturally*, as something that is a part of us, as if we could not behave otherwise.[6]

The other book, *Lepo Ponašanje*, Proper Behaviour, has a drawing on the front. The sentimental scene shows two toddlers in immaculate white giving one another a modest kiss in a pale yellow field of flowers. There are no allusions to unfettered behaviour, unless they are to be seen in the two playful butterflies, or in the two lambs nuzzling in the distance in the meadow. The back cover has a photo of the writer, a woman with a friendly smile, a modern hair-do and a rustic blouse. The blouse is not a random choice, as can be seen from the accompanying text. It contains a subtle hint for people who 'did not have the opportunity or did not live in a situation in which they learned to master the basic rules of decent behaviour in their childhood':

> Dušanka Bojičić-Bošković was born in Mrdenovac, a beautiful village near Šabac. She spent her infancy and early schooldays in her native village of Mrdenovac. She attended grammar school in Šabac with flying colours and completed her studies in Belgrade. For twenty years she worked as a successful teacher. Since 1986 she has spent all her time campaigning for more humane and *kulturni* (cultivated) human relations – proper behaviour in an attractive environment. Dušanka Bojičić-Bošković is the initiator, founder and president of the only Association for the Promotion of Proper Behaviour.

The rural background of the writer is mentioned twice. The village is 'beautiful' (an epithet that is less arbitrary than it may seem) and 'her own' (after all, it is her *native* village). And if we follow the rest of her career, it shows that it is not impossible to rise above that backward village background – because that is what practically every city dweller thinks about it. We can sum up the implicit message of a text like this one as follows: 'even though I was a village girl from the countryside, thanks to my study and successful career as a teacher I have risen to become president of the Association for the Promotion of Proper Behaviour'.

This book more explicitly targets Yugoslavian society. The foreword by the writer Miodrag Sijaković – 'A book for everyone...' – argues that old models of behaviour have disappeared and new, regulatory norms have taken their place. What we are offered in the public media and elsewhere is not enough, this writer claims:

> [...] it is as if that genuine bonton does not exist, that would regulate our everyday lives and ensure that we behave normally and in a cultivated fashion, instead of behaving repressively, arrogantly and in an extremely uncultivated fashion almost anywhere and everywhere.[7]

The proof that 'we (sic) behave badly' can be seen on every street corner, Sijaković claims. The writer is particularly shocked by bad language, the 'daily companion of our lives'.

Both books proceed to describe a programme of correct behaviour and proper actions. It is a highly ambitious programme that covers practically every aspect of life. There are rules and instructions for behaviour in public places ('we pay the bill discretely, without making a song and dance about it'), at home ('at any rate dubious decorations, such as cheap souvenirs, artificial flowers, etc., cannot form a part of the interior furnishings'), the correct way to pay a visit and to receive guests ('do not pay a visit if you have a cold or the flu'), the correct way to behave on holiday or while travelling ('you should not constantly eat in the train; it is best to eat once only, and then to eat food that we have prepared beforehand. Ready-made sandwiches, for example, but they too must be eaten discretely, without unwrapping all kinds of layers of paper, dropping crumbs or throwing away greasy leftovers. And we must take particular care not to eat anything with a strong aroma'), the correct behaviour between husband and wife, and between parents and children ('a little understanding makes life easier... So show a little understanding for men's "weaknesses", such as attending football matches or meetings with friends in a bar'), during time off ('it is very bad manners to insult the national or religious convictions of the players and their supporters during football matches'), at work ('do not stop your colleagues from working by chattering'), in letter-writing and using the phone ('if a telephone call is made in the room you are in, you should leave or behave in such a way as to make it clear that the conversation does not concern you' and 'if you should happen to become connected to someone else's telephone conversation [which often happens], it is bad manners to carry on listening'), giving presents ('we never give money as a present' and 'we do not give presents to someone we do not know very well, because it can be regarded as bribery, which is often not far from the truth'), forms of greeting, lending, tenants, domestic pets, the body and body care, dress etiquette, and behaviour during funerals.

Etiquette manuals like these provide an exaggerated version of an ideal. No one will submit to this programme entirely or study the books from A to Z. A friend from Novi Sad, to whom I showed the discovery of these books (not without a snigger at the deep depression in which the president of the Association for the Promotion of Proper Behaviour must have landed), was not at all amused that I regarded publications of this kind as material, and he denied their value and relevance. It subsequently became a standing joke to point out my blunders in the refined forms of behaviour every time I forgot to hold the door open, to help a lady into her coat, or committed some other faux pas. Books like these, however, are significant because – as is explicitly stated in the introductions to the books themselves – they are based on the assumption that a lot of people in this society are uncertain about how they ought to behave. The books play up to the idea that many Serbs in the city experience their own world as something foreign, a world full of words that they do not understand, rules that they do not know, codes of behaviour with which they are not familiar; a world which makes them feel awkward, makes them insecure, and constantly erodes their self-confidence.

These manuals, with their meticulous instructions about what to do and what not to do, also show how rigidly the ideal is adhered to. The fact that they are strange rules and strange words does not matter. The same applies to where the rules come from, who thought them up, and the extent to which they are related to the specific backgrounds of the users of these manuals, and the authors do not feel any need to comment on these matters. 'The rules for right and proper behaviour are the same all over the world' is the simple answer under the heading 'Abroad'. 'These rules are the result of a time-honoured process', they write elsewhere, and 'they have proved their worth'. And that's that. As for those whose background or childhood did not endow them with 'natural tact' and an 'embodiment of the rules' – sanctioned by sarcasm and a deep sense of shame – all they can do is to keep on practising and keep up appearances.

City in the making, city folk in the making

The insecurity, the lack of self-confidence and the feelings of uneasiness for which these manuals of etiquette try to formulate answers seem to be the direct products of society in an urban arena; the entire presentation of the manuals, the subjects discussed by them, and the various settings covered make it clear that the target audience is brand-new city folk. Nothing strange about that.

After World War II an explosive growth took hold of the cities all over Yugoslavia. Josip Broz Tito and his partisan army had emerged as the victors and wanted to launch the new socialist Yugoslavia into the modern age as soon as they could. A rapid industrialisation of the country and the setting up of a completely new and large-scale bureaucracy to plan and organise Tito's revolution were regarded as steps in the right direction. The loser was agriculture. The rural population were a symbol of the mentality, life-style and living conditions that the new socialist Yugoslavia was to leave behind.[8]

The postwar decennia saw a massive exodus of the rural population. Increasing numbers of the farmers who had characterised the city before the Second World War as 'an entity dangerous to body and spirit alike',[9] and who had described the bourgeoisie as 'parasitical and rapacious',[10] opted for life in the city when the war was over. In 1948 Yugoslavia was still one of the least urbanised countries in Europe. No more than 12% of the total population lived in communities of more than 20,000 people, and there were only two cities in the whole of Yugoslavia, Belgrade and Zagreb, with a population of more than 100,000. Thirteen years later the country already had seven urban centres with more than 100,000 inhabitants, and 19% of the population lived in communities of more than 20,000 people.[11]

The new city folk with whom Andrej Simić spoke in Belgrade in the Seventies almost all motivated their move to the city in terms of the primitive[12] living conditions and backwardness of the village, the lack of educational opportunities and jobs, the isolation, the hard work in the summers, the tedium of the winters, the gossip and social control. 'There is a conviction that residence in the nation's capital and employment outside of agriculture are more prestigious than the life of a peasant', Simić comments.[13] Many of Simić's stories recall my previous fieldwork in Vranje, in the southern part of Serbia, where I lodged with a young peasant with urban aspirations: the framed diplomas and certificates on the wall, the daydreams and endless stories about a business of his own, the undisguisedly scornful way he treated his parents-in-law, peasants from a neighbouring village, who came every week to fill his fridge with yoghurt, cheese, meat and vegetables, but whom he regaled non-stop with his stories about the backwardness of peasant life and how lucky he was that he had definitively left that dirty work behind him. He laughed at the neighbours who had built a shed for two cows as an annex to their city home. Unlike many of those who lived in the neighbourhood, he did not grow vegetables or fruit in his garden. And to the great consternation of his parents-in-law he refused to observe the good old custom that fresh city folks came back to the village to help out during the harvest. He wanted no more of that; he was a white collar worker with clean hands now.[14]

Studies of process of urbanisation in postwar Yugoslavia sketch a rosy picture of a society that was transformed with relative ease from an agrarian to an urban industrial one. Researchers like Bette Denitch,[15] Andrej Simić[16] and Joel Halpern[17] did not find the phenomena that characterise rushed modernisation and urbanisation in Third World countries: the impoverishment of the peasants who migrate to the city; the rise of slums; an increase in the crime rate as a result of uprooting and anomie. 'The city adjusts to the peasants, not vice versa' is the line taken by most studies, a process that is regularly referred to as the 'peasantization of the cities'.[18] Simić concludes his study of the postwar growth of Belgrade as follows:

> Many of those who assumed positions of great power following the war were immediately, or by birth, from the peasantry (e.g. Tito). The remarkable expansion of the economy, and the complete replacement of the ruling stratum of the nation, made very rapid mobility possible. In this respect, the peasantization of Belgrade has taken place not only among the proletariat but at all levels of society. Furthermore, even remnants of the old intelligentsia and aristocracy did not always lack ties with the peasantry, and shared with other segments of the population a nationalist fervor and a symbolic devotion to Serbian folkways. Thus, the migrant finds in the capital a body of belief and custom in many ways resembling what he has left behind in the village [...]. Finally, the modernization of the society is not simply a question of the transformation of a backward peasantry, but of an entire nation. Innovations have entered the society at all

levels, thus reducing the tendency for pronounced differentiation between migrants and long-time urban residents.[19]

Even if the egalitarian society acclaimed by those researchers in the Seventies in Yugoslavia ever actually existed – in an article from 1984, Simić makes several major corrections to his previous claims concerning a rapid and successful modernisation and urbanisation – the situation I came across in Novi Sad was drastically changed. The absorptive capacity of the industries and bureaucracies tailed off at the end of the Sixties, and the unabating influx of newcomers into the cities found it much harder to get jobs. Migrant labourers who returned home, privileged party executives and officials, and a rapidly growing group of entrepreneurs who successfully managed to exploit the economic reforms of 1965 brought the socio-economic divisions out into the open, notwithstanding all the public statements about a classless society. In one of the few empirical studies of social inequality in Yugoslavia, the sociologist Vesna Pešić distinguished four social strata in Yugoslavian society, each with its own characteristic life-style: the political and economic leaders with a luxurious and exclusive life-style, partly enabled through their privileges; the urban middle class (civil servants, intellectuals) with a life-style strongly orientated towards status; the working class (skilled and unskilled), with a life-style characterised by the difficulties of making ends meet, difficulties that are further exacerbated because they are no longer able to fall back on home-grown produce from the countryside; and finally the peasants (both farmers and peasant labourers) with a traditional life-style, though one that is rapidly changing.[20] Milena Dragičević-Šešić[21] and Ines Prica[22] refined the model and charted the urban subcultures. All the same, these authors resemble their foreign colleagues in pointing to the fluidity and vagueness of the structures that determine urban society in Yugoslavia.

To understand the uncertainty among many city folk about their new status, it is important to recognise the constant veiling of socio-economic differences through the use of an ideological smoke-screen that talks about equality and the classless society. The 'we-live-in-a-modern-urban-society' story, combined with the rhetoric of progress of state socialism, could flourish without hindrance, hardly contradicted if at all, questioned rarely or never. In what is still one of the best descriptions of Tito's Yugoslavia, Duško Doder comments:

> However imperfect Tito's socialism has been, one of its great accomplishments has been the introduction of what for want of a better term can be

described as the modern spirit. Deeply conscious of their country's backwardness, the Communists impressed upon themselves and others the absolute necessity of raising the cultural level of the population. The key
word was *kultura*, or culture, which was invested with a specific meaning.
The leaders have spoken about communism being the penultimate stage in
the evolution of man's society, yet until relatively recently their people
were in a preindustrial stage. So the leaders have stimulated a romantic
reverence for *kultura*, which in their minds embraces fields ranging from literacy and education to life-styles, literature and the arts. Which was, in effect, a drive for enlightenment, a yearning to cast off the inheritance of underdevelopment and move up to the cultural and economic level of
Western Europe. What else has been the purpose of a revolution? In trying to quickly bridge the vast gap between rhetoric and reality, the leaders
tried to make a kind of merger between the ideals of modern socialism and
the concepts of enlightenment.[23]

Education was singled out for special treatment. In the immediate aftermath of the Second World War there were three universities in the country; by 1975 there were 158 universities and colleges, and the number of
students per 10,000 inhabitants in that year was the third highest in
Europe (after Sweden and the Netherlands). 'In quantitative terms',
Doder acutely points out, 'the three decades of Communist rule produced impressive results'.[24] 'Education, obtaining diplomas, is one of the
major goals of the urban population', Pešić notes, 'because that is how
members of the urban middle class try to secure their position in that
class once they have attained it'.[25] All of the middle class groups distinguished by Pešić are enormously concerned about giving their children a
good education: 'This orientation is completely in line with the preoccupation with careers and social progress. This ambition can only lead to
results if you are in possession of several diplomas of higher education. If
you consider the behaviour of our middle class, especially the intellectuals, the conclusion is inevitable: parents' main concern is the career and
future of their children, right from the start. It is not enough for them
that their children *learn* properly, they have to be 'brilliant'. If a child
does not come up to the parental expectations, the parents are not only
extremely preoccupied but also insulted and ashamed'.[26]
     Although the socio-economic dividing lines of this society have come
into the open since the collapse of Titoism – the prewar bourgeoisie in
particular cannot help noisily showing off its claims to natural refinement
and high culture – I was struck by the fact that the term for city folk, *fin
čovek* or European is not protected or monopolised by a clearly distin-

guishable group. Anyone can appropriate the epithet or tinker with its meaning before flashing it around. So practically everyone I met demanded access to the label *fin čovek*: the woman with the moustache, the Gypsy musicians, the colleagues in the ethnological museum, the refined lady who could still claim kinship ties with the prewar bourgeoisie. And they all used the arguments and resources at their disposal to this end. While one waved his well-filled wallet in the air to back up his claim to urbanite status, another referred to the fact that his surname went back to the famous *Biographies of Novi Sad* by Vasa Stajić (a detailed list of the old Serb families who have lived in the city since the eighteenth century). Another's claim to urban status was his punk outfit, complete with safety-pins and Mohican hair-do. Others were just as vehement in declaring that it was not a question of safety-pins or money, but education and profession, and above all awareness of *kultura* as the only valid ticket granting admittance to the status of *fin čovek*.

Urban primitives

No matter how much effort my discussion partners put into telling the stories of their lives in a way that would make them members of an urban bourgeoisie, the contours of their story were much clearer when it came to what they no longer were: they were no longer peasants, people from the countryside, villagers. What they no longer were, or at any rate what belonged to their past, was a much more important point of orientation in the discussions than the label *fini ljudi* that had taken its place. My discussion partners from Novi Sad were thus not only concerned to convince themselves, one another and me of their refined manners, polite etiquette and familiarity with everything regarded as coming from the West; they were above all engaged in pinpointing signs and manifestations of the primitive in their direct everyday experience, labelling it, and avoiding confrontations with it.[27] They steered clear of contacts with primitives (*primitivci*), and uncontrolled outbursts or rude behaviour in their own group were corrected, sometimes with a joke, sometimes more seriously. Those areas of the city where society reveals its naked face – public transport, the market, public institutions, social services – were avoided as much as possible too. When this proved impossible – as was often the case, given the degree to which the norms for polite behaviour were tightened up – it was as if the evil influence of such an environment had to be exorcised by the incantation of a long litany of curses addressed to so many primitives.

As can be inferred from the entries in my diary cited above, when my discussion partners used the term 'the primitive' (*primitivizam*), the point of reference was primarily to a whole range of uncontrolled actions. The category could be applied to actions as diverse as constant cursing, un-limited partying, the wasting of large sums of money on unnecessary items, breaking the speed limit, mourning too loudly at funerals (the tra-ditional *kukati*), uttering wildly nationalistic opinions, exaggerating, singing (or enjoying) epic heroic poems, displaying greediness, and vio-lence. Less obvious manifestations of the primitive included people who bumped into one another in overcrowded buses; they were accused not of carelessness or clumsiness but uncultivated behaviour (*nekulturno ponašanje*). If someone tripped over an uneven curb or threshold, the first reaction was not to help them but to laugh at them: tripping up and falling down were seen as an unmistakable sign of lack of control. The corrupt practices of the politicians were discussed not in terms of illegal acts that should be punished, but in terms of civilisation: that behaviour was above all else *primitivno* and *necivilizovano*.

The label primitive was also continually used for certain social and ethnic categories in urban society. The prime target was the Com-munists. 'The primitives who came to power here have ruined our coun-try', was the comment of a woman who claimed relations with the pre-war bourgeoisie. 'Their children got grants to study abroad, but they didn't learn anything there. We can see that all too clearly today!' Incidentally, it was by no means always clear to whom the term Communists referred; it was a kind of amorphous mass which was some-times taken to include the new powers that be under Slobodan Milošević, sometimes not. Another striking category among the primitives were the *Gastarbeiter*. There were plenty of cases which were taken to show that they used their material wealth for nothing except the public display of their bad taste and ignorance of the rules of civilised behaviour. As some-one who tried to explain the codes for recognising *Gastarbeiter* to me put it: 'Just watch out for showy houses and a second-hand Mercedes parked in front, the wrong kind of shoes with white socks and men wearing a gold necklace, a signet ring, and one button too many open on their shirt: you can be sure it's one of our *gastarbajteri*.' It was also constantly repeated that *Gastarbeiter* are really peasants, the most primitive social group, and that they come from the most impoverished and backward parts of the country into the bargain. 'If something bothers me', an ac-quaintance confided, 'it's the confrontation with our *Gastarbeitern* abroad. Seeing them is enough to make you ashamed of being Yugoslavian.' The *nouveaux riches*, consisting of members of the former party elite and the former *Gastarbeitern* who have returned, also had a reputation for being primitive.

As I have already indicated, under socialism the peasants were regarded as everything that belongs to the past for a *fin čovek*. Drakulić gives a good example of the kind of stories that I kept hearing:

> A family had moved into the ground floor of our block of flats straight from the countryside. They had a small truck and had a thriving business in buying up vegetables from remote villages and selling them for two or three times the price on the country market. It was not strictly legal, but they got away with it, probably by bribing the officials like everyone else. It was rumoured in the flat that the woman had lit a fire on the floor of the bathroom because she had never seen a bathroom before. My mother had told me that after the war there were people who kept pigs or chickens in their bathroom, or filled the tub with soil to grow carrots or lettuce.[28]

All the same, people were less loud and clear in talking about the primitiveness of the peasants than of the other categories listed above. Perhaps this was partly due to the fact that the parents or grandparents of practically everybody in this postwar boom town had been peasants.

My discussion partners were the most outspoken when it came to the ethnic categories that were categorised as primitive. This label applied first and foremost to the Albanians. Their primitiveness was displayed in their clan mentality, their blood vengeance, their violence and involvement in the arms trade, their large families, and the archaic relations between men and women, between parents, children and relatives.[29] Still, Albanians were less prominent in the stories told to me by my discussion partners in Novi Sad than elsewhere in Serbia, where even people whom I got to know as liberal-minded cosmopolitans lost every sense of proportion once Albanians came up in the conversation. In Novi Sad the label primitive was applied much more often to the Serbs from south of the main rivers, Serbs from outside the Vojvodina: Montenegrans (who are also regarded as Serbs), Bosnian Serbs, Serbs from Croatian Krajina, and Serbs from the south of Serbia itself. These *Srbijanci* or *dodjoši*, as they are disparagingly called – the word literally means 'those who arrived' – settled here in large numbers as colonists after the Second World War.

The colonists were the butt of constant criticism. If it was not their patriarchal mentality, it was their primitive practices and customs, their lack of familiarity with Western civilisation, their martial, soldierly and warrior-like attitude and the corresponding contempt for honest work on the land, their aggressive bearing, their adherence to a clan, their preference for primitive songs and epic poems.

In the stories of the Vojvodina Serbs – who in many cases were themselves from the south, although from earlier colonisation programmes, by the way – the arrival of these *balkanci* was presented as nothing less than a catastrophe. An anthropologist from the Vojvodina who had research experience with these colonists told me:

> As ex-servicemen they were given the best land, but they weren't at all interested in agriculture nor in this country. They are from the mountains, you know. Today, forty years after they came, there are still colonists who ask me if I can explain why I love these plains! I ask you! They should just send them back. It's not good for them to be here either; they still sing about their fatherland. The saddest songs I have ever heard in my life were the songs of Montenegrans about their home country!

There are many stories which contrast the Serbs from the Vojvodina with other Serbs. On a number of occasions I was told the story about the peasant who was instructed by the village committee soon after the Second World War to welcome the colonists who had just arrived from Montenegro. An interviewee told me:

> Can you imagine it? How the chairman of the village committee puts on his best suit and says goodbye to his wife, frightened to death that he may not survive this welcoming ceremony at the station? It's true, we in the Vojvodina really felt as if they had come out of the jungle. Wild men! And the colonists, who had fought as partisans in the war and who had been prevented by all kinds of restrictions from taking any luggage to their new homes, simply confirmed this picture; they moved into the best homes – they used to belong to the Germans – but they didn't even know what lighting and electricity were! They used the parquet floors for firewood! And those big tiled ovens, you know, which were in all the German houses they occupied – they thought they were monuments in honour of Hitler! So they immediately cleared them out. They had no idea. They came from villages with five or so houses and our villages here in the Vojvodina were cities in their eyes.

This informant also added that most of all he would like to send all the colonists back home. A Hungarian woman who lived in the city said that the colonists had been domesticated by now. When she saw that I did not know the word *pripitomiti* (domesticated), she laughed and explained: 'You only use that word for animals, but in the case of the colonists you can apply it to human beings as well'. Somebody else confided that he felt much closer to the Hungarians than to the Serbs from south of the rivers. 'Look, you hate the Hungarians a bit, of course, but we still belong to the same Pannonian cultural zone'. 'Give me the Germans', another complained, 'in those days you could still get that lovely asparagus on the market. Since the colonists came all you can get is potatoes and cabbage. That's all they know'. A student from Novi Sad who studied in Belgrade said that it was terrible to be 'down there' (*dole*) – this is how people in the Vojvodina refer to Serbia. She looked at me with pity when I told her I had spent some time in Vranje: 'Vranje! Terrible! No, those colonists are worse than animals; you should hear them in the bus talking about the war. When you sit in the bus to Belgrade and hear them saying how they would love to wipe out all the Croats! It's only now that you can really see what kind of people they are, what kind of a country you're living in!' I asked her what it was like before the war, whether she saw it the same way then. 'No, then you would have just regarded them as uncivilised peasants', she replied.

Nevertheless, all these stark distinctions are less clear-cut than they seem. In fact, the distinct categories people used were undermined by the fact that, when I questioned them further, there was hardly anyone who could incontrovertibly and without a shadow of doubt lay claim to the title *fin čovek* as distinct from primitive. The vast majority of Serbs settled in the Vojvodina during the colonisation programmes.[30] 'What do you expect, everyone here is descended from peasant grandparents' was one of the mottos which the people of Novi Sad carelessly employed to comment on their own efforts. It was proof of insight, as most of my discussion partners themselves, in their youth or through one or both of their parents, (had) belonged to those social and ethnic categories which they now labelled as primitive. This made everyone vulnerable who laid claim to the title *fin čovek*. Because of their past or the background of their immediate family, each of them could be revealed as a *šminker* (from the German *schminken*, to make up). This has to be taken into consideration in accounting for the doggedness with which the claim 'we are citizens, urbanites, cosmopolitans' is bandied about.

Who we are and who we no longer are

Folklore – a middle-class reformulation of what is supposed to be characteristic of a particular people – is an interesting field in which to examine the elimination of the primitive that this society has imposed on itself. It is precisely folklore which features non-Western, non-urban and thereby potentially primitive elements such as traditions, rituals, peasants and peasant life. Although folklore is supposed to be an expression of a people's character, it is much more a formulation of what city folk prefer to regard as something they have left behind them.

Folk dance
A folk dance performance I attended in the Serbian Popular Theatre in Novi Sad – a modern, clean, white tiled building popularly referred to as the abattoir – offers a good example of such a polished and refined version of the cultural heritage. The folk dance ensemble presented a programme with songs and dance from various parts of Yugoslavia. The intention, according to the programme, was 'to preserve the authentic folk arts of the nationalities and peoples of Yugoslavia'. The stage was not just the setting for song and dance – an implicit story was narrated there as well. This story went: we are Serbs from Slavonia, we wear this kind of clothing, sing this kind of song, dance this kind of dance. We are Serbs from Bosnia, we wear this kind of clothing, sing this kind of song, dance this kind of dance. We are Hungarians from the Vojvodina. And so on. One category followed another, each with its own typical and distinctive features, customs and practices. And above all: no confusion.

The programme staged a friendly peasant life in a clean and pure world. Healthy young boys and girls with rosy cheeks, immaculate costumes without a crease, who smiled at one another in a forced way and nodded their heads towards one another in time to the music. The males are male. They walk past the girls in goose-step, holding their thumbs under their arm-pits to emphasise their broad chests. The girls are impressed. They stand in a row, hitch up their skirts and twirl them from left to right and from right to left with movements as lacking in spontaneity as their girlish screams. Ooh-yoo-yoo! Perfectly timed excitement. A heavily directed mating dance of male and female specimens of the peasant species.

This performance left no room for individuality, character or passion. The choreographies reinforced this impression of a sterile world, consisting of complicated patterns which showed each time how to transform a collection of separate individuals into perfectly coordinated groups: rapidly gyrating circles that scatter and combine again, rows that become entangled before dispersing into rotating couples. And if a single individual became separated from the group, it was as a pastiche: a bride, a bridegroom, a seductive girl, a young shepherd.

So-called authentic rituals, accompanied by so-called archaic song, were carried out during the performance. The women's singing was nasal and shrill, while the men produced a noise something like the bellowing of an ox. Exotic, strange activities that in this context meant no more than themselves: 'this is where an ancient, traditional ritual is being performed'.

Incidentally, I did not have the impression that the audience seized the prolonged invitation to see the exotic, stylised and sterile world on the stage as a reflection of their own world, or even of that of their parents or grandparents. Someone did whisper to me 'these are our ancient songs and dances', but that was all the person in question had to say on the subject. The audience was extremely enthusiastic, but the enthusiasm was more about the singing and dancing relatives who could be seen in the company than about any happy recognition of the *Volksgeist*. I was pleased to note that it was the slip-ups in the dance productions that the audience enjoyed the most. A headscarf that came loose in the whirl of a dance and swept over the stage, and the moment when the hat beneath it started to wobble ominously. A dancer who just missed another dancer's hand and risked going off the tracks in a rapid round dance. And the most applause went to the *tamburica* player who got lost in a solo and could not resume the thread quickly.

Ethnography

Other workshops where being a Serb is crafted to middle-class standards are ethnographic writings and the ethnographic museums. Just as order and ethnic purity have top priority in the folk dance performance described above, ethnographies almost exclusively present their own world as a mosaic of separate peoples and groups, each of whose special characteristics are described with great precision and attention to detail, but between which hardly any lateral connections are allowed to exist.[31] The ethnographic journals are full of hundreds of articles with titles like 'Several striking Christmas rituals among the Croats in the village of Golubinci', or 'Several specific details from the marriage rituals in the village of Morović in Srem and an analysis of the songs that are sung on that occasion'. Ethnographers who go further than strict description opt almost without exception for structuralism in its most formal versions,[32] not in the last place because these theories provide an opportunity to introduce a wider context without the need to take account of human beings in all their complexity. Questions bearing on the mutual relations between different ethnic groups, mixing, for example, are still to a large extent anathema, even in a province like the Vojvodina, where no less than twenty-six recognised ethnic minorities not only coexist but also interact. 'That is politics', I was told when I asked a colleague why there were no ethnographic studies of inter-ethnic interaction, 'we do not go in for that here'.

The representation of the 'spirit of the people' reaches almost surreal proportions in the Ethnographic Museum in Novi Sad. Dresses, coats and shoes of peasants from the Vojvodina, everyday clothing until recently, have been given a thorough going-over at the dry cleaner's before ending up on display in shiny showcases, aesthetically highlighted as the exotic remnants of a past that remains unspecified except for the fact that it is *past*. TRADITIONAL FOLK COSTUME. AN OLD SPADE. A PEASANT WAGON. If you visit the main market of Novi Sad, which is situated right behind the museum, on market days you can see similar if not identical dresses, coats and shoes walking around. What do you suppose a peasant woman's daughter thinks when she joins a school trip to the big city, visits the ethnographic museum, and sees her mother's or grandmother's dress hanging in a gleaming showcase to illustrate a dim and distant past?

Turbo-folk music
Perhaps the clearest expression of the concern to keep folklore pure can be found in the heated debates on the phenomenon of the *novakompono-vana narodna muzika*, literally 'newly composed folk music', which is as popular as it is hated. Unlike folklore, this turbo-folk is shamelessly commercial mass production. Both the text, music and visual presentation are an amalgam of West and East, of traditional and modern, of domestic and foreign. Traditional folk melodies accompany texts which refer to such present-day phenomena as foreign currency, weekend romances, tractors and bio-energy. Alternatively, a Germanic-sounding *šlagerska melodija* may accompany songs celebrating the place of birth, or even nostalgia for the traditions that are no more. Heavily sentimental texts about treachery and lost friendships are orchestrated like the cheery, swinging rumbas and cha-cha-chas of the Miami Sound Machine. Long-legged peroxide chanteuses in revealing dresses with plunging necklines sing the whining, deeply oriental love songs (*sevdahlinke*). The producers of this genre are not remotely interested in authenticity or the spirit of the people. All that matters is glitter, glamour and gushing emotion.

The *novakomponovana narodna muzika* music is hated by purists of every kind. For supporters of ethnic purity it is an unacceptable fusion. For those who want to keep folklore free of foreign taint it is too oriental. For those who favour the views on taste of the civilising ideal, it is too commercial and tasteless. Everyone hates the *novakomponovana narodna muzika*, and the violence of their reactions is astonishing. They refer to the absence of durable values, the lack of creativity and originality, they talk about plagiarism, and they speak disapprovingly of the presence of Spanish, Greek, Alpine and other foreign influences.[33] The music is described as scandalous, a disease of the mind, pseudo-music, kitsch, and musical padding.[34] It is interesting that oriental sounds are the object of particularly harsh criticism. Complaints were expressed about the number of Bosnian *sevdalinke* on Radio Belgrade, which posed a threat to the Serbian character of the programmes.[35] Another critic commented:

> The music contains elements which are entirely foreign to our mentality [...]. Oriental ballast, full of meretricious ornaments and inappropriate arabesques, which is completely foreign to our folk music. [...] under those corrupting influences, all our people, from peasants and workers to intellectuals [...] are no longer capable of enjoying the popular, genuinely authentic and sound folk music, music whose beauty lies precisely in its simplicity and monumentality, and not in the ballast of the complicated and confused Muslim world, their language, forms of expression and mentality that are not ours.[36]

An article in the daily *Vjesnik* refers to the quasi-arabic character of this music:

> The dominant character of the *novakomponovana narodna muzika* has no relation at all with the Slav musical traditions [...]. It is a case of the (sub)cultural expression of a genetic legacy of the presence of Ottoman armies and administrators in this part of Europe for five hundred years [...]. Those five hundred years of slavery and oppression are clearly expressed in the texts of *novakomponovana narodna muzika* which are primarily about love. Those texts contain oriental, archaic or degraded models for relations which are entirely overshadowed by sadistic and masochistic instincts, and which reveal the deepest strata of the memory of the oppressed raja [Christian resident in the Ottoman empire].[37]

A less condemnatory text puts it like this:

> A large part of the population is somewhere between the village and the city. They are no longer villagers, but they have not yet become city folk. I think I am not wrong in claiming that this music has combined the rural with the urban; it is no longer folk music, but it has not yet become what it should be: a music which – as an artistic form – is self-conscious, which is aware of its endeavour and of its existence [...]. Still, a people is like its songs.[38]

Several critical scholars[39] who asked themselves why this music gives rise to so much fierce indignation[40] conclude that the *novakomponovana narodna muzika* is a pitilessly accurate reflection of the social transformations that have taken place in Yugoslavia since the war.

This view is shared by Dejan Kršić.[41] In an attempt to clarify his view of the phenomenon of the *novakomponovana narodna muzika*, he states categorically:

> If the Israelis send someone to the Eurovision Song Festival, they make no bones about sending Ofra Haza, who sings songs from Yemen, of all places. But Yugoslavia, which is frightened of appearing underdeveloped, will never send someone like Lepa Brena [the most popular singer of *novakomponovana narodna muzika*], while you can already see how a group of foreigners like the 3 Mustaphas, for example, run off with Yugoslav folk music! [...] In the West they regard that music as exotic, and of course that cannot have any connection with us. [...] We are simply frightened, frightened of the terrible spectre that walks and bears the name 'the Balkans' – everyone is frightened of *janjeća čorba* [lamb's soup], of *musaka* and *baklava*, but still, secretly, they all tuck into this food, lick their fingers and cry out for 'More! More! More of this wild man's food!' [...] Everything which shows our real nature, and the culture that is really ours, is primarily a source of shame to us.[42]

Other stories about the same world

Fear of the terrible spectre that goes by the name of 'the Balkans'. 'Everything which shows our real nature, and the culture that is really ours, is primarily a source of shame.' Kršić's formulation reveals how important more or less incidental comments can be regarding people's motivations. This determination of a false bottom, of a reality behind the reality that dominates everyday life, coincides with the story in which my discussion partners have invested so much, the story that says 'we are a modern European world' as something false, unreal and incomprehensible. Kršić's observation also points to an important motive behind the exaggerated extent to which the people of Novi Sad try to purify their world of the primitive: fear and shame about 'who they really are'.

All the same, a question immediately arises in connection with these statements. How do lamb's soup, *baklava* and other greasy foods achieve the status of defining 'who we really are'? Why is *novakomponovana narodna muzika* 'the culture that is really ours'? And why is what is 'genuinely ours' so terrifying and shameful? Whose definitions of reality and unreality are being used here, and whose views of shame and pride? In other words, is it not simply that one story is being exchanged for the other?

I could never have realised the importance of Kršić's comments if I had not been confronted from the start with incidental remarks, casual comments, jokes and other marginalia conveying a very different story about the world in which my discussion partners live. The intensity with which they strove to live a middle-class life could not disguise a gnawing doubt about that life-style. Uncertainty about the place of Serbia in the community of civilised countries seeped into virtually every conversation, every action, every glance. Almost all my discussion partners issued contradictory statements like the ones provided by Dejan Kršić: 'Of course you don't stick to the rules and you mess around with this and that', 'of course we're in the Balkans, where nothing proceeds as it should and where nothing will ever change', 'of course there's nothing more delicious than bread with lard and cayenne pepper, or a roasted pig's head to pick at', 'of course there's nothing better than to throw away your money with a big party', 'of course we are temperamental and warm and know how to receive guests, while you in the West are cold and inhospitable', 'of course a Gypsy orchestra is much better than a classical concert'. This story, 'we are residents of the Balkans', could crop up in the most unexpected and everyday situations and discussions. The butcher in my neighbourhood in Novi Sad, for example, who had no plastic gloves but laid the meat on the scales with his immaculately clean but ungloved fingers, excused himself by saying: 'This is the Balkans'. The fact that buses and trains never ran on time, the inefficiency of the urban bureaucracy, the long queues in the post office, were all dismissed with the words 'five hundred years under the Turks' (*petsto godina pod Turcima*) to indicate a supposed condition of underdevelopment which was simply part and parcel of the country and its people. In other words, the attempt to present to the world the appearance of a modern European society was accompanied by a never-ending flow of common-sense comments to the effect that 'of course we know that this *fini ljudi* nonsense isn't for real, that we know its limitations, that in the last resort we aren't really like that'.

The terms with which this civilisation debate[43] is conducted in Novi Sad imply that the world can be broken down into two clear-cut, irreconcilable halves: a primitive world and a civilised world. On the basis of the discussion so far, we can present the main categories of these two mutually opposite clusters of stories as follows

primitive	*civilised*
rural	urban
peasant	middle-class
wild	civilised
uncontrolled	controlled
wasteful	economical
Balkan	European
oriental	Western
backward	modern
traditions (*tradicija*)	culture (*kultura*)

The clarity suggested by these terms (see introduction) does not correspond to the actual situation. Everyone in the city feels the pressure to make an uncompromising, unambiguous choice for civilisation, for control, for Europe and the West. The imperious tone with which the authors of the etiquette manuals urge their readers to conform to the rules of correct behaviour is one example, and so are the definitions of national character which could be seen in the folklore. Within the terms on which the civilisation debate is conducted, the option for Europe is bound to be a rejection of the lack of control, of the *primitivci*, of the peasants and the Balkans. 'The final paradox of the search for purity is that it is an attempt to force experience into logical categories of non-contradiction', Mary Douglas once said, 'But experience is not amenable and those who make the attempt find themselves led into contradiction'.[44] Contradictions. That is putting it mildly as far as Serbia is concerned. Opting for civilisation, for control and for Europe in a society in which the urban population has expanded explosively since the Second World War, soon comes to imply being ashamed of one's own background, a denial of one's own childhood, parents and relatives, and, as we shall see in the next chapter, of essential attributes of being Serbian. Therefore unambiguous choices are not made. To remove the impression that people in the civilisation debate take up fixed and unchanging positions, I shall provide a few portraits of personalities I came across in my fieldwork in the hope that they will throw some light on the variety of positions that can be taken up in this debate.

Vuk Konjević, a painter, had a long beard and long, dark hair, in accordance with the latest Serbian fashion. He looked a bit like the saints with their curly beards that he so keenly admired on the Serbian frescoes. He was a handsome man, although he was irritating and boring when he drunkenly told me about the Balkans as the cradle of Western civilisation. There had not been anything new since the Greeks and Byzantium, he claimed. 'What about the Renaissance?" I asked him. Wrong. The Romans, the Renaissance, and everything that came after it, were all nothing but plagiarism. The Greeks, especially Byzantium, were the real thing, the place where it all started. Tibet, that was an example of a different, *original* culture. But the West, the West was nothing but plagiarism.

Baltazar Schulteiss (the Germans constituted a substantial minority in prewar Novi Sad) appears in Aleksandar Tišma's novel *Suspicion and Trust* as the incarnation of a style of argument that became very familiar to me. Returning to the city that he and his fellow collaborators had been forced to leave at the end of World War II, he had few positive remarks to say about Novi Sad or the Serbs who were in control. 'Since his arrival here, he was disappointed by the clear and pronounced pleasure with which Milan [his Serb host and former acquaintance] vegetated in this Novi Sad, that in Baltazar's eyes was a city in decay which had sunk to the level of the most backward place in Europe and the world since the expulsion of the Germans and the rise to power of uncultivated proletarians [...]. What he had already noted in Vienna, but much more here, was that the city of his childhood had retrogressed, was in decay, and had collapsed into lawlessness, chaos and poorly organised activity, into an unjustifiable idling, into idle chatter over beer – bad beer, and coffee – primitive muddy coffee made in Turkish pans. But Milan Stepanov, the shining example of that backwardness and decay, one of its perpetrators and victims, sat cheerfully blinking, slumped in an arm chair on the verandah of the guild house he had inherited, with children who fawned on him and learnt irresponsible loafing from him to become – no doubt about it – just as guilty a victim as he was. Baltazar had come to this house to help and to rescue [...]; but Milan (and it was in his children's interests at the time, and thus in his own too) was barely interested in his efforts, assumed a kind-hearted, reconciliatory, nonchalant attitude, and left Baltazar alone with all the efforts and blows to which Milan turned a blind eye with aristocratic disdain, as if he was a rich man instead of a second-rate school teacher saddled with an irresponsibly large family.'[45]

Dragan Svilarović, scion of one of the prestigious ancient Serb families, wanted to break completely with 'those Serbs' because of the war. Dragan was one of the Serbs who could not see the expulsion of the *Volksdeutschen*, the 'most active and orderly sector of the population', as anything but a stupid mistake by the Communists. At the start of my fieldwork he criticised me (in a very subtle way, but barely hiding his satisfaction at reprimanding the ignorant Westerner) for my interest in the events connected with the Gypsy orchestra. In his view, it represented exactly what is primitive and exotic in Serb society. He phoned me to ask for advice: he would be leaving the country shortly and his friends abroad had asked him to take a few cassettes with Gypsy music. Well, since *I* was the expert in that field, and he claimed never to listen to it nor to have any idea of it, it would be nice if I could advise him on which cassettes and which Gypsy orchestra he should buy, or better still, if I would be prepared to record some items for him from my own music collection.

Dragan Svilarović was thrown into utter panic by the outbreak of the war and the subsequent mobilisation. He had already been through the trauma of making the acquaintance of his primitive fellow countrymen and of a soldier's life during military service. His only defence was to deny that he had anything to do with this war, these primitive tribal wrangles. He shut himself up in his study, read Goethe, and reflected on plans to assume the German surname of his Czech mother so that he would not have to bear the unmistakably Serb surname Svilarović for the rest of his life.

Later he fled the country and sent me letters full of nostalgia for Novi Sad.

'Where would a Westerner like you place us on the scale of primitive and civilised? No, you can be honest about it.' Goran Plavšić, ethnographer, kept asking me this question, even after I had made it clear to him that I considered it a stupid one. What authority did we have to draw up any universal scale of gradations of primitiveness and civilisation? Small talk in the staff room of the ethnological museum, with coffee and endless cigarettes. Satisfied and approving nods from the others at my reply. Exactly. Who can decide? The West again, no doubt? But Goran, I now realise, was not looking for pedantic courtesies or conventional pleasantries. He wanted to know what I really thought. He kept on asking, and returned to the point again and again. 'I know that you don't believe in a scale like that, but still, what do you think of the level of civilisation here in Novi Sad compared with Amsterdam?' Goran did not relinquish his belief in a scale of gradations of primitiveness and civilisation, not when the world around him caught fire.

Jasna Kuzmanov, who works as a civil servant in the city, invited me to the traditional Sunday lunch and served a roasted pig's head. 'You can't leave without trying roasted pig's head, because someone who wants to find out about us has to have eaten it.' Not that they ate it themselves all that often: in fact, I suspected that they had never prepared it before and didn't really know how to do it either, because the cleft head that proffered me its deathly smile from the platter was greasy, tasteless and rare.

I thought it was a practical joke against me and my anthropological explorations. Jasna, like many others, was very interested in the impressions that I gained of her country and her people. I had told her a week or so earlier about the Fellini-like scenes at the annual market in Šabac and described the big party tent to her, where rosy-cheeked peasants with trilby hats were served roast pig's head while a voluminous topless dancer wearing nothing but a goose-feather tanga slip circulated among the rough wooden tables to the sounds of a Gypsy orchestra. Not yet completely at home with the local sensitivities, I believe I said something about cannibalism. So now they were serving me pig's head. I thought I could regard this meal as a comic commentary on what I had previously said, so I greeted the dead head with loud cries of undisguised horror, soon followed by her two young children. This was not appreciated. The mood changed. Leaving the pig's head untouched was likely to be interpreted as an insult. To compromise, I was allowed to turn the head away so that it did not keep on looking at me all the time.

Milan Jovanović, one of the Gypsy musicians from the chic *Dukat* restaurant, stated that genuinely civilised people were hard to come by in this city. In order to be civilised, he claimed, you had to have grown up in a rich family where there was never any lack of money. Only then could you behave naturally as a *fin čovek*. Novi Sad was full of peasants with money who pretended to be important, and that was something completely different. He had nothing against that, mind, but they did it in what was obviously the wrong way. Well, he had no need to explain that to me, because I already had seen it by now in the bars. He did not want to be a *fin čovek* so much as a *dobar čovek* (a good person); but then he regaled me with an interminable story about the wealth of his father and grandfather, who had travelled around the world as musicians, and about the blue suit with a white shirt that he wore because his father and grandfather had done so too. 'It's not an act!' he emphasised.

Radovan Radović, a Serb member of parliament, believes that the Serbs suffer from a Europe complex. In a speech to the Serb parliament he stated: 'If we didn't have that complex, we wouldn't be concerned about that blockade [the trade embargo]. We think that European children are born in primary school, and that we are of lesser value, which makes us continually dependent on Europe. But it's absolutely not true. I've often been in

Europe, I've seen Europeans and their children. And when I look at those children, I'm convinced that you could never teach them more than sixty-five phrases in Latin, and I even doubt whether you could ever teach them how to measure the integral length of a graph. That is why I will never entertain the idea that any people at all are superior to us Serbs.'[46]

When I asked Dragana Divjaković, who runs an art gallery, about the image of Gypsies in the naïve painting for which Yugoslavia is famous, she dismissed the question with a wave and a sniff. Quasi-rhetorically, she wondered when a researcher would come from Europe to investigate contemporary painting in Serbia. She was convinced that it would not be out of place in the most famous salons in Paris, but it was being kept out by a conspiracy of the Western arbiters of artistic excellence. 'You keep on condemning us to that awful folklore!'

None of these people opts unconditionally for Europe or for the Balkans. The complaints about the Serbs by the German betray an implicit but unmistakable longing and jealousy; the descendant of an old Serb family who does not want a Serb surname any more writes strange, nostalgic letters about Novi Sad from abroad, a practical joke – or was it a joke? – with a pig's head to express what is authentically Serbian unexpectedly turned sour, the words of a member of the Serb parliament still reflect the formerly unassailable respect for European civilisation, and the painter who, fired by his nationalist feelings, accused the civilised West of plagiarism by situating the origin of everything in the Balkans; in an ingenious fashion, he too has managed to suspend the irreconcilable contradictions between Europe and the Balkans, and can now claim to belong to both.

These vignettes are intended to emphasise that, when my discussion partners distinguished between the primitive and the civilised, they were not only engaged in creating a 'We' and a 'They' group, they were also trying to reduce the confusion in the extremely contradictory stories which they tell about themselves. The outbreak of the war brought those divisive ambivalences in how my discussion partners saw themselves out into the open.

I shall go into this in more detail in the next chapter, which focuses on Thoden van Velzen's suggestion[47] that major social changes (like war) can be analysed by analogy with mechanisms like those described in psychoanalysis as periods of weakness in the social system. At such times, latent forces that are normally hidden may emerge to the surface. I shall show how the subterranean reservoir of people's images of themselves to which I have referred again and again in this chapter – a legacy of hundreds of years of subjection, as the Serb history books never tire of repeating, to more powerful and populous nations – was broken open by the war.

2 Borderland, Warzone

Novi Sad, Wednesday 26 June 1991. Terribly hot. In the daytime with K. and N. to the Danube. The war is announced by a drunkard on the Danube quay. A bottle of rakija in his hand, he calls upon the passers-by to join in the struggle. A Gypsy who walks by confirms his drunken message: war. The drunkard comes up later and offers us a drink. 'Courageous tourists', he says, 'to go on holiday in a country at war'. To restaurant *Dukat* in the evening.

The war was announced by a drunkard. I can still see him staggering along the Danube promenade. I'd sought the shade of willows and poplars on that June day with a couple of visitors who had dropped in on their way back to the Netherlands. We were down by the waterside, he was up there on the dyke. A middle-aged man, tangled hair, his belly protruding, his crumpled shirt hanging out of his clumsily fastened trousers. His hands up in the air, he waves a bottle of liquor. Paralytic. 'The war's begun!' 'To arms!' 'It's war!' I can no longer remember the emotion in his call, whether it was fearful or joyful. At first I had no idea what he was shouting, it was far off and it took some time for me to understand the words. I can still see a couple of boys, giggling as they cycle around the man on their bikes, the spokes dazzling in the sun. He ignores them, but the boys, on the alert despite their teasing, maintain a distance. A couple of passers-by look back, perplexed. Perhaps they have already heard the news and do not think this drunkard's shouts appropriate. But perhaps they don't know yet and are annoyed by this public display of drunkenness and disorderliness. A man with a transistor radio comes along the waterside and I ask him if I've understood it properly. Yes, yes. With a grin he says that the army has occupied the border with Slovenia, that the tanks have driven into the streets, that there's been some fighting, dead and wounded.

A drunkard announces the war, but that is all that changes. Nothing else to indicate that the war has just begun. It is sunny and warm, very pleasant to sit under the trees by the riverside on a folding chair. And it stays that way. Just as the Danube simply flows on, and the castle standing on the other side of the river just continues to stand there. As if nothing is happening. War had broken out, and I have to admit that I just stayed there in the shade of the river bank, without any special thoughts or feelings as far as I can recall. In retrospect, knowing what the war would bring, it is astonishing that there are no other jottings in my diary for the 26th of June except the extract cited above. No profound reflections on war and peace. No report of busy activities to chart the reception of the war among my informants. Not even a sign of concern or anxiety. But the completely irrelevant remark that it was a Gypsy who walked past and confirmed the drunkard's words. After hearing the news that war had broken out, I don't believe I thought much about it except something like 'well!' or 'be at home to see the 5 o'clock news'. I can't even remember it properly.

War. Ever since my arrival in Novi Sad, an alarming series of incidents with dead and wounded had taken place in Croatia. Slovenia and Croatia had announced independence months earlier, and it was obvious that they did not intend to revise their opinions. War was in the air. The question 'Is war going to break out?' in people's discussions had changed to the question 'Has it already broken out?' weeks before. In May, soon after the bloody events in the village of Borovo Selo in Eastern Slavonia, the question 'Has war broken out?' had already cropped up in a conversation with friends. We were surprised at the question and had commented that it was idiotic to suppose that the war had to have a clearly marked starting point. As if it was only a war after someone had said so, as if a war only exists after an unambiguous declaration of war. Besides, we argued, who was supposed to decide when it was war? The newspaper? The politicians? The well-painted lips of the impeccably bourgeois newscaster on Television Belgrade who had been telling us the most brazen and ugly lies and propaganda all these months? We had come to regard the question as meaningless ages ago: you *know* once war has broken out. And yet, somehow or other it kept cropping up in conversation. When a Macedonian soldier of the federal army in Split was lynched, when a blood-bath was perpetrated in Borovo Selo, when there were shoot-outs in the Plitvice region and Slavonia, each time the question came up again: 'Is it war now?' Although we knew better, it remained important to know exactly where peace comes to an end and war begins.

At last, this drunkard's call to arms meant that it was war. It had been said, and it would be repeated interminably all day long. By the newspaper, by the politicians, by the Television Belgrade newscaster, and by the drunken clientèle in the *Dukat* restaurant, where I went that evening as usual to be with 'my' Gypsy orchestra. Everyone said it. Amazed. Incredible. Angry. Frightened. But also to realise that saying 'it's war' did not cause an earthquake, that saying those words didn't cause a cloud to pass in front of the sun, or a squadron of planes to appear on the horizon.

My notes on the first days after the announcement of war contain a strikingly large number of references to drunkenness.

> 28 June 1991: Kets [a bar] is packed out. Met Marković, a journalist for Novi Sad TV and blind drunk. Completely devastated by the war violence. 'I support Yugoslavia, but it doesn't exist any more', he says.

> 29 June 1991: Had an evening appointment with V., but he didn't show up. Called today to apologise. He had got completely drunk.

> 1 July 1991: Zorka comes running up to me, her eyes swollen from crying, and is about to burst into tears again. 'How concerned your mother will be about you', she says. Then she bursts into a fit of rage and snaps at me, asking me to explain how the West can believe all those lies from Slovenia and Croatia. Then the tears start. She insists that I drink two generous glasses of brandy.

> 2 July 1991: Stevica [the accordion player] hasn't shown up at work for two days. The 'tart' [the owner of the restaurant where they play] came, wafted on a cloud of perfume, to ask where 'the colleague' was. 'We don't know', the others replied, but later they told me he'd been drinking for two days.

The war takes root in Croatia, the violence carries on, and the TV screens carry pictures that grow more atrocious every day. Mobilisation. Refugees and front-line troops come back with stories from the war zones. Someone reassured me with the remark that I need not worry. 'Nothing ever happens in Novi Sad', he said, 'this city is simply too petit bourgeois for war'. But his remark couldn't alter the fact that the world of the *fini ljudi* had already disappeared.

The return of the wild man

The violence, the bloodshed, the destruction, the emotions which came to dominate the news in the summer of 1991 seemed to drive the discourse on Novi Sad as being part of the Balkans from half-concealment to the surface of public life. My discussion partners increasingly made remarks to the effect that the total chaos, lack of control and wildness that had spread at such a pace in this part of Europe were due simply to the primitive character of the peoples of the Balkans. 'You see', people said to one another, 'you see, it's the eternal, unchanging Balkans, the land of blood vengeance, civil war and fighting between tribes, where the language of violence and the emotions has always had more appeal than the language of reason'. At first remarks like these seemed to be expressions of disbelief and astonishment. Later they took on a more serious tone.

Nowhere was the collapse of the discourse 'we are a part of the civilised world' clearer than in the letters and articles to the press in which Serbs tried to understand and explain what was going on around them. There are desperate appeals to listen to reason:

> *Reason is the victor*
> I beg you to print my letter as an appeal to all peace-loving and decent citizens to raise their voices on behalf of peace, liberty, unity and friendship. The achievement of national, religious and territorial interests through violence and the sacrifice of innocent men, women and children only leads to more hatred, vengeance and poverty. There is no prize that is worth so much and that can give mothers back their children. Weren't the lessons of the Second World War enough? And these stupid politicians who are sending our children to their deaths? I guarantee you: tomorrow, if peace is restored, you will see them organising their parties again in their palaces. You won't see them at our sons' graves.
>
> Mothers of whole Yugoslavia! Raise your voices against those stupid, uncultured and uncivilised people! Take one another to peace meetings. We must all be able to live with each other as good neighbours, because otherwise there is no civilisation, no liberty and no free market economy. Why make war if we can agree to live together?
>
> The intelligentsia is the foundation of every people. Do not allow that foundation to be undermined by stupid politicians! We don't need any outsiders to bring us peace, we must make peace by ourselves. There is no need to look for a culprit. There is no culprit, because there are innumerable factors that contribute to the evil that is overwhelming us now.
>
> There is no problem that sensible, civilised and tolerant people cannot solve. Reason is the greatest victor. All the rest is defeat.[1]

Others appeal to the traditional tolerance of the Vojvodina Serbs:

> *Stop stirring up a war*
> We protest against the policy that determines the programmes on Novi Sad Television. Recently those programmes have been characterised by

incitement to war and extreme nationalist broadcasts [...] Programmes of this kind do not contribute at all to a healthy patriotism. They reinforce the negative image that Serbia already has in Europe and will do immeasurable damage to Serbia. Public incitement to war and supporting religious and nationalist feelings of hatred and revenge is not in the spirit of the peace-loving and democratic traditions of Serbia. We call upon Novi Sad Television to respect the most elementary standards of decency and level of culture and civilisation of the citizens of the Vojvodina, to whom these broadcasts are primarily addressed, and we want to emphasise the well-known Vojvodinian tradition of tolerance and love of peace with regard to other nationalities and persuasions.[2]

Many are unable to see the war as anything but a return to total wildness. When Lord Carrington is appointed as peace negotiator, there are bitter comments on his previous diplomatic activities in Africa. 'Lord Carrington has already managed to calm down the heads of tribes before [...]. He is an expert in tribal disputes', is the comment on his appointment in *Borba*;[3] 'even in Africa people are laughing at us; even there they follow us in calling their troubles "Balkanisation"'.[4] Two other examples of commentary:

From The Hague to New York
After the anger and irritation with which Lord Carrington met the chairpersons of the Yugoslav tribes in The Hague [...] he is back with us, with a smile and with the optimism that befits an English gentleman when he is on safari among the 'barbarians', who are so keen on wiping one another out but are not insensitive to presents from all over the world.[5]

I want to be a Bush Negro
When I consider the monstrous behaviour of some Serb circles and those in power, I am ashamed to be a Serb. I shall therefore do all within my power to ensure that I get a different national status after my passport number: as far as I'm concerned, it may be Libyan, Angolan, Iroquois, Bush Negro, but never Yugoslav or Serb.[6]

There are masses of comments in which the *fini ljudi* describe this war as an anachronism, as a return to the past, as nineteenth-century, medieval, prehistoric, an impossibility on the eve of the twenty-first century. They make comparisons with the Thirty Years' War in Germany – 'the cities were besieged then as well, but at least they had the decency to allow the citizens to leave' (*Vreme*). Others make comparisons with the Wild West:

It reminds me of the Indian attacks on stagecoaches that drove through
their territory. If you drive along the motorway from Zagreb to Belgrade
today it's not much different... Historians will eventually write about how
a few tribes in the Balkans butchered one another, tore out one another's
eyes, and cooked one another on the spit.[7]

Some try to understand the outburst of violence in terms of a disease: the
cruelties and the urge to destroy are taken to be the results of madness,
drugs, alcohol, or disease:

I am not in favour of people sending us foreigners to keep us apart and
calm us down, but I can imagine how astonished people are at seeing a
barbarian country behaving inhumanly at the end of the twentieth century. And we are not barbarians, that's exactly the problem. But in that case,
what is poisoning us? It is as if no one is normal any more and people can
manipulate us as if we are crazy. We all seem to be ill. I'm not at the front,
I just stay at home in my room and type on my typewriter, but I'm ill too.
And what about the ones who send people to the front, or the ones who
are already there? My friends, doctors, talk about children being killed, losing their legs, their arms. It is all going on around us and everyone sees es-
caping into indifference as the only way out. Just as in Hitler's day when
millions of people died and at the same time people organised parties,
drank champagne, went to the opera in occupied Paris, and Göring listened to Beethoven. I think it's a terrible parallel, and I wonder where it
will end. The newspaper, the television, everyone of importance in this situation all bear an incredible responsibility and I'm not sure that they are
aware of its full consequences.[8]

Above all, however, the source of all the trouble is located in 'the primitive', 'the Balkans'. An essay by the writer Dragan Velikić talks about
the unchangeable primitive character of both Serbs and Croats:

Half a century later, the volcano of primitiveness has erupted in
Yugoslavia which is destroying Pompeii after Pompeii throughout the
country. The Serbs are not ashamed of their barbarians, they see the
strength of their ethnos and the triumph of their myths in barbarism.

According to Velikić, the Croats do all they can to get rid of their barbarians, but they cannot deny their own primitive character either, because the primitive is the source of their vitality. The Dinaric world,
which was divided into a Croat and a Serb part a long time ago, has re-

mained 'in everyone's veins', and both groups – 'still warm from wildness', writes Velikić – bear witness anew every fifty years to their genuine origins, their real belief: primitiveness. They take up arms and, instead of heading for the light, race in the other direction into darkness. A 'conspiracy of primitives' must be the basis of the tragic course of events, he concludes: 'They were successful in 1945, and I'm afraid that they are going to pull it off again this time – in 1991'.[9]

These attempts to find a point of comparison for the war seemed to reach an important turning point in November 1991, when Vukovar fell into Serb hands after months of bombardment. The *fini ljudi* were appalled by so much destructive force so close to home. When I went out in the street or into the shops, I did not hear anybody repeating the propaganda texts about 'liberation' and 'resurrection of Serb Vukovar', as was the case with so much other propaganda, which was repeated as a fact three days or so after it had been broadcast. All the same, that was not the post-Vukovar change I am referring to here. Before Vukovar the violence and destruction was blamed on (specified or non-specified) others, but after the pictures of the complete destruction of the city I was more often struck by the fact that the speaker did not distance himself from 'primitives' or 'peoples of the Balkans'. Homo Balkanicus, a subspecies of Homo Sapiens, had resurfaced in the annihilation of that city on the Danube. The middle class of Novi Sad might still only cherish their Serb identity and authenticity in folklore and museums, but *he* was not yet behind the glass of a showcase or in some museum, and had proved that fact a mere seventy kilometres up river.

'Aggression is simply in our genes', was one of the recurrent comments that I heard. Or: 'We Serbs have always been a warrior people'. An acquaintance made a wry joke that Europe 'must declare our country a reservation for pathological madmen'. People were ashamed when they remembered the comments that had been made here when the revolution broke out in Romania. At the time everyone had regarded the violence and chaos as a 'logical' consequence of the primitive state of that Gypsy country (*ciganska zemlja*). Nothing like that could ever happen here...

A strict foreman from the West

Weighing it all up, there were two factors which particularly struck me in the reactions to the outbreak of the war. The first reaction was the one described above as the return of the wild man of the Balkans: the apparent inability of the people I met to distance themselves from the violent course of events. 'We are simply wild', 'It's just that we're barbarians', 'we're uncivilised', people said time and again. The fact that people also said the war was the fault of others, of the politicians, of the colonists, the *primitivci*, the *balkanci*, the Communists, the Croatian fascists, the Germano-Vatican-Islamic pact, or of anyone else, did not affect the argument 'we're simply barbarians' in any way. In other words, these were the reactions of people who, against their better judgement, had hoped to belong to the civilised world, but who were now confronted with what they had always known.

A second striking reaction to the outbreak of the war was the attitude to the West. Sometimes I had a strong impression that this society was engaged in an ongoing dialogue with a strict, disciplined foreman who was situated somewhere in the West. It was as if they felt constantly under European scrutiny and had to justify their actions to Europe all the time. This impression was obviously partly determined by the fact that, as a researcher, I represented that very West. But even in my absence people still seemed to be keenly aware of the attention paid to them by the West. 'The whole world was talking about Yugoslavia again today' were the words used to introduce the latest horrors of the war in the Serb newsreel, or 'the events in Yugoslavia were on the lips of the most important leaders in the world again today'. A regular newspaper feature like *Svet o Nama* (The World on Us) carried extracts from the foreign press every day. In an open letter from eleven professors from the University of Belgrade, the writers expressed their concern at the image of the Yugoslav peoples 'who are regarded today as a barbarian and inferior civilisation':

> Europe will remember us as inhuman, underdeveloped and primitive tribes, as a horde of wild men who butcher one another. [...] This war has ejected us from civilisation, and it will take decennia, and probably longer, to regain our position among the civilised peoples.[10]

The press furnished other examples of 'feeling that one is being watched'. Newspapers and magazines were full of articles with a content and tone like the following:

> It is enough to see which ideas dominated the European media during the last few weeks of the 'sacred war' of the Balkan tribes, who are so proud of their knightly traditions and martial reputation. 'There are no lovely wars, but this one is exceptionally disgusting' – wrote a reporter in the introduc-

tion to a piece of journalism reporting Serb militia who killed prisoners of war with a shot in the back of the head, trucks piled high with mutilated corpses, plundered hotels, shops and houses, the shelling of hospitals and refugee camps... 'This is no gentlemen's war', wrote another war reporter, a British one of course, and he continued 'this is such a dirty war that it's not worth getting killed in it'. People are also talking about the 'drunken' war. Leaders of rival groups are described as 'alcoholics who can't leave the bottle alone'. Commentators note that 'the European peace proposals are rational', but they do not have much chance of success, given that the emotions of nationalism [...] are stronger than reason and logic.[11]

In the eyes of the world, the Yugoslavs will always be crazy wild men who have no place in today's or tomorrow's Europe.[12]

Besides such reactions of shame, there were reactions of a very different kind which can best be described as a radical acceptance of the primitivism which was so looked down upon in the past. The previous chapter contained a few examples of this crass reversal of values: the Serb member of parliament who wanted to shake off the Serbs' inferiority complex with regard to Europe, for example, or the painter who claimed that the origins of European civilisation lay in the Balkans. Vojislav Šešelj – Dr Vojislav Šešelj, as he likes to be called – leader of the radical nationalist party of Serbia, provided a good example of this attitude when he stated to foreign journalists that 'he would love to shoot the UN relief forces and throw them in the river Drina'. Šešelj's wild poses in front of Western cameras are just as much a part of the dialogue with the West as the concern of the professors about Serbia's reputation in Europe.

What accounts for this ashamed but resigned acceptance of a story that states that the people of the Balkans are just wild and belligerent, even by those who claim to embrace the ideals of the *fini ljudi*? What explains the fear of an all-seeing eye that registers every mistake and failure and will never fail to pass a negative verdict: *tiefste Provinz*, wild tribes, backward peasants? It is tempting to understanding the findings detailed above in terms of collective insecurity, identity crisis, collective inferiority complex, or similar psychological mechanisms, and I would certainly not want to rule out the explanatory force of such terms in advance. However, at this point in the present study such terms would confuse the issue rather than clarify it. For instance, there is the question of the sociogenesis of the two clusters of stories that circulate within the Serb community in Novi Sad. In attempting to get to grips with the world around them, why do the people of Novi Sad resort to a discourse that is so uncomplimentary to themselves and their world? How and why have the people of Novi Sad ended up in a discourse in which matters and types of behaviour that they regard as their own are at the same time labelled as objectionable and shameful?

Before dealing with these questions, I must first present a brief survey of the rise and development of Serb nationalism.[13] To a large extent the nationalist movement in Serbia produced the terms which the Serb city folk still apply to themselves and the world they live in. Without a closer look at the complex relation of the Serb nationalists to 'civilised Europe', on the one hand, and their 'Byzantine-Oriental' background, on the other, it is impossible to obtain a proper understanding of the dichotomies and ambivalences which dominate the civilisation debate in Novi Sad today.[14]

Refugees, Grenzer, *peasants and other wild men*

The early history of the steppes and swamps of the Vojvodina is shrouded in obscurity. At any rate, it is clear that the region always had a mixed population with both Slav and Hungarian elements, but the questions of who first arrived in the steppes – the Hungarians or the Serbs –, who were in the majority, who stayed the longest, and who became assimilated or converted are the subject of heated controversy – as seems to be customary in this part of Europe. For a historian who describes the presence of the Serbs in the Vojvodina within the context of Hungarian history, the Serbs are emphatically strangers on Hungarian territory, *Einwanderer* as Anton Hadžić bluntly formulated it at the end of the last century.[15] A work full of nationalist and anti-Hungarian sentiments like Dušan Popović's *Srbi u Vojvodini* (Serbs in the Vojvodina), on the other hand – my main source for historical facts and developments – states that the Hungarians are actually Slavs who have assumed the Hungarian language and culture.[16]

When it comes to understanding the dichotomies and ambivalences in the civilisation debate in Novi Sad, questions of the numerical predominance of one or other group of genes are less important than the fact that the districts which today constitute the Vojvodina were administered for most of their history from Budapest, Vienna and Zagreb. Serbs were a subordinate and peripheral minority on the outermost borders of the multi-ethnic Habsburg state. For centuries it was this factor that deter-

mined power relations in the region. It was also this factor which provided Germans, Hungarians, Croats and other population groups with
whom the Serbs shared their territory with the arguments to represent
the Serbs as an inferior and primitive group and gave them access to the
media with which they could publicise these views. Finally, it was this
factor which forced the Serbs who wanted to escape from their subordi-
nation to adopt strategies, arguments and terms which were borrowed
from the dominant discourse. In other words, the convolutions of my informants in wrestling with the question of whether or not they belonged
to the civilised part of humankind cannot be understood without considering the way in which power relations between Serbs and other groups
in the Vojvodina have arisen and been transformed.

For centuries the Vojvodina formed a part of the Habsburg Empire,
until it was annexed by the Kingdom of Serbs, Croats and Slovenians in
1918. Or rather, it was its outermost border, the ragged edge which had
to be contested time and again with the Turks. It was a vulnerable and
long border, difficult to govern and even more difficult to control. It was
thus the setting for much coming and going: victorious and defeated
armies, colonists and plunderers, garrison soldiers and refugees, mer-
chants and border guards; they all trudged through these muddy plains
and swamps. Some of them stayed, and came to know this world as the
country where – as someone once characterised it to me – it is better to
ask '*u čijoj kući živiš?*' (whose house do you live in?) than the usual '*čiji si?*'
(who are you? Literally: to whom do you belong). Houses here always offer a more durable and reliable point of orientation than their inhabitants.

On two occasions in history there seems to have been a virtually total
depopulation of this area.[17] The campaigns of conquest of the Turkish
Ottoman armies[18] in the first half of the seventeenth century drove almost the entire Hungaro-Slav population further north. A century and a
half later the movement was in exactly the opposite direction: an exodus
of groups who had settled here during the period of Turkish rule and
moved out in the wake of the defeated Turkish armies. 'After the period
of Turkish rule, there was nothing but a faint shadow left of what had
once been flourishing South Hungarian country', Szentklavan states. 'No
plough worked its furrow, no garden produced vegetables, no agricultural land was ablaze with variegated blossoms, no elegant towers rose
above dazzling villages to brighten up the landscape. The whole area was
a dark, horrible country full of monstrous lakes, gloomy forests and un-
inhabited wildernesses.'[19]

Of course, a description like this can only be a prelude to better times.
The repopulation and colonisation of these areas was tackled seriously in

the eighteenth century under Maria Theresia and Joseph II. It was particularly to Germans from the poor and overpopulated regions like
Ober-Rhein, Frankenland and Hessen that land and resources were
made available to bring the wasteland under cultivation. An explicit role
was played in this process by the idea that the industrious and hard-
working Germans could set an example for other groups.[20] Because it
was not just Germans who set out for the Vojvodina, colonists from
Hungary, Czechia, Slovakia, the Vlach territory, Galicia, Ruthenia and
the Ukraine also tried to build new lives here. Incidentally, there appears
to have been a very high mortality rate among these colonists: most of
the newcomers could take the place of their unfortunate predecessors
who had died from the plague or from the war against the Turks which
kept flaring up. All the same, 'where earlier only the bellowing of wild
oxen had disturbed the uncanny silence, now the sound of church bells
summoned the faithful to God's house.'[21]

The Serbs who entered the Vojvodina came from the south. They
crossed the Danube and the Sava and moved northwards, more often
under compulsion than on their own initiative. Soon after the famous
battle of Kosovo in 1389, when the Christian armies were routed and the
victorious expansion of the Turks in Europe commenced, the historical
sources mention groups of Serbs who sought refuge in these steppes, 'driven by the approaching Turkish Ottoman armies', as popular belief has
it. This theme of 'the flight to the north' was to become a recurrent element in Serb history from then on.[22] Of all these flows of refugees it is
the *Velika Seoba Srba* (The Great Serb Exodus) of 1690 which has gone
down in the annals of Serb history as the most dramatic. It is the story
of a failed campaign against the Turks by the joint Habsburg and Serb
troops, and the subsequent flight of 30,000 Serb families from Kosovo in
fear of the retaliatory expeditions of the Ottoman Turks. Led by patri-
arch Arsenije Crnojević III, they sought refuge in the south-eastern parts
of the Habsburg Empire to wait for better times when they could return
to their home country.

The reception of the refugees by the local Hungarian nobility and
population was nothing if not hostile, according to Popović,[23] and there
were groups of Serb refugees who soon turned round and went back to
Turkish Serbia – a statement which, in terms of Serb historiography, can
safely be regarded as the worst reception imaginable. To emphasise the
centuries of suffering and victimisation of the Serb people, Popović cites
extensively from a letter of 1699 in which an inspector of the Hungarian
Chancellery reports on the Serb refugees who had crossed the border in
large numbers:

This whole people is base and wicked to such an extent that one is justi-fied in saying that they are no more than woodlanders and wild men. They are heathen and sinners, prone to robbery, banditry, murder and all kinds of other wickednesses and crimes. Both the men and the women look for-ward to getting drunk every day, and wherever they go they bring con-tention and quarrelling. This people is mad about weapons. Even the or-dinary folk have a very large number of weapons in their possession. Most of them are schismatics, they hate the Catholics and are the bitterest ene-mies of the religion [...]. This is a people of nomads, they do not usually have a permanent residence, but stay one moment here, another moment there. These people have nothing positive to offer God, country or His Illustrious Highness. They are only interested in leading an easy-going life, wherever they can find it. Whether it is under the Turks or under anoth-er ruler is a matter of indifference to them. [...] Nowhere do they construct anything, but they live in huts and mud hollows made by their own hands so that they can move to another spot when it suits them. They prefer to stay in the woods and hills, where they can lie low and escape with their booty. [...] If they leave those areas, the fields they worked are empty, and they leave nothing behind them except earth and abandoned huts. This is a very base and unprofitable people.[24]

When the peace of Karlovitz was signed in 1699, the definitive border between the Ottoman and the Habsburg Empire was laid down and it was decided to institute the *Militärgrenze*, a long buffer zone between the two Empires. Many Serb refugees settled in the new border zone. In ex-change for the right of religious freedom, the right to choose their own local leaders, the right to cultivate land for their own subsistence, and ex-emption from certain taxes, they carried out services in the defence of the Empire as *Grenzer*. To the dismay of the Hungarian and Croatian nobil-ity, this entire zone came under the direct control of the Emperor in Vienna.

In spite of the advantages for the Habsburg Empire, there can be no doubt that, in their own terms, they had allowed a motley bunch of wild men onto their territory. Even Popović notes that – 'after years of wag-ing war and taking to flight [...] the cultural level of the population was very low, and it was therefore not easy to bring them to order'. The Austrian government was therefore obliged to implement in peacetime the same laws for the Serbs in the *Militärgrenze* which usually were only in force during a war.[25] These laws and regulations (and the first 'at-tempts at civilisation' which can be seen in them) could not prevent the *Grenzer* from rapidly acquiring a reputation as bandits and wild men. 'As a soldier the frontier peasant was difficult to control and discipline', reports historian Barbara Jelavich. 'At first he had been able to collect booty, and he continued to plunder even friendly territories. Frontier bands were also subject to frequent mutiny and desertion.'[26] The volunteer corps, a kind of ad hoc unit composed of *Grenzer*, who also served abroad, had a bad reputation which spread far beyond the limits of the *Militärgrenze*:

> They were called pandours, and in the West people still remember their wildness with a shudder. In 1744 several pandours, who had been taken prisoner by the French, were put on display, and people could pay to see them as something wild.[27]

A wild and martial character continued to influence the image of the Serbs for a long time. A late eighteenth-century travel account describes the Serbs of Slavonia as 'wild', but, the writer adds: 'they are not so backward and stupid as peasants in other countries can be'. Other positive qualities that are mentioned are astuteness, trust in leadership, a strongly developed sense of honour, hospitality, willingness to make sacrifices, a dauntless spirit, and a warrior-like nature. Another traveller from this period comments on the Serbs of the Srem region:

> They have a strong and healthy body that can endure anything, both heat and cold, hunger and thirst, flights by night and long, endless marches by day. This courageous and valiant people seems to have been born for war. Their whole life is cruel, and differs from the life of more refined peoples as heaven from earth! They prefer weapons to all else, with which they practise keenly from early childhood.[28]

Negative terms which recur in the descriptions of the Serbs are: ignorant, superstitious, naïve, strong-drinking and eager to exact vengeance. They were regarded as trouble-makers and plunderers 'who constantly became embroiled in disputes with their neighbours'.[29] Laziness was regarded as the worst feature of the Serbs. 'A people whose needs do not rise above those of animals is always lazy and hostile to work', was the terse verdict of one commentator.[30] 'This people prefers to laze in poverty rather than work for a good life', commented another. Travellers and commentators also noted an 'incredible' lack of interest in the future on the part of the Serbs. The Serb farmers in the Banat region were believed to sow the absolute minimum each year, 'preferring to live from what nature provided for them'. 'They are not concerned about anything, and all their efforts are devoted to producing liquor', remarked another commentator; 'they use manure mainly for their plum orchards in order to be able to produce even more *rakija*, and they pay little or no heed to having a permanent place to stay'.[31]

Notions of Serbhood and romantic nationalism among the Habsburg Serbs

> The houses of the Serbs, their cattle, their coaches and wagons, their saddles and bridles – they are all of the worst sort, worse than among all the peoples with whom our people coexists, even worse than among the Vlach. Their homes are dirty, and their surroundings are dirty.[32]

The word 'our' in this description of the Serb peasants heralds a revolution in the course of the civilisation debate. The speaker here is a certain Djordje Natošević, a Serb who reported on the situation in the Serb villages in South Hungary in 1866. It indicates that it was no longer just the established members of the Habsburg Empire – Germans, Hungarians, Croats and other, usually Western, travellers – who took the floor to announce the phenomenon of 'the Serbs' to the world; in the present case we see how Serbs speak about themselves (or rather, about the 'wild' members of their own group). The word 'our' marks a switch from being scrutinised to self-scrutiny, though self-scrutiny *through the other's eyes*, of course. This phenomenon of Serbs who are viewed and described by other Serbs in terms of the established indicates a development which was to take shape particularly in the nineteenth century,[33] and which has remained undiscussed so far: the rise of a Serb urban middle class. As we have seen, substantial Serb communities had developed outside the *Militärgrenze*, consisting of traders, craftsmen, higher officers, clerics and teachers.[34] Novi Sad had a population of around 13,000 at the beginning of the nineteenth century. 'The largest Serb city in the world', was how the folklore specialist, researcher in linguistics and language reformer Vuk Karadžic (1787-1864) described the city, and though it does not tell us everything, it gives us some idea of urban Serb society in the nineteenth century. Accounts of this world evoke a frontier town from American Westerns. Every report of unpaved streets covered with mud is matched by a reference to the rustling crinoline of ladies' dresses. For every description of cultivated Serb city folk who engage in *unterhaltovati* in German with punch and coffee, a *konversations-lexicon* within reach, there is a report of Novi Sad as a city where the houses are constructed without any arrangement, or a city with an oriental look.[35] It must have

been a world of enormous contrasts – *biedermeier* and the Balkans – where
the minuet, polka and galop were danced at the large city balls, while in
times of drought the peasants dressed naked young girls (*dodole*) in twigs
and leafage and sent them out into the wilds in the hope that this would
win the favour of the rain gods. A world in which the actors in the Serb
Popular Theatre prepared for the three-hundredth anniversary of the
birth of William Shakespeare while outside the blind bards, accompanying themselves on their one-stringed fiddles, intoned the epic poems of
Serbia's glorious past.[36]

The brand new Serbian middle class stuck closely to the Germano-
Hungarian example. Classes in the grammar schools in Novi Sad were
in German and Latin, and later in Hungarian as well. The rules of proper behaviour were inculcated in accordance with the popular *Deutsches
Sittenbüchlein.*[37] For further study and training the Serbian bourgeoisie
sent their children to the north, to the schools and universities in Szeged,
Budapest, Prague, Bratislava or, if possible, Vienna. 'The extreme snob-
bery of this young bourgeois society which had only just outgrown the
patriarchal and village social structures and life-styles is reflected in the
assumption of everything that was in fashion', is the verdict of Stana
Djurić-Klajn on the Serbian bourgeoisie in the nineteenth century.[38]
Vienna was the example, the highest rung on the ladder of civilisation.
That was where life was lived.

Although the urban Serbs took on a life-style that was largely influenced by a (Central) European model of civilisation, from the early
nineteenth century on there are also signs of a desire for national eman-
cipation and the preservation of a Serb identity. This concern to maintain a Serb identity in the sense of more or less deliberate attempts to
create a 'we group' was not in itself new. The Serbian Orthodox church
had constantly endeavoured to preserve the Serb community from mixing fully with other people in these plains.[39] Retention of identity was a
central point in the negotiations between representatives of the Serbian
Orthodox church and the Habsburg Empire on the settlement of the
Serbs in the *Militärgrenze.* And it was once again on an initiative of the
metropolitan bishop of the Serbian Orthodox church that the first Serb
grammar school was founded in Sremski Karlovci in 1792 with financial support from rich Serb traders, soon followed by the establishment
of a Serb grammar school in Novi Sad in 1811. The first attempts to develop a standardised language – Slavo-Serbian, an artificial language
based on ecclesiastical Slavic – date from the same period. The church
also contributed to the unity and identity of the Serb people by devel-
oping a commemorative cult which kept alive the glorious Serb past,

with its kings, emperors and constant battles with the Turks.[40] Ravanica, a convent in the Fruška Gora, the ridge of hills south of Novi Sad, contained the mummified remains of Czar Lazar, the Serb army commander who had been defeated by the Turks at the famous battle of Kosovo. The blind bards took part in this cult by travelling through the towns and countryside and declaiming their epic poems in every village and hamlet to keep the memory alive of the main figures and events in Serb history.

This concern for the maintenance of Serb identity and unity became linked to a new and much more powerful discourse at the beginning of the nineteenth century: nationalism.[41] The name of the German philosopher Johann Gottfried Herder (1744-1803) circulated in intellectual circles in Vienna, Budapest and Prague and he had an enormous influence on the development of the nationalist movements in Central and Eastern Europe in particular.[42] Herder's philosophy emphasised the organic link between a culture and the natural surroundings in which it flourished. The study of cultures, according to Herder, must give priority to that unicity of cultures and not – as was customary in his day – subordinate the different cultures to large-scale, pre-conceived intellectual frameworks to classify the human race.

This intellectual legacy had an immense impact on the (political) thought of the Habsburg minorities. Until then, the intellectual representatives of the various population groups in the Habsburg Empire, had been educated in the classicist traditions of the Enlightenment. They could only regard what was specific to their group as something primitive and irrational, and therefore as something to be looked down on and to be left behind. Herder provided the argument to regard what was specific to a people as something valuable and worthy of study precisely because it was primitive and irrational. Peter Burke notes that Herder's interest in the specific characteristics of a people coincided with a genuine cult of the wild and the exotic, a movement that he described as '*cultural primitivism* [...] a reaction against the Enlightenment, as typified by Voltaire; against its elitism, against its rejection of tradition, against its stress on reason. The Grimms, for instance, prized tradition above reason, what grew naturally over what was consciously planned, the instincts of the people over the arguments of intellectuals'.[43] In the early nineteenth century we can see how the intellectual vanguard of almost every population group in the Habsburg Empire assimilated Herder's research programme and proceeded to study its own language (and to purify it of foreign words), to write its own history, and to record its own customs and oral traditions; all of these activities were designed to arrive at a reformulation of national identity, what was specific to the people, its *Volksgeist*.[44]

Serb intellectuals were no exception. Herder devoted considerable attention in his work to Slav folklore, and he regarded the epic heroic poems of the Serbs as 'a good example of the *Volksgeist* in action'.[45] They did not miss the point. The Serb folklore and language specialist Vuk Karadžić worked entirely within the romantic nationalist tradition.

It is an irony of fate that Serbs discovered their national *Volksgeist* at a time when, as Burke remarks, '[...] 'artificial' (like 'polished') became a pejorative term, and 'artless' (like 'wild') a term of praise'.[46] The romantic celebration of the wild and the primitive seems to have been very influential on the limits within which the Serbs could develop their notions of Serb identity. Karadžić is a good example of the double programme on which intellectuals with a nationalist orientation worked. He published a collection of Serb heroic poems and achieved great success in Europe with these poems about *hadjuci* (freedom fighters) and the great and glorious medieval empires of the Serbs. Goethe, the brothers Grimm, Walter Scott, Pushkin – as every Serb will tell you today – were interested in these epic poems and extolled them. The reception of Karadžić's work in his own circle, however, shows that at home in a city like Novi Sad the Serb intellectuals had to take into account the sensibilities of the newly-fledged middle class. Their status as city folk was still a novelty for the urban Serbs. The romantic cult of the wild and the undomesticated as the ultimate expression of the *Volksgeist* may have been the done thing among the circles of intellectuals in Vienna or Budapest, but for people who had been forced to put up with the label 'wild' for so long, the romantic cult of the wild, the rejection of reason as false and artificial, and the glorification of the pure and uncorrupted rural life cannot have had much attraction.

Karadžić's idea of taking the ordinary spoken language of the people as the basis for the standardisation of Serbo-Croat met with a lot of opposition from the Serb middle class. In particular, the Serbian Orthodox church and its followers in the Vojvodina stuck to the traditional ecclesiastical Slavic as the basis for literature and cultural development.[47] But Karadžić himself was ambivalent about the romantic cult of the wild as well. The first part of his collection of folk songs, published in 1814, contains a preface in pastoral style, in which the songs are described as 'the songs which are sung by simple souls, naturally and without artifice', and he further explicitly mentions the fact that he had learned them when 'in the happiest conditions known to mortals, I kept sheep and goats'.[48]

However, Burke goes on to state that 'the preface was probably written tongue-in-cheek for the benefit of the educated reader; Karadžić was indignant whenever he was referred to as an uneducated goat-herd and had set his heart on an honorary degree from a German university. *He was not reacting against the rococo, or classicism, or against literacy'.*[49]

The case of Karadžić clearly brings out the emergence of a duality which, as I showed in the previous chapter, still determines thinking about Serb identity. The question of why the people of Novi Sad participate in a discourse about themselves in which matters and forms of behaviour that they regard as characteristic of themselves are at the same time labelled as objectionable and disgraceful seems to find its answer here. The way in which the idea of a Serb identity has arisen can best be understood as a process of bargaining. To put it simply: the Serbs distance themselves from their Turkish past and as Christians they wanted to be recognised as Europeans. But the Europeans whose recognition they sought were not at all interested in the 'European Serbs'. At the time when the Serbs were making a name for themselves in the cultural centres of Europe, those centres were going through a particularly strong wave of interest in the wild and the undomesticated. The Europeans preferred to see the Serbs as half-Turks rather than as half-Europeans. The attempts of the Serbs to behave as good citizens and convincing Europeans probably met with little more than some sarcastic smirks at their provincialism.[50] In short, the Serb identity that they constructed had to provide scope for the most diverse and contradictory wishes and desires. First of all, it had to be comprehensible and acceptable for the members of the Serb middle class, who wanted to leave the primitive backwardness of their fellow peasants far behind. Second, it had to be comprehensible and acceptable in Budapest and Vienna, where the negotiations on recognition (and the eagerly awaited political autonomy that was to result from it) would eventually be carried out. Finally, it had to be comprehensible and acceptable for the romantic nationalists themselves, who were not in favour of a return to the life of the past either and were reluctant to give up the position that they had now acquired.

The dualism in the notion of a Serb identity seems to have reproduced itself endlessly in the course of the nineteenth and twentieth centuries. Although more research is required on this subject, I would like to indicate the main lines of development in the civilisation debate.

Main lines of development in the civilisation debate

Herder's ideas were initially confined to small Serb élites in the large cities of the Habsburg Empire. New generations of urban Serbs, heavily radicalised by the experiences of the revolutionary year of 1848, increasingly turned to the romantic nationalist idiom to reinforce their demands for more self-government and more autonomy. 'The attitude of the [Serb] romantics to Europe was divided', states Miodrag Popović in his study of Serb romanticism:

> The romantics were those who disseminated [European] culture and literature in our environment and were at the same time the most vigorous opponents of the European societies and the attitude of the European states to the peoples of the Balkans [...].
>
> The romantics behaved like hurt children. Europe was their spiritual mother; she nourished them and taught them to love their own people and its history, language and traditions. But Europe's calculating attitude and indifference to the miserable fate of the Christian peoples in the Balkans aroused the wrath of the poets. Her cool arrogance embittered them even more, but their love for Europe grew along with that bitterness.[51]

The establishment of an independent Serb state south of the Danube and the Sava, first as a tributary vassal state of the Ottoman Empire, later as an independent kingdom, opened a new chapter in the development of the civilisation debate. The Serb monarchs were determined to transform their country into a modern European nation state and turned to a large extent to the Serbs from the Vojvodina to give shape to their ideal of Europeanisation. This made it possible for the Habsburg Serbs to reverse their status entirely: though they still had a reputation for being half-savages in their own country, in Serbia they now acted as *grands seigneurs* from Europe who advised the court on how a European court is organised, on European customs and practices, on the educational system, the demolition of the Ottoman Belgrade and the reconstruction of that city after the model of Vienna, Budapest and Paris. It must have considerably increased the pressure to live up to that civilised status in the eyes of the southern Serbs.

The kingdom of Yugoslavia was created after the First World War, when the Vojvodina Serbs were united with their fellow Serbs south of the rivers. This also meant that new discussion partners intervened in the civilisation debate. Serbs now found themselves in the same nation as Croats and Slovenians. Politically speaking, the Serbs dominated the new state, but they lacked the *cultural* capital of Zagreb and Ljubljana, where the citizens ostentatiously contrasted their 'civilised' Habsburg past with the Ottoman, Oriental and Byzantine background of the 'primitive' Serbs.[52] The chapters on her stay in Zagreb in the period between the wars in Rebecca West's *Black Lamb and Grey Falcon* (1941) present good illustrations of how (already at that time) the 'irreconcilable contradictions' between Croats and Serbs were constantly expressed in terms of level of civilisation. For instance, West describes how everywhere – in banks, museums, hotels – she was assured without asking that 'we are not as the Serbs in Belgrade, here we are businesslike, we do things as they are done in Vienna'.[53] An outing in the company of a Serb and a Croat led to constant discussions, because almost everything they visited proved to be the occasion for heated debates on the differences in level of civilisation between Serbs and Croats. During a lunch in a restaurant, her Serb companion praised to the skies what the Serbs had done for the other peoples in the kingdom, as well as the sacrifices they had made for the well-being of others. The Croat, barely disguising his contempt and waiting until his mouth was empty – 'It is a considerable part of the Croat argument that Croats do not shout in restaurants and do no speak at all with their mouths full', West notes[54] – replied to all that Serb exaggeration with a mere: 'Yes, I see it [...] but if you want to found a strong and civilised Yugoslavia you should have brought the Serb schools up to the Croat level instead of bringing the Croat schools down to the Serb level'.[55] During a visit to a medical centre in Zagreb, the doctors told West about the serious problems of tuberculosis in the city. One possible idea that might arise in the mind of the foreign visitor was immediately nipped in the bud: 'And this was not because they were Balkans. They said that with a sudden leap of fire to their eyes, which could be understood by anyone who has heard Germans or Austrians use the adjective 'Balkan', with a hawking excess of gross contempt. We English, they said, had had just as much tuberculosis at the beginning of the nineteenth century'.[56]

It is interesting to see how these constant references to the primitive character of the Serbs kept on producing movements that attempted to bring about a radical reversal of values in the ideal of civilisation. While the cult of the primitive had already prompted Serb poets in the nineteenth century to make statements like 'Serb folk knowledge should replace religion' and 'the day will come when people will realise that there were better poets among the Serbs in 1860 than among any of the hypercivilised peoples';[57] in Yugoslavia in the years between the wars, it was the movement associated with the poet Ljubomir Micić's journal *Zenit* (which was published in Belgrade between 1921 and 1926) which advocated the overthrow of the struggle for civilisation by the Yugoslavian elites of the time. The Zenit supporters made Barbarian Balkanism their ultimate virtue with slogans like 'Europe is an old woman, the Balkans is a young stud' and 'it's to our advantage that we have no cultural traditions'.[58]

After Tito came to power – to take a giant stride in this rapid historical sketch – the civilisation debate reared its head again in a different disguise. Primitiveness, backwardness and Balkanism, as I showed in the previous chapter, now had to be combatted in the name of a progressive and enlightened Socialism. The fact that the Communists also made use of anti-bourgeois rhetoric, especially in the first decennia, could not stop them from symbolising the dream of progress that they held up in front of workers, peasants and soldiers in the only form available: in the values, norms and life-styles that the Serbs had learned to idealise as European, urban and bourgeois. 'Progress', writes Slavenka Drakulić, meant that 'a modern Communist middle-class family – and which family did not want to belong to that category? – had to have a newly designed bathroom, with every separate component from the sink to the WC in the same colour, including the towels – exactly as they had seen it in the magazine *Schöner Wohnen* that was imported from Germany'. They called it 'socialism with a human face'.[59] Communist hardliners poked fun at Tito's socialism as *il socialismo borghese*.[60] This period also had its movements which elevated the primitive above the ideal of civilisation. In the 1970s, the period when the growth of prosperity reached its zenith, the extremely productive Yugoslavian cinema was dominated by a *crni talas* (black wave), a whole series of films that focused on the backwardness, violence and primitivism of the margins of Yugoslavian society. In the Eighties the rock music world of Sarajevo had a movement which expressly called itself *Novi Primitivizam* (New Primitivism) and tried to achieve a synthesis between the detested *novakomponovana narodna muzika* and Western rock idioms. One of the men behind this movement, Elvis J. Kurtović, formulated it in a few words: 'The problem of this country is primitivism. We can change the whole system and adopt capitalism, but we won't be like West Germany, we'll be like Turkey – primitive'.[61]

More is at stake here than the provocative showing off of marginal groups. The popular folk writer Dobrica Cosić – the 'former Communist people's commissioner, former Communist dissident, former writer and, for the time being, former president', as he was described by Blagojević and Demirović – soon afterwards made a name among wide sectors of the Serb population with similar statements.[62] The days of bathrooms with matching towels are over, Cosić writes. After condemning all the Yugoslavian orientated inhabitants of Serbia, as well as all 'liberals, pacifists, Europeans and cosmopolitans' as 'the scum of the Serb nation', he continues:

> The Serbs were always good and brave soldiers, victors in the war, but weak and timid citizens who do not know how to construct their lives. That is why, although the Serbs are the majority in Yugoslavia, they have fallen to the level of a subject, slavish mass. In peace and liberty the warrior degenerated into a coward.[63]

I have always wondered how remarks like these could win the ear of an urban population that had abandoned those ideas of Serb identity and tucked them away in folk dance performances and museums in favour of the life of a European citizen. The preceding account, in which I have shown how notions of identity, like a pendulum, oscillate incessantly to and fro between the two poles of the civilisation debate, has brought us closer to a solution to that riddle. Cosić's comments on the enfeebled and bourgeoisified hero of war are a new attempt to create a positive redefinition of the negative self-image that has been ashamedly hidden away.

For the civilisation debate that was conducted by the Serbs from the Vojvodina during my stay in Novi Sad, the rise of extreme nationalism and the collapse of Yugoslavia meant above all that they increasingly came to belong to the Balkans and became more and more isolated from Europe. The non-stop propaganda against the West in general, and against Germany, Austria and Hungary in particular, made it increasingly difficult to display any cultural or mental affinity with Central Europe or the former Austro-Hungarian Empire – one of the main arguments in the claim to a high level of culture on the part of the Vojvodina Serbs. Under these circumstances it could easily be regarded as treason. This was certainly the case for the ideas that I was still able to record at the commencement of my period of fieldwork: ideas that Slovenia and Croatia were the civilised part of Yugoslavia, while the Vojvodina had a much closer cultural and mental affinity with those federal states than with Serbia. The extent to which people were forced to adjust to the new stories which were being forged during my stay in Novi Sad can be illustrated from the following example.

When I left for the Netherlands, Sonja Svetović gave me an anthology of Serb folk stories – one of those books with an imitation leather binding and the title printed in gold letters with baroque ornaments on the spine, to make it look distinguished and valuable. She wrote a dedication, a citation from the collection, a phrase which had caught her attention in this fairly voluminous work: 'if we rise above ourselves and the situations we find ourselves in'. She had added: 'remember that, despite everything, now and then good people are to be found living here too'. She had carefully noted the page from which the citation was taken in pencil: page 41. I ought to read it when I got home, she said. Page 41 turned out to contain a passage she had underlined, a passage in which the editor of the anthology outlines the history of the Serb people in a few sentences:

> With or without humour, with or without fantastic elements, folk stories reflect the heavy, painful lives of the mass of the people. Suffering, a thousand disappointments, ups and downs, downs and ups, and painful steps ahead – progress on hands and knees, with strength and wisdom. Moments of despair on that road, when the oppression seems to be never-ending... but other moments too on the same road, and ever the hope that brings alleviation and the thought of victory, by which people rise above themselves and the situation they find themselves in, so that they can take on anything. That optimism and that heroism characterise these folk stories and represent their most important value.[64]

I was surprised that this woman, of all people, should give me a collection of Serb folk stories. In Novi Sad in 1992, such an anthology was one of a whole range of expressions and products in which the rediscovered Serb *Volksgeist* was articulated. There were books on Serb history, expensive-looking publications with illustrations of Serbian Orthodox monasteries, frescoes and glittering gold icons; video tapes of traditional Serb rituals, accompanied by expert commentaries by anthropologists; music cassettes with Serb folk music, epic poems or Slav religious choral music; table-cloths with hand-embroidered folklore motifs; calendars with beautiful Serb landscapes; and even cooking programmes which rescued traditional Serb recipes from oblivion. I could have expected a collection of Serb folk stories from lots of people, but not from her.

I had got to know Sonja Svetović as a cosmopolitan person, someone who scorned the 'euphoric nationalism', as she called it, and who also opposed the rapid rejection of Europe that she saw taking place around her. Although she was born and bred in a village in the Vojvodina, was good at playing the *tamburica* and was strongly attached to the traditional obligations of her *kumstvo*, her ritual ties of kinship, matters of this kind had a separate place in her life. She ran a software company and liked

to quote a lot from works of international literature. She had travelled
widely and enjoyed treating her guests to 'foreign' dishes which she managed to concoct from what she could find on the Novi Sad market plus
the dried herbs and spices that she brought back from her trips abroad.
By discussing one of her favourite subjects – the superficiality of US culture – with me and an English acquaintance we shared, she felt she was
where she wanted to be: among Europeans.

But now, on the eve of my departure from Novi Sad, she gave me a
book that centred on the adventures of Serb peasants, valiant warriors
and villainous Turks, powerful emperors and golden-tressed woodland
fairies. No Ivo Andrić, no Danilo Kiš, no Aleksandar Tišma, but an anthology of folk tales.

It was only upon reflection that I realised that this gift was not so
strange after all. During our many discussions of the political situation in
the country, Sonja Svetović had hardly been able to vent her rage, fear
and dissatisfaction with the developments in Serbia except in terms of a
continual berating of her country and her people. With the fervour of
someone who has begun a desperate offensive against the campaigns in
the media which consisted solely of Serb self-aggrandizement, she continued to talk about the backwardness of the country, with its crude, simple and underdeveloped population. People like her had no expectations
any more, here in the Balkans. She saw only darkness ahead for the next
few decennia, and considered emigrating to South Africa: 'South Africa!
One of those countries where I wouldn't even have considered going on
holiday two years ago!'

Looking back on these discussions, her choice of a book of Serb folk
tales as my leaving present, the dedication she wrote in it, and the reference to the passage on page 41, are moving and eloquent. The dedication – 'remember that, despite everything, now and then good people are
to be found living here too' – still bears a trace of the shame felt by someone who can image exactly how the outside world will judge her people's
actions. At the same time, however, the gift bears witness to the fact that
she will spend the rest of her life in a different story, and reveals the first
wary explorations of possibilities for not only judging but also understanding that same people.

Novi Sad: the reality as it is told

This chapter began with a discussion of how the outbreak of the war facilitated the sudden emergence of a cluster of remarks and stories in

which the people of Novi Sad no longer represented themselves and the world they lived in as modern, civilised and European, but as wild and crude. Although I had previously heard similar comments on the unchanging wild nature of the Balkans, in retrospect they proved to be no more than the tip of the iceberg; the manifest expressions of a much more comprehensive system of hidden, subterranean views and ideas that my discussion partners entertained about themselves and about the world they lived in. The only way to fulfil their longing to belong to civilised Europe proved to be on condition that they labelled matters and forms of behaviour which they felt to be characteristic of themselves as disgraceful. Vice versa, their eagerness to be regarded as Serbs seemed to be possible only by rejecting civilisation as false, artificial and foreign. In other words, the civilisation debate forced my discussion partners to constantly deny and amputate essential (and often highly cherished) parts of their own personal and collective biography.

The lack of any kind of synthesis of these two clusters of stories was astonishing. The painter Vuk Konjević – whom we met in the previous chapter – made it clear that there were individual *bricoleurs* in Novi Sad who managed to weld these two worlds together in an ingenious fashion, but meetings with figures like him could not take away the overwhelming impression that my discussion partners in Novi Sad had nestled in stories in which they would always see themselves as half-strangers.

The question of why my discussion partners were so adamant in opting for two diametrically opposed clusters of stories – a circumstance that is bound to bring about a great inner division – was the pretext for the history lesson of this chapter.

That lesson taught me, first and foremost, that the terms and concepts with which my discussion partners were able to construct a story about themselves and their world were not the terms and concepts of their choice. The fact that the people around me had hardly any ammunition to counter the newly activated story about their wild character and undomesticated nature is connected with the fact that the fixed dichotomies which dominate the civilisation debate in Novi Sad are the result of a historical process in which the subordinate position of the Serbs on the periphery of Europe has been a very important determinant. All the ideas about human agency – the ability of people to gain control of processes of signification in a creative and inventive way – that are so popular in current anthropology are thus in need of an important corrective. 'Culture controls the definitions of the world for actors, limits their conceptual tools, and restricts their emotional repertoires', Sherry Ortner once said.[65] With respect to the way reality is told in Novi Sad, my discussion partners were certainly bound by the limits of their own conceptual frameworks; they were prisoners of a historical legacy of mutually opposed and irreconcilable stories about themselves and their world.

Note that this holds true of reality as it is told. Because my discussion partners knew that there are other sources of knowledge about and insight into people and the world beside the stories I have been discussing. And they meticulously protected those sources of extraordinary knowledge from the norms and values imposed by the dichotomies of the civilisation debate.

PART II
Beyond the world in stories

3 Lessons from the Reform School of War

> Ideal, ideal, ideal
> knowledge, knowledge, knowledge
> boomboom, boomboom, boomboom.
>
> – Tristan Tzara, *Sept Manifestes Dada* (1924)

There are two kinds of knowledge about our world, my discussion partners in Novi Sad managed to bring home to me. The first type – knowledge about people and the world in the clear concepts and orderly discourses which have been developed for that purpose since the Enlightenment, knowledge about what a European thinks, feels, does and does not do (and knowledge about how an inhabitant of the Balkans behaves and thus how a European does not behave) – has been discussed in the previous chapters. The next few chapters will concentrate on the second type of knowledge; a murky and obscure knowing, muted and marginalised, and accessible only to those who are 'in the know'. Following Michael Taussig, I will label this second type of knowledge 'implicit social knowledge': '...a non-discursive, essentially inarticulable and imageric knowing of social relationality and history'.[1]

In its vagueness and intangibility, implicit social knowledge is everything that the anthropologist who has embarked upon an empirical fact-finding mission would want to avoid. Yet to do so would be to deny the enormous power of implicit social knowledge as a motivational force in the lives of individuals and groups. For clarity's sake let us take a concrete example which clearly contains a reference to this domain of a different type of knowledge.

'You don't know our history', I was told (rudely at times) in Novi Sad on a number of occasions. It usually followed reports that Serbia had been under attack again by the representatives of the world community for war crimes, broken pledges, or yet another meaningless signature to yet another meaningless document. Sometimes it followed a remark of mine that my discussion partner found too critical.

'You don't know our history' was not an incitement to engage in in-depth research. In fact, I more often had the impression that my interest in the language, culture and history of the Serbs provoked irritation. 'You don't know our history' was thus above all a statement of fact.

Don't waste your time trying to understand what's going on here, seemed to be the implicit message, because learning the language, reading books or knowing the facts won't enable you to understand our history.

In a parenthesis in his three-volume history of the Serbs in Vojvodina, Dušan Popović indicates how the knowledge of that history is a question of empathy, so that really knowing that history becomes a prerogative reserved exclusively for the Serbs. 'The life of a refugee was never pleasant', the historian wrote on the Great Serb Exodus of 1690, when 30,000 Serb families fled from the Turks and left their home country to seek refuge in the Habsburg Empire:

> Finding a safe refuge in a foreign country in the middle of winter, without a roof above your head, without food or heating, was not easy. Today we can still feel the misery and misfortune of our people and their leaders, which still echo in a few summary but highly painful accounts, that all begin with lamentations like 'Oh', 'Uvi', 'Ole', 'Avaj' and 'Lele'. Our people never went through a worse time in history, and we feel those events more than we can show them, because the documents are scarce and only present one side of the picture.[2]

'We feel those events more than we can show them'. 'Oh', 'Uvi', 'Ole', 'Avaj', 'Lele'. Wordless exclamations that, in Popović's eyes, contain more meaning for Serb history than the 'scarce' documents that 'only present one side of the picture'. No room for an intruder there.

Above all else, the expression 'You don't know our history' seemed to be used to distinguish between two kinds of knowing and understanding. One was the Enlightened, rational, European way of understanding, a system of knowledge in which both Serbs and non-Serbs can participate. The other was the exclusively Serb way of understanding, non-rational, incomprehensible and inaccessible to every non-Serb.

My informants provided me with dozens of other examples of this reference to an exclusively Serb domain of knowledge about what kind of a place the world is. The obscurantist remarks about the Serb or the Slavic soul, for example, or the descriptions of a feeling that was labelled with a Serb borrowing from Turkish, *dert*. 'Untranslatable', I was told, and although some people were prepared to say that it had some connection with *Weltschmerz*, it seemed to owe its significance above all to this emphatic untranslatability. This mood can only be expressed in Serb, they explained, and 'foreigners like you can't understand it'. And then there was the mass of remarks in the margin of discussions, a quietly spoken but non-intermittent flow of phrases, comments, asides and little jokes which referred to very different views of people and the world than the ones my discussion partners wanted a visitor to the 'Athens of Serbia' to see.

This implicit social knowledge was not just exclusively Serb. It was also considered to be truer. The exaggerated tones in which people who strove in every aspect to live the life of a European would speak about 'the decadence of the West' which 'has somewhat lost its picture of reality' is a good example of the conviction that Serb knowledge has a higher truth value than the views of the Europeans. Another example is provided by the bitter sniggers which met my indignant comments on the fact that the Yugoslav politicians did not keep their promises, ignored their earlier agreements, and did exactly what suited them best at the time. 'Every child knows that.' In this sense too, remarks like 'You don't know our history' marked a boundary: the boundary between the world of the *prazne priče*, the 'idle stories', on the one hand, and the world 'which we all know for what it is'.

Prazne priče was the reply of my discussion partners when I told them something they disagreed with. 'Idle stories.' And they said it in an inimitable way, with the look of people who know what 'idle stories' are. I soon learned that the expression was not only a stopgap to undermine someone else's convictions but referred more generally to the human capacity to make up stories. The phrase *prazne priče* – as well as the poise with which it was uttered – is rooted in all those grand narratives which had been made up in the last two hundred years: nationalism, pan-slavism, modernism, Communism, humanism, fascism, Yugoslavism, Stalinism, Titoism. They were all enthusiastically welcomed only to be worn out, labelled a lie, and swapped for something else, something new. *Prazne priče*. Idle stories. Yesterday's truths are today's lies, while tomorrow's story is already in the making. Never have I heard so many people so often contest the verity of this or that phenomenon by adding the label 'so-called' (*takozvani*). Never have I heard such blunt denials of someone else's identity ('they think they're Croats, but really they're Serbs...'). Never have I heard people talk so heatedly about 'facts' (*činjenica je*, 'it's a fact that...') while their faces betrayed their confusion at the lack of facts. Never have I seen people making such fine distinctions between 'the truth' and 'the real truth', 'who we are' and 'who we really are', 'the world as it is' and 'the world as it really is', 'what people say' and 'what people mean', 'the wording' and 'what you can read between the lines'.

This chapter is about this largely hidden knowledge that is clearly presented as something Serb and true. What do the obscure and significant comments about an exclusive Serb knowledge refer to? And in the view of the Serbs, what confers on this knowledge a higher truth than the world of the stories?

It is no easy matter to answer these questions. After all, implicit social knowledge is a reservoir of insights that are not contained in a society's canons; knowledge that is not embodied in the language of newspapers, books or academic journals; knowledge that you will not be able to find under any of the key words in a library catalogue; knowledge that is not included in the regular syllabuses of schools and universities. A knowledge that goes the rounds of this society like a scent that finds its way into everything and everybody.

It is no easy matter, but it is not impossible. By now a growing number of anthropologists have come to assign a central place to the layered nature of knowledge. The insights and perceptions that they have developed can offer valuable clues as to how this field of hidden knowledge can be explored. As stated earlier, a parallel comes to mind with what Michael Taussig in his study of shamanism in Latin America called 'implicit social knowledge', knowledge that is generated by the collective experiences of successive generations. This knowledge gained by experience is often impossible to articulate, says Taussig, but all the same it determines 'what moves people without their knowing quite why or quite how, with what makes the real real and the normal normal, and above all with what makes ethical distinctions politically powerful'.[3] Clifford Geertz' statements on common sense as 'an interpretation of the immediacies of experience [... that] pretends to reach past illusion to truth, to, as we say, things as they are'[4] also throw light on what I mean by 'implicit social knowledge', while further points of entry for an exploration of the layered nature of knowledge can be found in the work of Hans Peter Duerr, James Fernandez and the Dutch anthropologists Bonno Thoden van Velzen and Wilhelmina van Wetering.[5] During years of fieldwork among the Bush Negroes in the east of Surinam, the latter were continually confronted by 'seemingly isolated pronouncements on the nature of a "hidden reality"', by 'strange institutions that play no discernable role in the field of practical action', and by 'images carrying great emotional charge' that could not be explained in the terms and stories that dominated manifest public life. By not brushing these expressions aside as irrelevancies but by systematically recording them, the two anthropologists were able to obtain a picture of a hidden reality that influenced the actions of their discussion partners beneath the surface of public life. They label the totality of these expressions a collective fanta-

sy, 'a corpus of fantasy images, usually developed in response to some ur-
gent need, to widespread feelings of alienation, when older normative
structures have broken down while alternative structures fail to com-
mand people's allegiance'.[6]

Victor Turner's comments on cultural performances as the drawing-
board on which creative actors sketch the designs for living that seem
more suitable or interesting to them are also intended to focus on the
products of the imagination and fantasy.[7] Turner also offers clues on
where to look for the knowledge and insights to which I have given the
label 'implicit social knowledge'. Jokes, films, carnival masquerades, literary products such as books, poems, fairy stories, dramatic performances, children's games and sports events are conceived as settings in
which knowledge that is normally unspeakable can be articulated. They
are play frames which temporarily suspend everyday reality and enable
people to view the world from a different angle.

Another important area to which my discussion partners referred
when they indicated that they had access to different sources of knowledge came from a totally unexpected quarter: the war. During most of
my fieldwork period and while writing this study, I was reminded day in
day out of what war is, how war can disrupt and wreck human lives.
That daily confrontation with the realities of war raised the question of
where people – supposing they survive it – can accommodate their acquaintance with this world of inhuman experiences. But at the same time
this issue presented a compelling answer to my questions about the hidden domain of knowledge. This was the volcano where the *fini ljudi* established their civilised world. This was the potential of human cruelty
and human misery that people knew or suspected to exist beneath the
stories that constitute the everyday reality of Novi Sad. This was what
made all those remarks about 'the emptiness of stories', 'a Western lack
of sense of reality' and comments like 'you don't know our history' so real
and convincing.

On the sense and nonsense of stories

> So Philip sat in the café and watched the people passing along the street,
> musing how strange and enigmatic indeed that movement in the street was
> – People passed by carrying within them a mixture of boiled fowls' legs,
> wretched birds' wings, cows' buttocks, horses' haunches, while only the
> night before those animals were cheerfully swinging theit tails, the hens
> squawking in hen-coops on the eve of their death, and now everything had

found its way into human intestines, and all this movement and gluttony could be summed up in one word: life, in western European cities at the end of an old civilisation.

That is how Miroslav Krleža, another writer with Pannonian roots, described what the civilised world looks like once the story about people and the world starts to fall apart.

The protagonist in Krleža's *The Return of Philip Latinovicz* (1932) suffers from a disturbing ailment: now and then he is overcome by a state in which the link between perception and meaning is dissolved. 'For quite a while Philip had noticed how all objects and impressions fell apart into details under his gaze' is how the author describes this remarkable condition of Philip Latinovicz. 'He became absorbed in these details, but was unable to give any profound sense to all the details around him'. The reader is given a glimpse of this absurd world in dissolution through Philip's eyes: 'Strange indeed are human cheeks, stiff, hard, as if chiselled, while chains and stuffs and furs all hang on human bodies like superfluous ornaments and mingle with skirts, hair, spectacles and eyes in a strange unravellable tangle...'

It speaks volumes that the condition first manifested itself during the First World War:

> ...only in the most critical days of the war, when everything was breaking up and when nothing else was noticeable save a blind piling up of quantities of material – and since man by himself is nothing but an insignificant and petty quantity – only in those gloomiest and loneliest days did it happen that Philip forgot himself in what was going on, losing sight of his own existence...

People reduced to the dimension of a string of intestines containing smoked chicken heads, a phantom decked with spectacles and tissues: here they are again, those banal and inescapable truths that are generated in wartime and which pursue people afterwards. *I am reality*, war says. Blood in the snow. Brains against a wall. As we have seen, those were the essential truths on which Aleksandar Tišma, the writer from Novi Sad, could and dared to base his account of his understanding of people and the world. After seeing that blood and those brains, Tišma *knew*, and it was that deduction that struck me so: the perception (brains, snow, blood, wall) and the conclusion ('*Therefore* I know what ethnic madness is, I know how crazy people can become').

Experiences obtained in the terrible reality of the war, in which these confrontations with the most brutal violations of the integrity of the human body – violations of what is perhaps the ultimate story we have to tell about ourselves: the story that says that we are more than just skin, bones, blood and brains – seem to bring about an utter alienation. Such wartime experiences undermine the foundations on which stories are built like a serious form of concrete rot. They transform the stories that people inhabit into draughty flats ripe for demolition, into slums where the holes in the floor constantly reveal a subsoil of mud.

In their novels, writers like Krleža and Tišma return time and again to the war, and to the absurdity of the stories that dominate a postwar reality. Eugen, the Jew from Novi Sad in Tišma's *Suspicion and Trust* who survived the camps to live a life in retreat in the plundered home of his parents, is described as someone for whom everything he has ever heard, read or thought has been stripped of sense and meaning. The stories he used to consider his own have been smashed to smithereens by his camp experiences. His head is still filled with an incessant jumble of 'rattling consonants, nasal, broken, screaming, wheedling, whispering, panting, blubbering and bleating vowels'. Eugen no longer has a vocabulary of his own, just the words and stories of others, '...just brain cells that transfer their twitchings to his throat, his jaws, tongue, palate...':

> He has nothing. No language, no thoughts, no decisions, no consciousness, no love or hate. But he does feel hungry if he doesn't eat for a long time, shivers if he hasn't got any clothes, cold if there's no heating, tired if he sits or walks too long at a stretch, sleepy if the evening is gone, erections if he lies down in bed.

The insight that beneath every word, idea and story all that is left is something that might be called 'physical experience' or 'bodily awareness', is also a recurrent feature in the work of Danilo Kiš – another native of these plains (from Subotica, to be precise), sufficient reason to mention him here.

Kiš's 1972 novel *Hourglass* contains a passage on implicit social knowledge among the 'notes of a madman' (a certain E.S., a resident of Novi Sad who works for the railway, who once awaited his death on the frozen banks of the Danube in January 1942, survived his execution and disappearance beneath the ice, but died there and since then bears the riddle of *death* which makes him ill and crazy):

> What are all man's strivings, all that goes by the name of history, compared to his vain and ludicrous attempt to combat the absurdity of universal death, to give it any other meaning than the one it has. The most

cynical philosophers try to console the public by giving meaning, with the help of some higher logic or clever turns of phrase, to the meaninglessness of death. But what, to me at least, remains an inexplicable mystery is this: how has man been able, despite his knowledge of death, to go on living and acting, as though death were something outside him, as though it were a natural phenomenon. The trembling that has taken hold of me in the last few days has enabled me, despite my paroxysms of fear, to understand the nature of my sickness; namely, that from time to time, for reasons quite unknown to me, and with heaven knows what motives, I become lucid. Then the knowledge of death rises up in me, of death as such; in such moments of diabolical illumination, death, death *an sich*, assumes its full weight and meaning, which most people (deluding themselves with the help of work and art, whose meaning and *vanitas* they obscure with fine phrases) do not so much as suspect, until it knocks, clearly and unmistakably, at the door, scythe in hand, as in medieval engravings. But what terrifies me (knowledge brings no consolation) and adds to my inner trembling is the consciousness that my madness is in reality lucidity, and that what I need if I am to recover – for this constant trembling is unbearable – is precisely madness, lunacy, forgetfulness; only lunacy can save me, only madness can make me well. If by chance Dr. Papandopoulos were to ask me about the state of my health, about the origin of my traumas, my fears, I would answer clearly and unmistakably: *lucidity*.

Although Kiš once claimed not to want to be a writer who flatters his readers by 'embellishing ignorance', but who attacks the reader (in which he is completely successful), it should be noted that it is the carefully protected (and protecting) rules of the literary genre – this is fiction, this is a novel, in spite of every insight and recognition – which make possible such reflections on the human condition. For this knowledge, this awareness that every meaning can ultimately be reduced to blood in the snow and brains against the wall, cannot serve as the foundation on which to build life, existence, society, future, hope, or belief. Kiš's lucid idiot is clear about that: insight into naked death, knowing what it is, is a sure road to the asylum. It is absolutely impossible for a human being to bear the resulting alienation.

Let us leave the site of my fieldwork in former Yugoslavia for a moment and turn to a more general consideration of the sense and nonsense of stories. '[Man] can adapt himself somehow to anything his imagination can cope with; but he cannot deal with Chaos', says Susanne K. Langer on the primary importance of stories that confer significance. 'Because his characteristic function and highest asset is conception, his greatest fright is to meet what he cannot construe – the 'uncanny', as it is popularly called'.[8] Anthropologists have repeatedly emphasised the total dependence of people on stories that convey meaning and significance. 'The thing we seem least able to tolerate is a threat to our powers of conception, a suggestion that our ability to create, grasp, and use symbols may fail us', Geertz notes in his essay on religion. 'Man depends upon symbols and symbol systems with a dependence so great as to be decisive for his creatural viability and, as a result, his sensitivity to even the remotest indication that they may prove unable to cope with one or another aspect of experience raises within him the gravest sort of anxiety'.[9] The work of anthropologists like Mary Douglas, Edmund Leach and Barbara Babcock is also permeated with the idea that the interpretative frameworks within which people confer meaning on their experiences are intended to keep absurdity and, in its wake, the ultimate alienation at a distance.[10] Stories that convey meaning and significance must be kept free of ambiguity, equivocality and multiple interpretations. After all, incoherences of this kind always provoke the uncomfortable suspicion that the stories we inhabit are not as immutable as the ten commandments but arbitrary and interchangeable. 'Whatever is felt to be abnormal is a source of anxiety', Leach remarks on the taboo, one of the mechanisms to keep stories beyond doubt. 'Abnormalities which are recurrent and frequent become hedged about by cultural barriers and prohibitions which have the force of signals: "danger: keep out: don't touch!"'.[11]

It is not difficult to see how these mechanisms, intended to elevate fictional realities beyond any doubt, operate in every life. We create protective stories to defend ourselves against alarming and potentially alienating insights of the kind which the Yugoslav writers mentioned above try to reach in their work. We create stories to confer meaning and significance about who we are and who we aren't, what the world is, what you can expect in it and what you can't. They may be grand stories, they may not. We say: my work is important. We say: we are a happy family. We say: people tend to be reasonable. We say: there will never be a second Auschwitz. We say: this is a worthwhile relationship. We say: this is how God wanted it. We say all kinds of things, and then we call those stories reality and do all we can to protect that reality against overly lucid insights. We create rules and forms of behaviour that anchor the story in praxis, we build institutions to guarantee the survival of the stories and to ensure compliance with them. We eliminate chaos and the like from our field of vision. It's all in order to avoid having to question those stories, expose them to doubt, undermine them with dissident ideas. It's only within clearly demarcated limits that we create safety valves and therapies for the inevitable tensions and conflicts that arise in the psyche as a result of the limitations of the story. We make stories everywhere all the time. The fact that we are so little aware of it is perhaps the best indication of what is at stake in the wording of reality: the story seduces us with the soothing illusion that there is no story at all, but a natural, divinely ordained or scientifically demonstrated reality.[12]

The skill with which we have learned to question our stories and keep them intact at the same time is evident in the social scientific institutes themselves, where so many have fallen under the spell of the deconstruction of reality. Taussig has raised some stimulating questions on the arbitrary questioning of the relation to reality of this or that story in the universities of the West. 'With good reason postmodernism has relentlessly instructed us that reality is artifice yet, so it seems to me, not enough surprise has been expressed as to how we nevertheless get on with living, pretending [...] that we live facts, not fictions'.[13] It is strange that we all find ourselves somewhere between 'the real' and 'the really made-up', he remarks. We disguise, we mask, 'we act and *have to act as if* mischief were not afoot in the kingdom of the real and that all around the ground lay firm. That is what the public secret, the facticity of the social fact, being a social being, is all about. No matter how sophisticated we may be as to the constructed and arbitrary character of our practices of representation, our practice of practices is one of actively forgetting such mischief each time we open our mouths to ask for something or to make a statement'.[14]

Back to what was once Yugoslavia. The reports from a besieged Sarajevo demonstrated how in times of war stories about people and the world disintegrate, how the war unashamedly and brutally imposed on a new generation of Yugoslavs its banal insights into what people are like in the last analysis and what the world is about. Zlata Filipović, a 13-year-old pupil in Sarajevo, wrote in her war diary:

> 27 May 1992. A bloodbath. Ghastly. That's Vašo Miškin Street today. Two grenades fell in the street and one on the market. Mummy was so close. She ran to grandmother's house. [...] A few minutes later we saw her running over the bridge. She was shaking when she came in. I've seen people killed, she said.[15]

Šefko Pašić, a hairdresser from the badly hit district of Dobrinja in Sarajevo, stated that he was in shock for days after seeing a mutilated corpse on the street for the first time last year. 'But now', he says, 'I walk past a couple of corpses every day and don't pay them the slightest attention: the most abnormal human experience becomes normal in Dobrinja'.[16]

But from the same Sarajevo there were also reports of how people stick to stories, incredible reports about how order is created even in the madness of that city that is blasted by bombs and snipers every day. Zlatko Dizdarević, editor of the Sarajevan daily *Oslobodjenje*, provides a telling example in his diary of the war. The sirens announce another general alarm. Dizdarević is forced to stay under cover while the alarm goes on and on. He notes how crazy it is to announce a general alarm – a period with a beginning and an end – in a city where there is permanent danger and where life and death have been a question of luck for months. Still, he is bound to admit that the inhabitants of the besieged city resist the absurdity of their situation. A new philosophy emerges, a new logic:

> When one of the grenades, one of the thousands of grenades, exploded near by, I chanced to hear an absurd conversation between two of my colleagues who were squatting on their heels:
> – I knew it was going to fall here. Igor's there, he had to get away from here.
> – Good God, how do you know it was going to fall here? How could Igor know?
> – Of course he could, you know a thing like that, everyone does...
> It is accepted that 'everyone knows'. No one even suspects that knowledge of this kind is pure stupidity. No one can ever know anything about this madness, because it's impenetrable. But we're brought up to look for the logic behind everything all the time, in a black and white world. We've always known the answers. That's why we felt so strong, virtually invincible. That makes the chaos that has overwhelmed us all the more painful, and fatal for some of us. No one has an answer to the real questions that arise today.
>
> We don't understand what's going on, nor why, nor who has a chance of surviving and who has almost none. Where will the grenade land? Where is it safe? Who will get hit by a bullet? Who was born under a lucky star?
>
> No one should be surprised that everyone here, without exception, is looking for a logical explanation, for a rule in the absolute chaos which seems endless. Those who succeed think they know a lot: where and when you can get through, which roads are out of bounds, what you can do without any risk, why the grenades fall here and not there. People like that

know the rules of life, rules which make it more likely that you'll win the lotto than get hit by a sniper's bullet. But a lot of bullets whistle through the air in everyday life in Sarajevo [...].

A morning when there's not a break. The grenades are falling near by, perhaps more than ever before. The official alarm goes on and on, so does the personal alarm. We assess our chances, we run risks and we keep on hoping. We have to find the strength for a personal matter: to give up lying to ourselves and continuing to search for a logic that doesn't exist. If we find that logic, tomorrow we'll find an explanation and a logic for those who have shot our entire logic to bits.

But I have to leave, the noise is getting unbearable. Besides I know perfectly well that a grenade will soon fall on the spot where I'm sitting now. They won't fall where I'm going. I wouldn't be a real cold-blooded and wildly optimistic Sarajevan if I didn't know that. And I'm just as certain that it will soon all be over.[17]

The oppressive dilemma that emerges from this passage is the utter incompatibility of knowing about the chaos (this is chaos, this is the domain of arbitrariness, there is no place for thought, desire or hope here), on the one hand, and realising that this insight is unbearable (if I give in to that realisation, it will all come to an end, so I still think, desire and hope all kinds of things, despite my better judgement). These two insights are here juxtaposed, unmistakable, irreconcilable, insoluble. Before the war Dizdarević had never given any thought to the relative character of reality: 'We've always known the answers. That's why we felt so strong, virtually invincible'. And the dilemma arises now not in connection with some abstract reflection on the constructed character of known reality, but in connection with a keen observation of what he sees happening around him in a human society under fire.[18]

In an Amnesty International report, a peasant from the Croat village of Hum describes the killing of his 60-year-old father. Although he uses few words, a small but eloquent gesture is proof of his awareness of the sense and nonsense of stories:

There was an enormous bang when someone threw a smoke-grenade into our house. We went outside, at the front of the house... The police shouted at us to go back in... everyone except my father... then we heard a shot and I and my mother knew what it meant... My father was lying on the ground and the whole wall was covered with his brains. I covered him with a blanket so that the children wouldn't see it...[19]

Towards an account of the damage war can cause to stories

> A trauma usually has a number of components. It causes physical damage
> which can lead to permanent health problems. It entails material losses
> which can have a permanent effect on the way of life of those involved. But
> the most serious effect is usually the psychological and mental effect. What
> happened should not have happened. If it happened all the same, every-
> thing the victim believed before was incorrect. The victim's world, ideas,
> feelings and convictions are all damaged, subjected to a heavy blow, some-
> times wiped out for good. People cope with serious shock in different ways.
> [...] But what has been destroyed cannot be repaired: fundamental trust in
> a meaningful world with people who are to a large extent worthy of that
> trust.[20]

The people of former Yugoslavia share our need to package life in stories that give it meaning and significance. All the same, I think there are
reasons to speak of a difference between the stories of those of us who
live in the political, economic and cultural centre of Europe, and the stories of the inhabitants of former Yugoslavia, the eternal periphery.

The stories with which Europeans set themselves in the heart of the
civilised world, to cite just one example, have served as a guide for action for centuries. The stories relating to the key notion that we are
civilised become encapsulated in an ever tougher protective layer. They
can take some knocking. 'Davon geht die Welt nicht unter, die wird ja
noch gebraucht', sang the star of the Third Reich, Zarah Leander, in a
bright *drei-viertl Takt* while the cities of Germany were being bombed.
Although the European Jews had to learn that 'the house of civilisation
proved no shelter' as George Steiner put it,[21] others were not tempted to
abandon their belief and confidence in civilised Europe. The Dadaists
and Surrealists had already discovered the indestructibility of these stories about European civilisation when they came back from the trenches
of World War I. In his discussion of the furious disillusionment and de-
moralisation of poets like Bréton, Éluard and Péret, Van Spaendonck argued that they had probably set their sights on an inevitable change after the war:

> The war was a reform school that would implacably separate the genuine
> from the false. It was reasonable to expect that killing and plundering on
> both sides on such a scale would inevitably lead to a bitter discussion of the
> civilisation which had made it possible. But the end of the war brought lit-
> tle more than minor shifts of emphasis within a world which was rebuilt as

it had been in the past – boundary corrections, reparations for the defeated, a new set of white masters in some of the colonies. In the meantime the
relations of power were safely anchored in their traditional supports. The
reconstruction was inspired by the cult of the family, religion, money and
the fatherland.[22]

This is not the place to go into detail as regards the question of how, despite so much evidence to the contrary, the story about the civilised West
can continue to exist as a framework that confers meaning and significance. But if my suppositions are founded, and stories like this owe their
resilience, their correspondence to truth, their compelling force to a large
extent to their age, to the investments made in them by successive generations, and to their capacity to accommodate, convince and inspire
generation after generation, then we can only state that the story of civilisation in countries like former Yugoslavia took much less time to hard-
en.

We have already seen in the foregoing chapters how national boundaries, ideologies and political systems in this part of the world – 'the no-man's
land of the world order', as Alain Finkelkraut so aptly described it –,[23] have
replaced and succeeded one another at a brisk pace. Here I would like
to recall the fact that all those states, ideologies and political systems had
their roots in the experience of war. They were installed with blood, and
they were wiped out again with blood. In this sense the horrors of war
marked continuity for the Yugoslavs. They were the chorus repeated after each verse of the song. In this way too, the war could call to the survivors: I am reality, I am the firm ground beneath your feet, the certainty
among all uncertainties.

What is war, and what is its role in the stories that people live by?
Provisional though they are, we can at least isolate a number of main
points in an attempt to get to grips with these questions.

The recurrent war
'The past is a foreign country', runs the well-known aphorism from L.P.
Hartley's *The Go-Between*. Not for the South Slavs. They know the past.
It's just like the present; they don't do things differently there:

> All around lie the ruins and remains of two thousand homes, grass grows
> in the streets, the walls are covered with moss, and ivy winds its way
> around the doors and windows. Shops, houses and green areas have dis-
> appeared, and their owners have left for the world outside or been killed
> in the war. Many streets were nothing but broken window-panes, broken

walls and burnt beams. The streets looked like huge piles of stone and rubble, side by side. [...] Since almost the entire city had been burnt down and
the Serb population had abandoned it, the houses which had not yet been
destroyed by the fire were plundered by the troops from Petrovaradin and
the people who stayed behind, mainly Hungarians. The new city council
sold the possessions of the Serbs who had fled. Those who stayed were the
prey of illnesses and other calamities.[24]

Villages were not just captured; they were in large part destroyed. The
inhabitants were driven out (where they had not already fled), and their
houses burned. Woe betide the man of military age, or the woman of 'enemy' national identity, who was found alive in the conquered village.
Rape was ubiquitous, sometimes murderous. Victims, now wholly dis-
possessed and homeless, were obliged to take the roads or the mountain
trails by the thousands, in a frantic search for places were they could at
least lay their heads. Great streams of pathetically suffering refugees
could be seen on many roads of the peninsula. Little pity was shown for
the sick and the wounded. Prisoners of war, if not killed outright, were
sometimes driven into outdoor compounds or ramshackle buildings and
left there to die of hunger and exposure. There was in general a total
hard-heartedness toward the defeated, whether military or civilian. Some
of this was carried beyond just the level of neglect and indifference and
into the realm of sickening and deliberate cruelty.[25]

These descriptions are not taken from the recent war in Bosnia. The first
is a description by a visitor to Novi Sad in 1850, one year after the bombardment of the city by Hungarian troops. The second is a summary of
a report from 1913 in which an international committee of investigation
presents its findings on hostilities during the First Balkan War. A sad reminder that the recent war is the fifth war of the century to have been
fought here after the two Balkan Wars of 1912 and 1913 and the two
World Wars. And that its horrors are a match for the large-scale bloodbaths, cruelties and mass migrations of its predecessors in the twentieth
century – not to mention earlier centuries.
   This element, the recurrent war, is one of the aspects that would have
to be dealt with in an account of the damage war can inflict on stories
about who we are and what the world is like that we live in. Homes,
houses of prayer, businesses, livestock, agricultural land, villages and
towns are destroyed and rebuilt, over and over again. 'Two wars per
generation' was the disturbingly sober comment on the recurrent war by
an old peasant woman in a village in Hercegovina that had been razed

to the ground. 'That's the way it goes here' is what she seemed to be telling the camera crew that found her amid the ruins.

The large-scale war
An account of the damage caused by war to stories that confer meaning and significance would also have to include the vast scale on which the Balkan wars are conducted. When they discuss the many wars of the past, Serb historians often use metaphors like 'storm winds that raged over the Balkans': an image that brings home the fact that everybody and everything was affected. In the words of the 1913 report of investigation: 'war is waged not only by the armies but by the nations themselves....this is why these wars are so sanguinary, why they produce so great a loss in men, and end in the annihilation of the population and the ruin of whole regions'.[26] Unreliable as they often are, the statistics at any rate all tell the same tale of mass destruction. One out of three Serbs was killed during the two Balkan Wars (1912 and 1913) and the First World War from war violence, hunger or epidemics. The figures for the Second World War are just as shocking: the official postwar statistics refer to 1,706,000 victims, 305,000 of them soldiers. This accounted for almost 11 per cent of the total population of Yugoslavia at the time.[27]

The total war
Besides statistics, an account would also have to list all the points which make the defeat of the victims a total defeat. War violates people's physical, mental, social and material lives. The survivors become acquainted with the experience that everything that had gone into making up their lives, everything that had offered a foothold and given life meaning and significance – their family, their relatives, their friends, their house and home, their photo albums and favourite chair, their money and possessions, their livestock and land, the lovely view from the bedroom window, their city and their country, the spot where their ancestors lay buried – all of it had proved unable to stand up to the war. A letter from a woman in Sarajevo to her brother in the Netherlands: 'To think that I could ever long for simple things like something to eat and especially: lying for hours in a warm bath. Incredible. Now I dream of filling the bath and emptying a whole bubble bath into it. What a prosaic wish!'

Belief in humanity and feelings of honour and self-respect seem to become totally disjointed. A refugee in a Dutch shelter to a psychologist:

I'm glad you're here. I can talk to you, I can't talk to the others here.

Perhaps they've been through even worse. No one is forced to listen to me. You listen to me. Now I can get it off my chest. After more than thirty years you come to the Netherlands, to the end of the world, and there they care about you [breaks down]. They give you food and clothes to wear. But someone who was your colleague for 25 years, with whom you worked, went out and shared the best years of your life, put on a *četnik* uniform and murdered eighty Muslim children. She deceived me. We're a deceived people.[28]

All those relations and all those matters which were taken to be natural and taken for granted reveal their essentially illusory character in the war situation. Like a soap-bubble, they can burst at any moment:

Do you really feel like an exile, a homeless person?
– Yes, I'm a homeless exile, because the first time I was forced to go into an air raid shelter the idea of 'home' was somehow destroyed. Whether we've actually lost a roof above our heads or not, whether we're actually exiles or not, the simple fact that many have lost a roof above their heads and have been driven out of their homes, that the same thing could easily have happened to us, and still can – all that makes each of us a homeless person. A house, the whole idea of home belongs to the peaceful cultures. We live in a war culture: and in a culture like that there is no room for a home, for a warm, comfortable chair, our books, a future.[29]

A war anecdote, one of the many stories that circulated during my fieldwork in Novi Sad, provides another clear example of this insight. A woman doctor, a Serb from Borovo Selo, one of the hot spots in East Slavonia, not far from Novi Sad, had been married to a Croat for five years. One day she found a note on the kitchen table with the words *'Srpsko Ciganko!* [Serb Gypsy], I don't know how I managed to stand you for five years.' He'd gone off with the children. The woman – 'an intellectual!', my informant emphasised – arrived in Novi Sad completely broke. She had lost everything, absolutely everything. Now all she wanted was a weapon so she could go to the front to kill – 'or get killed', my informant wryly added. It is characteristic that this story was so popular in Novi Sad (and elsewhere: soon afterwards I found an almost identical version in a magazine which was supposed to have taken place in Zadar, Dalmatia). The story summed up perfectly the experiences of my discussion partners: fundamental principles on which their lives had been based, such as belief in Yugoslavia, in "Brotherhood and Unity", in Serbs and Croats living together, in a family life, in the ideal of a good education and job, but above all in the possibility of keeping emotions under the control of reason, turned out to have been unfounded.

The desecrative war

The account would also have to point out how nothing is sacred in war. War teaches that every conceivable taboo can be broken, and every taboo is broken. And where there are no longer any taboos, war teaches, no one is spared the effects of the storm: no man, no woman, no child, no pensioner, no one who is ill or mentally deficient, no journalist or nurse. All rules have been suspended, all arguments for sparing them have lost their validity, all violations are allowed. Nuns are raped, child convoys are shelled, the mentally ill are abandoned to their fate without food or drink, hospital patients are taken from their beds, dragged off to a field and shot. Cultural monuments and libraries, historic buildings and sacred places like houses of prayer and cemeteries: they can all be destroyed, and they are all destroyed.

The shameless, importunate war

Attention would also certainly have to be paid to the public character of the violations, the undisguised way in which the cruelties are manifested. The killings are not confined to the fields of battle, nor do they take place only behind the walls of concentration camps – protected and protecting frames which keep overly lucid insights at a distance – but they penetrate deep into the scenery of everyday life. The terrors of the war may take place in streets and village squares, in hallways or farmyards. The residents in those districts of Novi Sad where the German and Hungarian troops had done most of the butchering during World War Two were still able to point out the pieces of décor which had played a part in that murderous game. When I passed a restaurant in the centre of town with a Gypsy musician, he suddenly pointed to the ground to show me where the bodies had lain during the Second World War. An old man I got into conversation with on the municipal beach beside the Danube reminded me that this recreation area was the spot where the razzias had reached their bloodiest climax. These kinds of incidents made me realise how a street, a beach or a city like this is never the same:

> Those back streets, overgrown with grass and lined with squat, low houses, almost entirely inhabited by Serbian agricultural workers and small tradesmen, were scenes of the greatest cruelty when the Hungarian troops arrived. The soldiers, carrying out their raids, were not in the least restrained by the sight of such modest means, such neglect. There, among

the houses with damp walls, faded flowers in the windows, the image of the killings still hovered, muted. The people who in the evenings came out to talk at their gates still pointed to the lampposts from which their neighbours had been hanged, and to the darkened windows of the homes from which a friend had been led away. For these people, there was no topic of conversation more lively.[30]

Although Novi Sad itself was not the site of hostilities in 1991-1992, unprecedentedly detailed pictures of the horrors found their way into its living rooms. The television set, still ornamented with emblems of bourgeois culture like crochet-work and floral decorations, offered the prospect of endless series of images of death, destruction and corruption. The programming did not display the slightest degree of reticence. Viewers were not warned that some of them might be shocked by the pictures; the cameras of Belgrade Radio-Television and Novi Sad Radio-Television zoomed in shamelessly on cut-off noses and ears, eyes that had been put out, and other mutilations that had been perpetrated on the faces of dead soldiers and civilians. One evening-length programme was completely devoted to the shocking images of a bloodbath somewhere in Croatia: despondent people on a farm collecting the limbs of their relatives that were scattered all over the place and putting them in a coffin. Corpses, besmirched and arranged in the most humiliating attitudes and positions, were put on the air without any excuse.

The cruel war

In addition to these allusions to the recurrent, total, public and desecrative character of war, our account would probably also benefit from an extensive and detailed description of the cruelties and misery that the South Slavs were forced to witness during the war. I could cite from the naked descriptions of cruelties recorded by the committee of investigation of the Carnegie Endowment for International Peace in 1913; or from those compiled by present-day organisations like Amnesty International, Helsinki Watch or Helsinki Citizen Assembly; or from the detached and sober record of violence and torture in Tišma's *The Use of Man* or *Škola bezbožništva* (The School of Godlessness); or the feverish war lyrics that the Montenegran writer Miodrag Bulatović wrote in commemoration of the Second World War:

> Taliano, Taliano. Oh, my Taliano, my little soldier, how desperately he resisted when, naked and bloodied as he was, they stole his manhood from him. These Greeks or Serbs did it as they would to a bull or a ram. A cou-

ple held him in their grip, the others crushed his testicles with sticks and
stones. When they had bruised everything beyond repair, they started on
the soles of his feet. They roasted them, whispering incomprehensible
words in tender tones. Then they pulled out his nails, asked him something, and started to cry. Oh, my Taliano, my little soldier, they tore the
skin from your shoulders and made you filthy with ash and soil![31]

The unspeakable war
When all is said and done, it seems pointless to try to outline an account
which could convince the reader of the damage that war causes to stories that confer meaning and significance. How many pages of sensa-
tional details and lists of the cruelties, the bloodbaths and violations of
every conceivable taboo would it take to even approximate the experience? How many words would it take to get the awareness of the war
across? How many words to match all the reports on Yugoslavia that
have appeared in the newspapers and on television? And how many to
break down the wall of defensive reactions that has been erected against
those pictures and reports?

As I reread the passages you have just been reading, time and again I
was tempted to scrap the most poignant examples and illustrations. I
found them too crude, incompatible with the stylistic conventions of
moderation, control and good taste. My reaction was often one of: 'OK,
I know it by now, it really is terrible but I'm not in the mood at the moment'. It was precisely those reactions, the desire to purge my text of ugly
and disturbing material, that made me decide to keep these passages:
they are yet another illustration of the forces that are constantly at work
to protect those cherished stories ('the world is a tasteful entity', 'my
longing for peace and quiet is justified') from what threatens them.

All the same, I still find Danilo Kiš's decision to say something about
war experiences effective and tasteful. Note 53 of the madman in his
novel *Hourglass*:

> That feeling that my own I has left me, the way I see myself through an-
> other's eyes, that relation to myself as a stranger*
>
> beside the Danube while I stood in line. It was the same feeling...

The author adds a footnote:

> *Incomplete. A page is missing.

Just enough information to make the reader realise that the madman wants to compare his present sense of alienation with his feelings and experiences during the razzias in Novi Sad in January 1942, when he and all the other victims stood in line waiting to be executed and had to watch their unfortunate predecessors being thrown beneath the ice of the Danube. And nothing else except the comment that there is a page missing. Did that page contain a description of or reflections on the events on the banks of the Danube? Was it ever written at all? Was it torn out later? Was it unsatisfactory, merely evidence of the shortcomings of words? Kiš does not provide a direct answer to these questions. In fact, the missing page already says enough about how war nestles in fictional reality.

The silence of the victims...

The unspeakable nature of war experiences, the hard confrontation with the limitations of language as a way of expressing experiences, is perhaps the point at which the war affects the survivors' image of humanity and the world the most. The characters in Tišma's novels become alienated from language through their experiences. Kiš's madman tries to find salvation from lucid insights and knowledge in his madness. But it is not just writers who realise that language cannot accommodate the experiences of war victims and refugees. The refugees who were interviewed by journalists for practically every news programme during the war were often unable to reply to the questions except by remaining silent.

There's nothing surprising about that. How could anyone tell the story of what it felt like to spend three months in a cellar in Vukovar while the bombs crashed down on your city, your home and your life? Or the story of how life was reduced to endlessly waiting for rain to get fresh drinking water, waiting for the neighbour who dared to buy something to eat on the black market during a lull in the fighting, or waiting for the interminable cold rains to finally stop so that the cellars could dry out? How could anyone tell the story of the settling of accounts that took place after 'liberation', of the relief at leaving that damp and chilly cellar and the fear that the 'liberator' still might kill you because of where you come from? How to tell the story that what others see as the ruins of a city smashed to smithereens was your city, your street, your local shop, your home?

'Three months in a cellar': that endless, interminable period of fear reduced to five words, spoken in the twinkling of an eye. What is lost in the translation of experience into language? What tense corresponds to something that took place as an event in the past but which is still present in every way, here and now? All the inevitable choices called for when you put an experience into words – the choice of terms that suggest transparent meaning where ambiguity would be more appropriate; the choice of a sequence of words that immediately entails a hierarchy: terrible to fearful to hunger and thirst to boredom – is that the right sequence? It was probably all those things at the same time, undifferentiated, an inextricable tangle of impressions and feelings. Letter from Sarajevo:

> Sarajevo, 8 September 1992. It's difficult to write in conditions like these, no matter how much you love someone, because things sound so normal and rational in a letter. How can you convey the fear, the panic and the little bit of sensibility that we still have? We live every day with God's misfortune, death stares at us and we stare back. We grow less and less afraid, we are moved and alarmed less and less by this tragedy. We grow less and less human, more and more like animals who can only follow their animal instincts: stay alive! So what should I tell you?[32]

Refugees interviewed by journalists do not just talk about their experiences. At the same time, and perhaps more, they are talking about the inability of words to give meaning to those experiences. They sum up their experiences in a flat tone. Registering facts, without any further attempt to interpret them. Sometimes gasping for air between sentences. Sometimes in tears. Sometimes talking as if what they have been through is of no account. All in the same flat tone:

> We had everything, we all lived comfortably, we had our own house, we had everything, everything, we had a higher than average standard of living, you know. And now we've got nothing, now we have to start all over again from scratch. We don't even know how to go about it. What can I say to you? I don't know, it's indescribable. I can't find any words for it. How we feel is something that we only know in our soul.[33]

I feel humiliated.
– Why?
– Because I have to do this. It's difficult to explain exactly what I feel.
The twenty-year-old doesn't look up while he talks. He has a jerry-can sawn in half that he slowly fills with water from one of the few taps that still work in Sarajevo. Then he pours it into another jerry-can.
– Who's fault is it?
– Above all the politicians.

Modriča was attacked from all sides. [Pause] Everyone was in the shelters, terrified. In the end our town was occupied. A lot of women had been left there on their own. Many of them were forced to walk through the town naked. They had to dance on tables and serve naked. They had to liven up the men with *četnik* songs. [Pause] The men were of mixed ancestry and didn't distinguish between Serbs, Croats and Muslims. They murdered and raped indiscriminately. They all did it, young and old.

– Do you feel relieved now, after your abortion? As if a heavy burden has been removed?

– [Irritated] You journalists and everyone who interferes with me here, you think it doesn't bother me. But I have a very difficult time at night.[34]

Various people interviewed in Bosnia:[35]

I was taken prisoner in Foča on 20 April. I was in a camp near Foča until 11 September. I survived those traumas, I don't know how, you can imagine what it's like being a prisoner in a camp. [Shrugs his shoulders] Well, now I'm on the move, I haven't seen my wife and children for seven months. I can't find them anywhere. They won't let me through.

What am I supposed to do? Where am I supposed to go? What am I supposed to say?

– Just tell us what happened.

– We had to leave Jajce. It was torture. My children are split up all over the place. We wanted to go to Split, but they wouldn't let us through. Now we're here. What else am I supposed to say?

We had a car but we had to leave it behind in a village. We had to continue on foot, with young children and old people. We went by cart, we walked, or even got a lift on a tractor. People died on the way. Old people who couldn't keep up. Children too. When we reached the fort we saw how the children were buried there. We were exposed to grenade fire on the way. It's...I mean...indescribable.

It's very depressing to work here when you can't do anything. In six months' time or so, when people feel a bit freer, they'll feel the backlash of what they've been through. At the moment they're more or less anaesthetised. They're free. In a few months we'll see how they come to terms with their situation. There are twelve-year-old girls here who have been raped. You wouldn't believe it if you saw them. They can't express themselves. They can't say how they've suffered.

There was a man with a motorbike. The Serbs tied his testicles with a rope to the bike and drove off. They were torn out. They cut off noses and ears. These aren't incidents. You can hardly believe it really happens. But a woman here has recorded their statements. When I see them, I think: have they been through that? I can't comprehend it. That they've been through such terrible things.

Men were killed, women raped, beaten, butchered. What else is there to say? Everything was burned down or stolen. There was a lot of killing in Prijedor. What else? One-month-old babies were murdered. 2,500 people were killed in three or four hours.

For those who have been through the experience of what war can do to human lives, silence seems the most appropriate response to their experiences. The young woman who turned up alone one day at a refugee shelter in Croatia hadn't spoken a word for days. The Red Cross took care of her, washed her, gave her clean clothes and combed her hair. Now she just sat on the bed, staring into space. No one knew who she was, where she belonged, where she had come from, what she had been through. She did not speak.

Perhaps her silence should be interpreted as a sign of impotence. Perhaps the language of reason simply does not have a vehicle by which to express the experiences she had been through. But perhaps this mute woman in the Croatian refugee camp didn't want to yield her experience to the words and thoughts of others, for others to give it meaning and significance, the lying propagandists and the historians, who would steal her pain, her loss to embellish their own stories.

However that may be, the propagandists and historians, unlike the refugees, are never short of words, meaning or significance. Suffering is one of the colours in their palette. They appropriate the suffering of the common people, they homogenise and instrumentalise that suffering, use it as heavy ammunition to defend stories that in the first and last instance are theirs. For the silent woman in the refugee camp, the refugees from Jajce, the old peasant woman in the ruins of the village in Hercegovina, or any other victim of this war, all they are left with now when they draw up the balance is a list of losses. It is highly debatable whether they will recognise their experiences in the selection of important facts and memorable events which the chroniclers of this war will parade; and it is most unlikely that the victims will recognise themselves in the interpretation that those chronicles make of their experiences.

...and the words of the propagandists and historians

When I contrast the scenarios of the experiences described above with the war as it is represented in Serb historiography, journalism and propaganda, the dilemma which faces this society time and again rises to the surface: unspeakable experiences whose potential to undermine stories entails their exclusion from the stories that accompany the postwar reconstruction. They persist only as a subterranean knowledge.

Closer analysis of the 'translations of war into narrative', as Nancy Huston has called them,[36] offers insight into how people are tempted to move into these stories and into the negations that this requires.

Tito's lovely war
Perhaps the clearest example is provided by Tito's 'good news' about World War II. A precise study of Yugoslav historiography after World War II still has to be written, but Mark Thompson's concise characterisation as 'euphemisms and suppressions' seems adequate for the time being.[37] It is difficult to deny that there was a lot of suffering during World War II, that a lot of sacrifices were made, and that the country was transformed into a gigantic mess, even for the Titoist historians. But public commemorations only had room for the painful experiences that people had been through if the terrible character of the enemy and his inhuman behaviour had to be highlighted, or the perseverance and immeasurable goodness of the partisans. There was no place for suffering as an autonomous experience that deserved attention in itself.

'Comrades! Dear Guests!', was how Tito greeted the people of Titovo Užice in Serbia during a speech on the twentieth anniversary of the People's Revolution and Liberation War:

> Twenty years have passed from the days when the best sons and daughters of our peoples began writing the most glorious pages of our history with their blood. Those are great historical days so vividly remembered by all who took part in or witnessed those momentous events. Memories of these days will always be proudly transmitted from generation to generation. The past will provide a shining example to future generations, of how the peoples of a small country, determined to defend their land's freedom at all costs preferred death to servitude under the fascist invaders. And today when attempts are being made to minimize the glory of these days and years, to belittle the sacrifices made on this soil and throughout our country which suffered untold hardships during the four years of war, a great and mighty truth which cannot be concealed or dimmed by any means

blazes forth from these pages of our history.

What does the Twentieth Anniversary of the Liberation War and People's Revolution we are celebrating mean for the peoples of Yugoslavia? Twenty years in the life of a people are not much as peoples live for centuries and millenniums. For our country and peoples, however, these twenty years mark a historical turning point, a rebirth and the beginning of a new epoch which opens new vistas and the broadest prospects for the all-round development of all social forces in our new socialist society.[38]

The speech is indicative of the space that was left for war experiences in postwar Yugoslavia: not a word on the experiences of the war victims discussed above. Where the war was commemorated, as Mosse has also shown in his study of coming to terms with the war after World War I, it was 'in remembrance of the glory rather than the horror of war, its purposefulness rather than its tragedy'.[39] Glenny refers to 'the comic-book legend which the wartime struggle became at the hands of the Titoist historians',[40] and Drakulić recalls the lovely war of the partisan films from her childhood when ever brave, intelligent, humane and victorious partisans always introduced the spectacular massive attack scenes with a cry of 'Hurrah, comrades!'[41]

However, although the drama of the war could be deployed to underline the grandeur of the Yugoslav peoples in general and the partisans in particular, the most important feature of the past for Tito's partisans lay in the fact that it was definitively over. Commemorations like the one in Titovo Užice were in the first and last instance about the new start and the break with the past. 'Yesterday is over' was the slogan of the utopian idealistic rhetoric used by Tito's followers. 'Forwards', 'Progress' and 'We look to the Future' were the slogans of the new order. Metaphors like 'the Way', 'the Horizon', 'the Dawn', 'the Youth', 'the Spring' and 'the Enlightenment' also testify to a ban on retrospection. Anyone who lingered too long on bad memories could be accused of the specifically anti-socialist sins of defeatism, weariness, pessimism or lack of spirit.[42] That intrinsically positive quality that was assigned to what was over is perhaps best illustrated by Tito's answer to the question of why the whole people always greeted him at all times, places and weathers: 'It is because our people see that we are making progress, *that it is nowhere as it used to be*'.[43]

Like the logic that the Sarajevans developed on where the bombs will fall, the Titoist histories of the war provided a necessary story in which the victims could accommodate their painful experiences. In the aftermath of the war, when reconstruction and the return to normality were the central issues, these histories offered a framework which might confer meaning and purpose on the pointless suffering, ungrounded fear, total loss or all the other unbearable experiences that the war had imposed on people:

> Even for the postwar generation in Yugoslavia, the war was not a purposeless, meaningless shedding of blood, but a heroic, meaningful experience which was more than worth its one million victims. We stuck to this idea because our whole upbringing, lessons, textbooks, especially history books, speeches and newspapers were permeated by it, as if there had hardly been any history before 1941.[44]

Glorious defeat

In the last war it was once again the epic heroic poems of the Serbs, and the notions derived from them of the Serbs as a people that is destined to suffer, that formed the framework within which meaning and significance were conferred on the wartime experiences. During the period of my fieldwork in Serbia, a commonly cited motto was that of the popular writer Dobrica Ćosić: '*Srbi ginu u miru a dobijaju u ratu*' (The Serbs gain in peace and lose in war). So the ultimate experience of being a Serb can only be achieved in total defeat. To understand something more of the logic behind this sinister view of history, I shall look more closely at one of those events from history.

The myths and legends associated with the Battle of Kosovo in 1389 are exemplary in this respect. The story of how the mass of Serb troops under Czar Lazar were defeated by the superior Ottoman Turks – the story of the collapse of the medieval Serb empire and the commencement of five hundred years of darkness – occupies a significant place in Serb mentality, thought and feeling.[45] This story seems to have served as the model for the present-day collection of Major Serbian Events which the Serbs have compiled from their history: the Great Serbian Exodus of 1690, episodes from the First World War such as the Battle of the Drina river and the Solunski Front, the genocide of Serbs by the Croats during World War II. Each of these stories is one of the destruction, defeat and sufferings of the Serbs.

The Serb anthropologist Dušan Bandić has made a study of the Kosovo myths. He concentrates on a key passage in the myth in which an event is described that takes place on the eve of the Battle of Kosovo, at the moment when the assembled armies are preparing for the fight against the powerful Turkish army. That evening a grey falcon – the messenger of the Mother of God – offers Czar Lazar a choice: he can opt for the kingdom on earth, in which case victory over the Turks is guaranteed, or he can opt for the kingdom of heaven, in which case the armies will be defeated and all the Serb land will be overrun. After long meditation, Czar Lazar chooses the latter; in the famous phrase of the epic poem: '*zemaljsko je za maleno carstvo, a nebesko uvek i doveka*' (the earthly kingdom is of short duration, while the kingdom of heaven is everlasting and eternal).

This preference for earthly defeat and heavenly rewards is certainly astonishing. Why did Lazar have to die such a tragic death in order to enter heaven? Why couldn't he enter the kingdom of heaven as the victor of a battle against the infidel, as is common enough in Christian mythology? And how could he make this choice in full awareness of the consequences, namely that not only he and his army would be defeated, but also '*sve ono što je medju Srbima najvrednije*' (everything that is most valuable among Serbs)?

Bandić, whose interpretation makes use of ideas with a heavy nationalistic colouring, offers the following solution. The fates of the Czar and of his people are in a certain sense identical.[46] Lazar sacrificed his life and his kingdom to achieve higher spiritual ends. He did not do so out of free will, but was offered what was in fact an impossible choice by the higher powers (the Mother of God). And that, the anthropologist claims, is the historical fate of the Serbs:

> The Serbs have achieved genuine freedom through self-sacrifice. This is not the same as freedom in the conventional, everyday meaning of the word. They obtained freedom where their commander led them, in the kingdom of heaven. And that kingdom, as we have seen, is situated in themselves, in their soul, in the consciousness of the people. That kingdom is out of reach of any conquest at all. The Serbs could maintain their independence in this kingdom. They were subjected, but they were never enslaved. That is how they save their 'soul'. And that is how things still stand today. [...] The traditions on the fate of the Serb ruler Lazar are a poetic image which enables the Serb people to represent its own history, or rather, by means of which they could indicate their historical destiny. In their epic poems, the Serbs have represented themselves as a people that had to die in order to live, that had to relinquish earthly claims, but not heavenly ones. Such a picture of their destiny is perhaps naïve but – in the widest sense of the word – it is not incorrect. The myth shows the fate of a small people who are exposed to the whirlwinds of history that rage over the Balkans, a people condemned to struggle for survival against much

larger and more powerful peoples. A people like that can only survive in the way the legend indicates: by retaining its identity and independent spirit.[47]

These myths also assign a very positive role to war experiences. War, they imply, cannot be won by us. But war does provide the ideal condition in which to test being a Serb in its ultimate form: because the most complete way to be a Serb is to prefer death to a life of slavery.[48] No matter how archaic these ideas about the Serb 'soul' that can only flourish in independence and liberty may be, and no matter how sharp a contradiction there is between a sense of self-pity blown up to such baroque proportions, on the one hand, and the hard facts of Serb aggression in Bosnia and Croatia, on the other, it is not difficult to see that these myths too, in which total defeat offers spiritual victory, can provide a foothold in an acceptance, albeit an uncomprehending one, of the recurrent catastrophes which plague the peoples of the Balkans.[49]

No better Serb than the Serb who has laid down his life for the Serb cause. That is also the message from which people who were afflicted by the recent war were supposed to draw hope. The in memoriam for the 'volunteer' Srdjan Ignjatović, killed during the 'liberation' of Tenja in East Slavonia on 7 December 1991, ran:

> Loved among his comrades, known among his fellow villagers for his dedication, Srdjan could not turn a deaf ear to the call to aid his people. Brought up to the idea that in a case of injustice one should side with the underdog and always defend the truth, Srdjan unconditionally joined the volunteers from Prokuplje. The cheerful lad from Prokuplje, as his fellow combatants at the front came to know him, wrote to his parents: 'Dear father and mother, do not be alarmed. I have courageous comrades and we are bound to win, because death cannot touch the victor'.
>
> Two days after his mother Slavica and his father Milinko received this optimistic letter, they heard the news of the death of their only son. An incalculable pain now reigns in the home of the IgnjatoviÆ family, a black banner waves on the roof, black cloths cover Srdjan's new moped, and we find the mourning parents and sister beside a freshly dug grave in the small village cemetery. The plans to marry a girl from his village will never come to fruition.
>
> Srdjan Ignjatović, like all the other heroes who preceded him, has taken his place in the legends of a people who, because of the wishes of others, have had to pay with their blood for the most elementary freedom for centuries.[50]

Incalculable pain, lives cut short, disillusioned fiancées are essential in-
gredients of life in the Balkans. That seems to be the message to the general public. But if the parents of this young man are prepared to give up
their sorrow to the moral of this story, then, however meagre the consolation may be, their loss is at any rate no longer total. There are gains to
balance out the losses.

Truths and other lies

'We can tell any truth or untruth', George Steiner once remarked on our
ability to make up stories, and he was referring to both the creative potential of that fact and to the risk of nihilism. And yet, he claimed, there
are worlds of experience that cannot be accommodated in any story.

The people of former Yugoslavia have come across both facets of our
ability to make stories in the recurrent war. The mute, silent version of
the victims of the war betrays the alienation that occurs when there is no
language or story at hand to confer sense and meaning. The histories
produced by the Titoist historians or epic poets show how, after the war,
fictional reality enters a completely different but no less alienating crisis:
people are introduced to the unlimited potential of the lie.

The following selection of statements requires no further comment:

> I have never been anywhere where people lie so often and so openly. Take
> the cease-fires – they're like confetti. You know, very high-ranking people
> look at you and tell you that they haven't got any troops in, say, Bosnia-
> Hercegovina, and you know damned well – in fact, they know that you
> know – that it's a lie.
>
> (*Lord David Owen, EC negotiator in an interview with the BBC on his role in
> the negotiations with the parties in the Bosnian conflict*).

> I didn't say that war is better than Communism. What I said was that it's
> degrading to human dignity to live under a Communist regime because it
> reduces you to an idiot. Under Communism you had to swallow and de-
> fend opinions which did not agree with your convictions. Against your bet-
> ter judgement you had to betray principles. That is no longer the case. Even
> though there's a war going on, even though there are irrational forces on
> the loose at work, it's still no longer necessary for individuals to sink so low
> that they have to say the opposite of what they think. That's why I'm con-
> vinced that the situation now is better than under Communism.
>
> (*Aleksandar Tišma*).[51]

Oh, stupid Mile,
Why do you so lie so?
Say something true for once
Then you'll get a plush hat.

I walk the road in hunger.
Ajao! People! What a wretched soul I am!
Ajao! God! How terribly poor I am!
I don't even have a father.

If I may not lie either,
I might just as well do myself in.

(*Miroslav Antić, from the collection of poems Garavi Sokak*).

They're lying! They're lying!
They're saying that time heals all wounds!
Oh! How they lie!
My God, how they lie!

(*Hit single by the Serb singer Miroslav Ilić, Lazu da vreme leći sve!*)

I was moving inside a multi-storeyed labyrinth of deception. The free-wheeling pandemonium of events was actually controlled, until almost the end of 1991, by a handful of people who knew just what was happening, and ensured that the rest of the nation was fed an irresistible diet of lies. And the nation guzzled these lies so avidly that it turned into a lie. But I can't deny it was fascinating, pruriently so, to be in Serbia as the war escalated through late summer. I pictured myself as a doctor in a science fiction film, shrunk to the size of pollen dust and injected into a psychotic patient to observe the exploding synapses, fizzing ganglia, and rogue chemical invasions.[52]

(*Mark Thompson, A Paper House. The Ending of Yugoslavia*)

The lie is more readily accepted than the truth.

(*Serb proverb*).

I recently went to that grave and saw that my mother had laid a floral garland on that red star. She had bent the flowers so that you couldn't see the star any more. It made me very sad. It's only a small cemetery and everyone knows that it's the only grave with a red star. Still, she wanted to use the flowers to prevent the grave from being vandalised. I didn't dare to talk to her about it. We cover up the past and don't dare to stand up for our memories. We keep our mouth shut. We don't have the guts to say: 'This is my past and who are you to say I've been in the wrong for forty years'?

(Writer Slavenka Drakulić on her father's grave, the only one without a cross but with a red star in the small Croatian cemetery)[53]

Give me eyes that don't cry!
Give me a woman who doesn't mess around!
Give me wine that doesn't lie
And a song to love for free!

(Hit single by the Bosnian singer Haris Džinović, Laže me noćas ona).

I have spoken with hundreds of party members but have never found one who, when speaking privately, was a true believer. The hum of propaganda has created the facade of party conformity but Marxist political lingo has been so overused that it has been drained of all meaning. Party members openly have their children baptized and hold church weddings. [...] Undoubtedly, among 1.4 million party members there must be some true believers, but it is difficult for any outsider to discover who they are or whether in fact they exist. I have inquired into this aspect of Yugoslav life with greater persistence than it probably deserved, asking numerous Yugoslav acquaintances whether in their circles they knew of any true believers. Once, a Slovene engineer whom I befriended responded by saying that he had long thought the arm-waving circus posturing of a young colleague reflected sincere idealism until he had an intimate talk with him and discovered a cynical young opportunist. An even more stunning admission came from an old communist, who is a federal judge and the author of a series of books on 'socialist legality'. He had spent some time in Sweden on an exchange program and came to the conclusion, as he told us, that 'Sweden is the only place I know of where you have socialism. We and the Russians only talk about socialism without knowing much about it.'

(Dusko Doder, The Yugoslavs)[54]

The only truth about the war in Yugoslavia is the lie.

(War correspondent Micha Glenny)[55]

In this chapter I have followed the constant references of my discussion partners to a different domain of knowledge – an exclusively Serb knowledge, a knowledge that is truer than the stories that determine everyday reality, drawing on the reports and images of the recent war which once again plagued the territory of former Yugoslavia.

The inspiration derived from the war has provided a number of important facts. War is a world of experience in which the artificial nature of the world as we know it is revealed. 'All those stories are nonsense' is the lesson of war. *Prazne priče*. But at the same time the war says something else as well: 'I am reality'. To put it in other, less reifying words, war teaches people a knowledge based on experience that is simply undeniable. Dead is dead. Pain is pain. Broken is broken. Gone is gone. That's true. All the rest is idle talk.

The alienation that finds its way through the lessons from the reform school of war into fictional reality has been identified time and again in the books of writers like Krleža, Kiš and Tišma. But how many writers does a population have? And what do the rest do, those whose lives have taken such a course after the war that they do not arrive at the studied and concentrated formulations of the writers?

4   On Mud and Gypsies, or On People and the World as They Simply Are

The aim of the preceding chapters was to show that the South Slavs became acquainted with a world of experience during wartime that was no longer allowed once the return to normality was the main item on the agenda. The knowledge about people and the world that had been acquired during the war now had to be repressed and consigned to oblivion. This was the only way for the South Slavs to find the energy, courage and decisiveness to construct a new world on the ruins of their existence. And it was the only way that the story designed to flesh out that new, postwar world – a story of reasonableness, mutual cooperation and solidarity, (self-)control, hard work, frugality and progress – could be protected from the mocking of experience and an absurdity that throws everything out of joint.

However necessary this may have been, though, the question was whether people were really capable of this act of repressing and forgetting. There was certainly no lack of good intentions. The earnest attempts of the *fini ljudi* to purify themselves and their surroundings of the signs of wildness, and the showy way they claimed their place in civilised Europe, are examples of this endeavour once and for all to subject the 'primitive' peoples of the Balkans, with their never ending conflicts and bloody wars, to the laws of civilisation. However, I also suggested that the insights into people and the world that were acquired during the war persisted beneath the epidermis of public life. In a non-stop (and, as the war continued, growing) stream of asides and off- the-record-comments, my discussion partners in Novi Sad displayed a fundamental mistrust of the feasibility of their own civilising project. Their fragmentary remarks echoed the implicit social knowledge that had been acquired by successive generations of South Slavs: war and destructive conflict are recurring phenomena, everything is ephemeral, even those things we regard as natural, unchanging and divinely ordained.

The dilemma facing the peoples of this part of Europe could be formulated as follows: there is a permanent tension between the social and psychological need to forget the terrors of the war, and the impossibility of doing so, of forgetting what war can do.

So far I have concentrated on the first part of this thesis: the need to deny and forget, the erection of façades, and the mechanisms and strategies that are deployed to that end. The following chapters will focus on the second aspect of the thesis: the impossibility of erasing the empirical knowledge acquired during the wars in the Balkans. The main issue is the question of how people incorporate the lessons of the war in their lives. How are insights into the beast that lurks in man and the experiences of the war taken into account in their vision of society?

Questions like these make it clear how important it is for anthropologists to pay attention to the imaginary worlds that people create as well as to the discourses that dominate public life. The imagination takes over where everyday life in Novi Sad allows no scope for the lessons of the wartime experiences and pulverises implicit social knowledge to a fine dust that permeates every pore. In nightmares, dreams and daydreams, in the arts and other expressive genres, people abandon the everyday in order to create room for the imagination. As indicated in the introductory chapter, these fantastic imaginary worlds can be conceived as the drawing-board on which creative actors sketch the life projects which seem more or less appropriate to them. The fragments from the literary works of Krleža, Kiš, Tišma and Bulatović provided an example of an imaginary space of this kind in which the world is transformed in order to make contact with the implicit social knowledge that comes from experience. The imaginary world that the Serbs have woven around the figure of the Gypsy is another striking example.

Analogy: the world at war and the world of the Gypsies

The idea that the imaginary world spun around the Gypsy figure offers a haven for unspeakable wartime experiences was more or less imposed on me by the circumstances of my research. During the day I collected or studied material on Serb images of Gypsies and Gypsy life; the evening news and the morning paper contained virtually identical images and scenarios. Take *Ciganska Torba* (The Gypsy's Pouch) from the collection of poems *Idu Cigani* (The Gypsies Go By) by Ivan Glišić:

stare šešire	old hats
cipele tesne	cramped shoes
koru hleba	a crust of bread
u zlu to treba	useful in evil times
u žedne, bose	when the days are thirsty, barefoot

i gole dane	and naked
pred torbom cige	even the Emperor stops
i sam car stane	beside the Gypsy's pouch.[1]

This is not the Emperor familiar from Serb epics; a ruler who reflects on the pros and cons of the earthly and heavenly kingdoms on the eve of a decisive battle against the Turks. This Emperor has been reduced to the proportions of a hungry man looking for a crust of bread in a spot which can be regarded as the refuse heap of society: a Gypsy's pouch. In less turbulent times I would probably have skimmed over this passage; now the war revealed a layer of meaning in the text which does not require any further comment for anyone who has been confronted with images from the war in Croatia and Bosnia.

This collection of poems is illustrated with photographs that enable the reader to form a picture of Gypsy life. They show wagons with what looks like a hastily put together plastic covering. Gypsy men, women and children are shown on or around the wagons, their hair unkempt, wearing no less than four layers of clothing. Their few possessions are scattered here and there. Other photographs are of a Gypsy camp: Gypsies ostentatiously doing nothing, children running about, Gypsies trying to escape the heat of the sun in the shadow of a car. People warming their hands around small fires in an oil drum, or cooking in the street. The photographs in this collection, which was published before the war broke out, are artistic photographs of Others, of Gypsies. After the outbreak of war, exactly the same images appeared in the reports on the war on television and in the newspapers. But in those reports it is Bosnians, Croats and Serbs who are moving in the same wagons, with the same layers of clothing, their scanty possessions in plastic bags, cooking in the street, idling around and waiting in refugee camps, warming their hands around small fires in oil drums.

Let us take another example. The story *The Gypsy and the Lie*[2] suggests an analogy at a more philosophical level between the world of wartime experience and the imaginary world associated with Gypsies:

> It is said that the Gypsies once led honourable and respectable lives, like every other people in this world. Truth was their most sacred Good. During one of their trips they ended up in a wood. This wood turned out to be the kingdom of the apes. Before the Gypsies had properly realised this, the apes had surrounded them, and they led the head of the Gypsies to their king. The king of the apes addressed the head of the Gypsies:
> – I know that you and your people are devoted to truth. So tell me what

you see in my kingdom and tell me what my subjects look like.
– I'll tell you, the head of the Gypsies replied, if you swear that nothing in
    this world is dearer to you than truth.
When the king of the apes had made this solemn promise, the head of the
Gypsies said:
– In your kingdom the tails are longer than the heads. What I see in your
    case I see in the case of your subjects too. You've always been apes, and
    you will always remain apes.
The king was enraged when he heard this and he ordered his subjects to
tear the Gypsies and their leader to pieces.
Ever since, Gypsies are liars and the truth no longer exists, because it was
torn to shreds by the apes.

This story offers an explanation for the alleged duplicity of Gypsies. In
addition, more or less in passing, the last sentence provides an explanation for the lack of any truth in the world. The truth no longer exists, because it was torn to shreds by the apes. This explanation seems to refer
to what I argued in the previous chapter: no story can stand up to the
destructive beast in man.

This account of the demise of stories that confer meaning and significance during times of catastrophe also seems to be the main theme of the
story 'The Gypsies and the churches of cheese':

Once the Gypsies had stone churches. The Serbs, on the other hand, had
to be content with churches made of cheese. But when the Gypsies were
going through a difficult time and went hungry, they exchanged their stone
churches for the churches of the Serbs. The Gypsies immediately ate their
churches of cheese down to the last morsel. That is why the Serbs have
churches but the Gypsies do not.

This story too has more than one layer. At first sight it offers an explanation for the alleged absence of religious institutions among the
Gypsies. In the light of the war, however, it turns out to contain a deeper meaning: when life is reduced to a struggle for bare survival, religious
systems collapse. If you're hungry, the physical laws of survival take
precedence over everything else. Then you forget your belief, and if you
can get your hands on a church made of cheese, you eat it.

These examples suggest that these Gypsy stories are not just read and
narrated to say something about Gypsies and Gypsy life. They also offer
a haven for the painful and unwelcome insights of the Serbs themselves

that I referred to in the previous chapter as implicit social knowledge. This seems to be confirmed by the many Serb myths and stories, jokes and films, books and songs in which the main role is played by a Gypsy. These Gypsy stories are full of references to the world of experiences that the Serbs themselves came to know in times of war and disaster.

A reconstruction of the fantastic imaginary world associated with the figure of the Gypsy can thus offer insight into the question of how the Serbs accommodated their wartime experiences in their view of people and society. Viewed in the light of their collective fantasies about Gypsies, Serbs appear to be preoccupied with what lies behind the civilisation debate, the taboos, silences, questions that scream for attention but have to remain unspeakable and unspoken in everyday life. A reconstruction of this imaginary world of the Gypsies can also reveal how Serb society makes constant efforts to get a grip on the world that is simply there, the world lying out there in the rain and the mud, irrespective of what it is supposed to be like according to the prescriptions and labels of the civilisation debate.

I shall start this reconstruction by presenting a limited selection from my material on Serb images of Gypsy life which clearly bring out the analogy between the images, scripts and scenarios of a world at war and the images, scripts and scenarios of the fantastic imaginary world of the Gypsies. These snapshots of an imaginary world will largely speak for themselves.

Snapshots from an imaginary Gypsy world

How we had to flee
'Nothing, absolutely nothing, can move our houses', writes Tomislav Dretar, a poet who chose 'the Gypsy' and 'Gypsy life' as his motif and adorned his collection with the eloquent if somewhat bombastic title *Bol, Ciganska Rapsodija* (Pain, A Gypsy Rhapsody).[3]

Naše kuće čvrsto	Our houses are solid.
Na svom mjestu stoje	They stand in their place.
Našim kućama krov je nebo golo	The naked sky is their roof.
Našim kućama tlo je sag zemaljski	The carpet of the earth is their floor.
Našim kućama ognjište je sunce	The sun is their hearth fire.
Naša kuća jedno oko ima	Our house has only one window.
Našoj kući zid je zima	In our house, the winter is a wall.
Druže	Comrade,
Našu kuću nitko srušiti neće.	No one will destroy our house.

A more trivial example can be found in *Čergo moja, čergice* [Tent, my little tent], one of the many unashamedly sentimental songs on Gypsy life which form a part of the Serb bar repertoire.

Čergo moja, čergice	Tent, my little tent,
od čadjava platna	of smoke-stained cloth
Ti si meni kućica	You are my little home
srebrna i zlatna.	of silver and gold.
Gospodski su dvori	The houses of the lords
nepomične stene	are made of immovable stone.
a ti pratiš cigana	But you follow the Gypsy
kuda god se krene.	wherever he goes.
Moja živa vatrica	My lively little fire
što mi kuću krasi	that adorns my house
Svetluca mi vesela	My cheerful light
nikad se ne gasi.	will never die.

The advantages of a tent as against houses of immovable stone. Mobility. The light that will never die. As kitsch as can be, though perhaps the term is inappropriate here: refinement – another lesson from the reform school of war – is not the most appropriate way to express the world of experience to which this poem refers.

How we lost everything time and again
The war also forces us to look at Aleksandar Petrović's 1970 sketches of Gypsy life in the Vojdovina, *Skupljači Perja* (The Feather Collectors), through new eyes. The main themes of this film are loss and the futility of hoarding fortunes. The main character, a Gypsy who operates as a go-between on the goose-feather market, is caught up in an endless cycle of earning money, gambling money away and wasting it. His woman (mother? aunt? who knows?), a withered figure with a clutch of children, is depicted as a genuine monument to the recurring disaster that strikes the peoples of the Balkans. Time and again she is forced to look on as her only tangible and cherished possession, an enormous television set from the year dot, is taken to the pawnshop by the Gypsy gambler to pay his debts. Her ranting and raging are invariably rewarded with blows.

How we were thrown under the ice
The same film contains a scene which seems to refer unmistakably to the

razzias in Novi Sad in January 1942, the same events that haunt the works of Danilo Kiš and Aleksandar Tišma. In this scene, the feather collector, the main character in the film, has just killed a man. He carries him on a donkey over the frozen landscape along the banks of the Danube. It is a white, flat plain, only interrupted by the grey of frozen pools, pollard willows, undergrowth near the river, and the odd Gypsy hut. Tremulous women's voices murmur Serb hymns in the background. When they reach the river, the Gypsy slides his victim over the frozen surface towards a small round hole in the ice. The corpse disappears in it. It is a casual scene lacking in heavy dramatic content, but it acquires a strongly sacral character from the religious hymns and this muted white world. Nobody from Novi Sad with a historical awareness could miss the allusion contained in this scene on the banks of the Danube: the victims of the razzias in Novi Sad – Serbs, Jews and Gypsies – were thrown into a hole in the ice to disappear beneath the frozen waters of the Danube.

How we were victimised

A primary school textbook used in Novi Sad contains the story *Ciganski Slavuj* (Gypsy Nightingale) about how Gypsies were deported to the concentration camps by the Croatian *ustaši*:

> While the prisoners sat on the grass, hungry and tired, the ustaši drank plum brandy and ate bacon. And when they had eaten and drunk like animals, they summoned the old Gypsy.
> The officer said: 'Granddad! Hey, granddad! Play us a tune! If you play well we'll let you go... if you don't... see this gun?... we'll kill you. Come on! Show us which instrument sounds better, the violin or the pistol!'
> 'I'm not frightened of your pistol, young man, but we Gypsies can only sing when we're free.' The old Gypsy touched the strings of his instrument a couple of times and then stopped: 'Can you hear how scratchy the violin is? A Gypsy violin can only make scratching noises in the face of rifles and pistols. The violin can only make music in the moonlight.'
> The *ustaši* grew impatient. They fired, and the old man fell face down in the dirt. Mejra screamed. There was granddad, spread-eagled in the mud, one hand still clutching his violin. The column moved on. Mejra and her grandfather were left behind on their own.

Mejra's grandfather turned out not to be dead, but mortally wounded. Like all the dying Gypsies in the Serb storybooks, he used his remaining strength to draw one last song from his violin:

The old Gypsy drew his bow across the strings slower and slower, so that Mejra did not even notice how the last tone died away. When she looked into granddad's eyes, she saw the scenes of tents, endless roads, spirited horses, moonlight and campfires flare up in them one last time.

In the wood the *ustaši* officer said:

'The old man's croaked'.

The birds cried in the trees. The frogs joined in. Crickets packed up their violins and hid deep in the grass. Bears and bloodthirsty wolves retreated further into the dense forests of Bosnia, because even bigger beasts were travelling along the road – homo sapiens.[4]

The children of Novi Sad are asked to analyse this text on the basis of questions like: 'Reread the description of the prisoners of war on the grass and the *ustaši* eating. What feelings are aroused in you towards (a.) the *ustaši* and (b.) the prisoners of war?', 'Who are the people the writer describes as animals?', and questions for which, as far I could tell, *my* informants at any rate did not come up with much of an answer, like 'What does music mean to the old Gypsy?', and 'Explain what he means when he says "We Gypsies can only sing when we're free"?'.

How we had nothing

I asked two classes in a primary school in Novi Sad to write an essay on how they imagined Gypsy life. This is one of them:

How I imagine Gypsy life. They're strange people. They aren't bothered by anything. They spend the winter in a tent. The children warm their hands around a small fire. Gypsies always have lots of children and are very poor. They move house every other day. You often see them with their old bikes near the refuse containers. They don't have a job, clothes or warm shoes. People take pity on them, so they leave their old things near the containers. The Gypsies collect them and take them home. They don't have bath foam. They take a shower by throwing a bucket of water over themselves. If they go shopping, they often fill their pockets. And they beg in the streets, even if it's only for a dinar. They don't have an easy time, because they don't have any nappies for their children or prams. They haven't got any swaddling cloths to wrap their children in either. If they're lucky, they sometimes find an old cart. But almost always they find one piece after another and put their own carts together. Gypsy children play with mangy dogs while we take our poodles for a walk. They eat the bread we've thrown away. They come to school with worn out bags. They don't have any lunch with them and they're hungry all day. There are good ones and bad ones. Some of them swear at you all the time or jump around you. Then they say it's not fun to play with us. Personally, I think they're people too, even if they do have a black skin. You ought to love everyone in life. Black and white.

How we suffered
Suffering is not just the hackneyed picture of the crying Gypsy boy. It exists in every shape and form, and in overwhelming quantities. Farewell, loss, fickle women, an unjust world. But usually it's just there, an unavoidable part of life, without explanation or any specified cause. In the epilogue that Sreten Vujković wrote for the collection of poems *Pain, A Gypsy Rhapsody* – a quasi philosophical text – the Gypsies are commended for their unique capacity to achieve an equilibrium between 'reality as it is' and 'their emotional experiences in life':

> There is not a single people that has been so forced to elaborate strategies of survival (Jews belong to those peoples too). That is probably why Gypsies are so clever and inventive, because no other people (person) is the pawn of incalculable and blind forces day after day [...]. Pain is the main character in the theatre of Gypsy life. They are a people among whom history is constantly repeating itself, and so among whom pain is constantly repeating itself. Or rather, their present is never ending, and so their pain is never ending as well...[5]

The question of who is being discussed here immediately arises in the case of a passage like this one because of its obvious echoing of the laments of Serb propaganda. A newsreader on one of the Sarajevan channels made the comparison explicit. He began with a report of new atrocities on the East Slavonic front with a reference to what he presented as a Gypsy proverb: 'It was already bad, but it can always get worse'.

How we beat the cold
One of the schoolchildren wrote: 'Gypsies are most afraid of the winter, rain and wind, because then they're cold'. Another wrote: 'Some catch a cold and die'. One girl explained: 'When Gypsy children are born they're immediately thrown into cold water, and afterwards if the wind blows or it rains they are never cold'. The tricks and devices which offer marginal victories over an unlivable reality in a war of anti-heroes and losers. The imaginary world spun around the Gypsies has a place for this as well. One of the popular stories in which a bright Gypsy outwits every-

one is *Cigan i Pop* (The Gypsy and the Pope), in which a frozen Gypsy manages to get the dignitary to part with his duffle coat. They meet one winter's day: the Pope shivering with cold in spite of his warm winter coat, the Gypsy cheerful and unaffected even though he is dressed in little more than rags. Surprised at what he sees, the Pope asks the Gypsy whether he isn't freezing to death. The Gypsy manages to convince him that living out of doors has taught Gypsies that rags are the best protection against the cold. This arouses the Pope's greed, and they decide to exchange garments. Once the Gypsy has put on the Pope's warm coat, he takes to his heels as fast as he can.[6]

How we beat hunger
These too are victories over circumstances. The story *Ciganska Želja* (Gypsy Wish) contains an imaginary feast which could only have been thought up by someone who knew what hunger was:

> 'If we had fat and flour, we'd go and borrow a pan in the village to bake pita bread', a Gypsy woman once said. A Gypsy child replied: 'And I'd take the pita to the oven to bake it'. Another of the children, making the gesture of putting something in his mouth, added: 'And I'd eat it like this!' The Gypsy boxed his ears for him. 'Hold on a minute! Just look what a big piece you took! Do you want to eat it all by yourself?'[7]

A Gypsy family looking for food in a garbage can. Drawing by Janko from Novi Sad (9 years).

How no one can keep the peoples of the Balkans down
The final snapshot is perhaps the most remarkable in the series. It is a curious report published in the Belgrade daily *Politika* on 16 December

1991 which shows how the fantastic imaginary world of the Gypsies is also used for propaganda purposes. The report mentions a new stage in the propaganda war between Belgrade Radio and Television (RTB) and the Croatian Television Broadcasting Company. 'Kitsch, melodrama, and false sentimentality', according to the writer of the article, dominate Croatian commercials that propagate peace. He commends the reticence that Belgrade Radio and Television has demonstrated so far in this propaganda war. Now that Belgrade Radio and Television has taken up the Croatian challenge, however, the journalist has the following to say on the Serb reply:

> The idea emerged that someone had to react, so Belgrade Television created a suitable commercial too. In the editing room scenes from the present war were mixed with shots from the final scene of the film Who's Singing There Like That? It was the scene in which two young Gypsies accompanied by a Jew's harp sing a lament on the day that World War II commenced with the German air raid on Belgrade on 6 April 1941. But as the idea behind this commercial wasn't entirely clear, and, it transpires, there wasn't enough assurance of the need to broadcast a commercial of this kind, it was soon taken off the air.

The journalist is referring to the wonderful final scene of the 1980 film by the Serb director Slobodan Sijan, *Ko to Tamo Peva?* That film is the story of a bus on the road to Belgrade on the eve of the Second World War. It is filled with passengers, representing a cross-section of prewar Serb society. When it reaches Belgrade, the Germans score a direct hit on the bus. All the Serb passengers – the peasants, the town folk, the young married couple, the singer who dreams of a career in the capital – are killed. Only the two Gypsy musicians who got in at the start of the ride have survived the air raid. They emerge from the smoking rubble, shake off some of the dust, and then sing their melancholy song on the still smouldering wreck of a car:

Nesrećnik sam	Ever since I was born
od malena!	I've been wretched!
Od sve muke	Every sorrow
pesme pevam!	I turn into song!
Željeo bih, majko mila!	I wish, dear mother,
Da sve ovo samo snevam!	I was just dreaming!
Jao! Jao!	Alas! Alas!

The fact that the Serb propaganda picked out this scene and suggested a connection between the Gypsies singing their lament on the smoky ruins of a shelled Serb town and 'the sad fate of the Serb nation' is remarkable. The journalist's comment that 'the idea behind this commercial wasn't entirely clear' is just as remarkable – but more about that later.

Once my attention had been drawn to the analogy (and put on the alert for other clues), I was also confronted by casual remarks by victims of the war who compared their sorry situation with the world of the Gypsies. 'We've become Gypsies, without a home or anything else', was the direct reply of a young girl to a BBC reporter who was filming in a Croatian refugee camp. 'It's as if we were Gypsies', a woman shouted to the cameras of a Dutch current affairs programme as she hesitantly reached towards her head and poked a few fragments from her blitzed house in Dubrovnik together with her foot.[8] A woman in Novi Sad commented: 'Gypsies show the most sense these days'. And an actor was planning to get all the Gypsy musicians from the Vojvodina together on a large stage in the centre of the city. While several camp fires burned on the stage, the Gypsy musicians were supposed to join together to sing the popular *Ama, devla, chororo* (Oh God, poor soul that I am), one of the best-known Gypsy songs. When I asked him where the idea came from, his cryptic reply was that something like this seemed necessary during this time of war.

The Gypsies as guardians of implicit social knowledge

These snapshots from the imaginary life of the Gypsies lead to the suggestion that it is the role of Gypsies in this society to act as the guardians of implicit social knowledge. Those parts of the South Slav world which could not be accommodated in the story designed to shape the postwar order were relegated to the Gypsies. However, the snapshots still do not tell us anything about why *Gypsies* were chosen to play this role.

As the story 'The Gypsy and the Lie' showed, Gypsies have a reputation all over Serbia as arch liars. They are regarded as storytellers who are not to be trusted. 'Don't listen to them, they're lying to you' was the advice I received on more than one occasion when someone discovered that I was talking with Gypsies.

Sociologists of knowledge may recognise this as a well known strategy of those who control the mouthpieces of a society. After all, it is a com-

mon manoeuvre to discredit insights that are unfavourable to you by at-
tributing them to a group at the bottom of the social ladder. Old wives'
gossip. Drunkards' talk. Peasant wisdom. Fish market facts. Gypsy chatter. All the same, we can say more about the role of guardians of implicit
social knowledge that is attributed to the Gypsies. And that is certainly
true of a society like Novi Sad, where the mouthpieces tend to change
hands and where the interchangeability of truth and untruth is familiar.

We can begin by noting that the labelling of Gypsies as storytellers and
liars has never prevented the Serbs from consulting them. Serb ethnography provides plenty of examples of Serb suspicions of the extraordinary knowledge to which Gypsies are thought to have access. The best
known and most eloquent example is the fact that Gypsy fortune-tellers
could build up a clientèle. Serbs and other non-Gypsies consulted them
for their crystal-gazing, for the protective amulets they made, and for
their skills in curing people and livestock.[9] Dušan Bandić notes that
Gypsies possess a 'magical force' that can be used to positive or negative
effect. Contacts with Gypsies were held to be enlivening and strengthening: sick children could be fortified by giving them a piece of bread from
a Gypsy beggar's pouch or by feeding them from a Gypsy woman's
breast.[10] In Montenegro it was believed that if a child's first nourishment
was from a Gypsy nurse, it would later develop great endurance.[11] If a
Serb child was slow in learning to talk, the parents were advised to steal
a piece of bread or something else from a Gypsy beggar's pouch. The
child would soon to learn to talk, because Gypsies talk rapidly and they
talk a lot. There was a popular belief that if a child could not walk (while
he was old enough to do so), he should get a beating in the presence of
a Gypsy woman. That would teach him to walk soon enough. And a
horse-breeder should have intercourse with a Gypsy woman, because
that would make his horses strong and healthy, just like those of the
džambasi (Gypsy horse-dealers).[12]

Although fini ljudi characterise notions of this kind as primitive super-
stition, Gypsies can still use their 'extraordinary knowledge' to advantage
among the city folk. Time and again as I walked in the city centre, I saw
Gypsy women stopping passers-by and taking their clients to a bench for
a consultation, where they would calmly predict what the future had in
store. A few of my informants confessed (not without embarrassment) to
having had their palm read by a Gypsy woman. Despite protestations
along the lines of 'It didn't mean anything, you know, it's always the
same story about a long journey and an encounter with a man', they
weren't entirely convinced. For instance, a woman with a position of responsibility in the urban bureaucracy told me that she had felt something

uncanny when a Gypsy woman called out to her that she was dressed as a woman but behaved as a man. Another interesting case of a 'Gypsy' who managed to turn his extraordinary Gypsy knowledge to good advantage was a certain Raoul Amon, a successful businessman who dealt in herbal cures and cosmetics and had an office in one of the suburbs of Novi Sad. Persistent rumour had it that he had learned the recipes for his herbal medicines from his mother, and that she was a Gypsy. Whether this was true or not, the point is that the 'Gypsy mother' was combined with an exotic, non-Serb name like Raoul Amon to increase confidence in the efficacy of his cures.

The practices of musical bewitchment by Gypsies in the bars will be dealt with in the following chapter. It is sufficient here to state that considering Gypsies as the guardians of implicit social knowledge fits into a familiar pattern. Gypsies were never just liars; they were also sought for their wisdom. But the question still remains: why *Gypsies*?

The question can be formulated with more precision if we start with what the madman in Danilo Kiš's *Hourglass* realised: some insights into reality drive you crazy, so crazy that you are only prepared to confront them in a disguised or masked form. At the same time, that disguise must not go so far as to make them unidentifiable. In other words, expressions of knowing always strike a delicate balance between recognition ('Indeed, that's how it is!') and bewilderment ('Interesting, you know, but what's it got to do with me?'). The question of why the world of the Gypsies was chosen as the repository of implicit social knowledge can thus be formulated more appropriately as: how can Gypsies provide the disguises which enable this delicate balance between recognition and bewilderment?

Disguising and revealing:
the mixture of the worlds of self and other in the Gypsy neighbourhood

A visit to the Gypsy neighbourhood, on the outermost edge of the urban and village community, may throw light on what I mean by terms like disguise and revelation, recognition and bewilderment. Seen from the point of view of the Serbs, the Gypsy neighbourhood is a zone of fusion. It is a world in which what Serbs regard as belonging to the worlds of self and other exist side by side. That may sound a bit theoretical, but if you make the trip from the centre of any Serb city to the Gypsy neighbourhood, you will gradually find yourself in a transition zone. The fusion becomes perceptible because, the further you go from the centre, the more

frequently elements crop up in the familiar, orderly world that do not belong there. The streets that still look familiar – 'these are houses like ours,
cars like ours, roads like ours' – are increasingly interrupted by cooking
pots producing strange aromas, washing lines with strange-looking,
brightly coloured washing hanging from them, pigs rooting about, ghet-
to-blasters with strange oriental music, wrecked cars, mountains of waste,
and a stratum of mud and dirt that grows thicker and thicker. People
from the more central parts of the city can just recognise the contours of
their own world in this transition zone; the rubbish heaps barely reveal
the source of the rotting waste.

It is interesting to see that this phenomenon of fusion is picked up and
blown up in the representations of the Gypsy neighbourhood in the
works of South Slavic film directors, writers and ethnographers.

Vision 1: the film director
Right from the start, *Dom za Vešanje* (Time of the Gypsies), the Gypsy epic
by the Sarajevan director Emir Kusturica (1988), presents the viewer
with a landscape that has been aptly described by a French reviewer as
extra-urbain – 'not really a city, not really the countryside, but both at the
same time, a ruined urbanism, a social structure in a situation of ecstasy'.[13] You can't tell whether the houses are not quite finished or falling
down. There is no street grid. The continual comings and goings are
governed by nothing except an untidy pattern of intercrossing wagon
trails, interspersed with deep puddles. The film director Aleksandar
Petrović also depicted the world of the Gypsies as one big mud pool in
his *Skupljači Perja*: tiny little houses with wet feet and hollow-eyed windows, and curtains flapping outside through the broken window-panes.
Both films show mud everywhere. Both films show animals everywhere.
Every notion of the wild and the domesticated, which were so carefully
kept apart in the civilisation debate, is here in disarray. Stubborn mules,
recalcitrant goats tugging at a rope – or are they pulling their goatherd
along? -, fighting, growling and barking dogs, copulating turkeys, a cat
running howling through the street, a string of rattling tin cans tied to its
tail.

In both films remarkably large gaggles of geese are permanently in the
picture. Their unsullied whiteness, their precise goose-step and their
sense of community are a constant reminder of exactly what is missing in
this world.

But although both directors have delighted in portraying a wild,
strange and colourful world, they have taken care not to take the exoti-
cism too far. The foreignness is constantly injected with things and de-

tails that are very familiar to a Serb viewer. Amid the feverish succession of images with which Kusturica introduces the Gypsy neighbourhood, the camera suddenly pauses at a shot of a scene in the distance, the very ordinary scene of a boy buying a loaf of bread at the baker's. It is only a second's pause, but it achieves its effect: normality is just around the corner, don't think we're far from home.

The film is full of references of this kind. This isn't just any old rubbish, waste and junk, it's the rubbish, waste and junk of our society. As if by accident, casually, Kusturica's camera picks up a wagon with two Gypsy musicians riding on it. It must be a part of what was once a travelling circus stage – or a disused platform for political speeches, because you can just make out a portrait of Tito and the Yugoslavian flag with the five-pointed red star in the background. The appearance of this wagon has nothing to do with the narrative development in the film. There is no clue as to where it has come from or where it is going. The only message conveyed by this phenomenon seems to be that everything – even the portrait of Tito – eventually ends up in the mud.

The television sets blasting out their programmes in the ramshackle Gypsy houses are another clear example of the representation of the Gypsy neighbourhood as a domain in which the familiar and the unfamiliar are juxtaposed and intermingled. In the Gypsy house that Kusturica reveals to his audience there is a programme on genetic inheritance (*in search of the secrets of life*, is what we can barely make out), a popular-scientific educational programme like those that people watch in the tidy middle-class homes in Novi Sad. The fact that none of the Gypsies pays the slightest attention to the programme is beside the point; the viewers of this scene are once again forced to confront the strangeness of their own world or the familiarity of this strange world.

In short, the world that the film directors have created for their visit to the Gypsy neighbourhood is never simply a strange, different world. It is at the same time their own world: in decay, in a disorderly state in which nothing is where it belongs, but still their own world.

Vision 2: the ethnographer
The representation of the Gypsy neighbourhood as a combination of elements derived from the worlds of self and other also determines the image of Gypsies that is drawn in Serb ethnography. Unlike the film directors, who exploit this hybridisation to create poetic images, the Serb ethnographers – preoccupied as they are with arranging and labelling the specificities of the cultures of different peoples – regard this phenomenon as something problematic. They seem to be able to interpret

this fusion in no other way than as proof that Gypsies have no culture of their own. Of course, they do not put it as blatantly as that, but the suggestion is constantly present in their texts. Tihomir Djordjević wonders how Gypsies manage to exist as a group at all:

> They don't support one another, they don't help one another, and in fact they are not very keen on one another. And yet they have remained Gypsies. They do not share a common belief as the Jews do, because they are all indifferent to religion. They are by no means everywhere distinctive from others in terms of language. Many of the Vlach Gypsies in Romania and Serbia, to take an example close to home, speak nothing but Romanian. Gypsies are often physically indistinguishable from their neighbours as well. In many cases they have lost any ethnic specificity, and yet they have remained Gypsies![14]

In an article entitled *Cigani kao nosioci kulture* (Gypsies as vehicles of culture), the same author already anticipates the disbelief that this title will occasion among his readers by opening with the exclamation: 'What next? Gypsies as vehicles of culture?'[15]

The ethnographic literature also keeps on returning to what it is that makes Gypsies *Fremdkörper* in society. For instance, there is the fact that Gypsies came from abroad, from the Orient, and that they do not really belong here. The same goes for the fact that Gypsies have no history: 'until the second half of the eighteenth century no one knew exactly where the Gypsies came from', Djordjević states in his article *Ko su to Cigani?* (Who are the Gypsies?). 'What they said about themselves was either some fantastic story from their oral tradition, which did not yield anything credible, or simple fabrications to which only naïve people attached any credibility'.[16]

Ethnographic discussions of Gypsy clothing are another good example of the tendency to deny the Gypsies a culture of their own. In her study of Gypsies in the Vojvodina, Mirjana Maluckov comments that it is typical that they do not make their own clothes: 'Gypsy women do not weave, embroider or sew', she declares with barely concealed disapproval. Gypsies have their clothes tailored (whether in the style of their surroundings or not), wear second-hand clothes that they have been given, have purchased, or have earned in return for work, or they wear clothes that they have obtained in other countries where they went to trade or to work as migrant labourers. The Gypsies who have stayed abroad during the last few decades, Maluckov claims, have gone along with every fashion of modern dress, from nylons, jeans and plastic raincoats to the maxi and mini fashions.[17] Vukanović sketches the confusion that can be caused by wearing other people's clothes when he writes on the dress of European Gypsies:

> It consisted of a combination of different models and styles, depending on the items of clothing that could be obtained. As a result, their dress became one great incoherent motley *(jedno veliko neujednaćeno šarenilo)*. Gypsy women wore long or short men's coats, while men wore some items of old-fashioned Turkish dress combined with European clothes. There were Gypsies who wore combinations of city clothing combined with peasant *opanci* on their feet and a black broad-brimmed hat, Serb forage-cap or Turkish fez on their head.[18]

'Well...you know..., you don't really have typical clothes like that', remarked the curator of the ethnological museum in Novi Sad as she guided me, a representative of the Novi Sad Gypsy community and his wife around this temple of ethnic specificity. She rather shamefacedly had to admit that none of the mannequins in her showcases was dressed in Gypsy clothing. Don't get me wrong: I'm not saying that this was a malicious or deliberate and systematic exclusion. It is simply that the curator did not conceive of Gypsies as having a culture of their own. It was not until she stood in front of the showcase in the company of two Gypsy representatives that she became painfully aware of the fact.

As far as Gypsy music is concerned, ethnomusicologists constantly point out the collage of foreign and familiar elements; Gypsy music is a copy of music from elsewhere, Serb songs are combined with oriental-sounding melismatic decorations and Western harmonies. Djordjević comments on Gypsy musicians as performers of Serb music:

> They decharacterise and gypsify it. They change primitive folk music as they choose, and they interfere with the most essential aspects of this music: they change the details as they think fit, or if these details are already attractive, they overemphasise them or add decorations which sound gentle and beautiful at first, but which have no place in that music. That is the Gypsy quality of folk music.[19]

Andrijana Gojković had the following to say about an experiment in Budapest to train young Gypsy musicians to become serious, academic musicians:

> Many of them imposed their own expressiveness on the classical music,

and they ruined those works, while their own repertoire, that they had ex-
celled in interpreting before they entered the academy, lost a lot of its
colour, expressiveness and interpretation. They couldn't handle the new
music, they couldn't give the old music the sheen it had once had, and
what was left in their music was nothing but enormous confusion.[20]

Statements on religious and ritual practices among the Gypsies confirm
this picture: if the Gypsies as they appear in Serb ethnography display
any religious awareness at all, it is often for the wrong reasons, because
they do not understand it or because it is in their practical interests. The
colleague who told me that Gypsies had borrowed certain rituals from
the Serbs – going from door to door to receive gifts – and continued to
perform these rituals long after the Serbs had abandoned them, immediately added an explanation: they only did it as a way of collecting money. 'What kind of Muslims are you?' I heard someone ask a Gypsy musician, 'you haven't got any mosques, you celebrate the name day of our
St Georg (*Djurdjevdan*), you drink alcohol, and yet you still call yourselves
Muslims?' They do not really embrace any religion, Djordjević claims;
for them religion is 'merely a form, and they are always prepared to
change it: often they don't even know themselves what their religion is,
and then they just say whatever suits them'.[21]

   In the light of these considerations, it comes as no surprise that the anthropologist Mirko Barjaktarović considers that the Gypsies will soon
cease to exist as a people: 'What we can finally say with certainty is that
Gypsies in Yugoslavia, no matter how much they enjoy the freedoms enjoyed by every other people, do not have any prospects of remaining a
separate (strange and exotic) element in our society for much longer'.[22]
Gypsies are not concentrated in a particular region, he continues, but
they are scattered all over the country; besides, the prejudices against
them will disappear in the new Yugoslavia, so that biological mingling
with other peoples will be facilitated:

> Moreover, there is no question of a national awareness among the Gypsies,
> nor are there cultural traditions on the basis of which they could establish
> claims as other peoples in Yugoslavia do.[23]

Vision 3: my discussion partners
To close this account of the combinations of the worlds of self and other, of the familiar and the strange, that various Serb visitors perceive in
the Gypsy neighbourhoods, let me note that my discussion partners in

Novi Sad also repeatedly showed that they regard Gypsies as a people who lack culture. Despite their obvious presence and visibility in the urban arena, the Gypsies were often excluded from descriptions of the different elements that went into the multi-cultural melting-pot – 'For centuries we've been living at peace with one another' – of Novi Sad or of the Vojvodina. (As an outsider, I was regaled with these descriptions on several occasions by *fini ljudi*, who thereby hoped to display their cosmopolitan spirit and remoteness from narrow-minded nationalism.) Serbs, Hungarians, Romanians, Slovakians, Ruthenians, *Bunjevci* and *Šokaci*, even Croats, all featured in the story of centuries of peaceful co-existence in the Pannonian steppes. But not the Gypsies. Once again, I'm sure the omission was not intentional. When the pattern came home to me and I pointed out to someone at the next opportunity that she had forgotten to mention the Gypsies, they were generously added to the list. 'Of course, Gypsies too!' The fact that they were not mentioned spontaneously was not because my discussion partners denied the Gypsies a place in the multi-cultural society of the Vojvodina, but because they do not belong on a list of different cultures.[24] The fact that Gypsies were regarded as a special category by my informants could also be seen from the surprised reactions of some people to my use of the term 'Gypsy culture'. Gypsy culture? Do you call that culture? The idea of a Gypsy culture seemed to be a contradiction in terms. An acquaintance of mine was amazed when he heard that the language of the Gypsies was regarded as a language by the linguisticians. 'Gypsy language? I knew they can curse heavily, but a language...?'[25] Another discussion partner who was better informed, or at least wanted to give that impression, went on for ages to try to convince me that the language of the Gypsies was not really a language at all. Instead, he argued, it should be regarded as a collection of foreign words that the Gypsies had borrowed on their way from India to Serbia.

To sum up, Gypsies in Serb cinema, in Serb ethnography, and in the statements of my informants do not represent a culture that is clearly different and specific to them. It should rather be regarded as a collage of both familiar and unusual elements drawn from different semantic fields.

Let us return to the starting point of this preliminary exploration of the world of the Gypsies: why is it *Gypsies* who are capable of articulating implicit social knowledge in a way that both discloses and conceals? It is easy to see how the view of the Gypsy world as a collage offers the delicate balance between bewilderment ('it's tragic, you know, the fate of the Gypsies, but it's no concern of mine') and recognition ('Alas! Why has fate set us in this angry and cruel world?') which is called for by expressions of that knowledge. Secure in the awareness that they are dealing with others, with Gypsies, Serbs can get much closer to scripts and scenarios from their own collective experiences than they would be able to do if they were directly and unambiguously confronted by them under their very eyes.

Anthropologists like Victor Turner and Bonno Thoden van Velzen consider that such a composite, layered phenomenal structure is characteristic of the disclosing and concealing function of the collective fantasy. In connection with carnival masks, Turner points out that masks are not just donned to conceal: 'The masks, disguises and other fictions of some kinds of play are devices to make visible what has been hidden, even unconscious [... devices] to let the mysteries revel in the streets, to invert the everyday order in such a way that it is the unconscious and primary processes that are visible, whereas the conscious ego is restricted to creating rules to keep their insurgence within bounds, to frame them or channel them, so to speak'.[26] Thoden van Velzen writes about the often enigmatic products of the collective fantasy in a similar way. The collective fantasy masks the insights that it contains. Through scrambling techniques, processes of distortion and mechanisms of veiling, the first impression made by the collective fantasy is one of incomprehensibility. But there is more to it than that. Thoden van Velzen points out that the grotesque and fantastic forms that appear in the collective fantasy are deliberate visual puzzles: 'They beg, as it were, to be understood and deciphered'.[27]

All the same, it would be incorrect to present the fantastic imaginary world that is woven around the figure of the Gypsy too much in terms of a puzzle or enigma, of something purely cognitive. The imaginary world of the Gypsies emits taproots to (and nourishes itself on) the emotions and instincts.[28] This seems decisive for the strongly affective, emotional charge of the fantasies associated with Gypsies and causes recognition to lead to identification and glorification, bewilderment to lead to repugnance and hate.

Disguising and revealing: the disturbingly strange

Gypsies represent not only fusions of familiar and strange elements which can be found in the iconography of their appearance and social life. For the Serbs, Gypsies also embody a combination that Julia Kristeva (following Freud's discussion of the uncanny) has called 'the disturbingly strange', 'the "otherness" of our "ourness", which we do not know how to handle'.[29] In other words, Gypsies represent what we are although we are not allowed to be it.

A brief discussion of the role of the figure of the Gypsy in the education of Serb children reveals how early in life the foundation is laid for this mechanism of projective identification. Serb children's first encounter with Gypsies is in the context of the prohibition of uncontrolled behaviour. Children who swear or who argue constantly and noisily are compared with Gypsies. Troublesome and complaining children are warned that the terrible Gypsy will come to get them, or that they will be given to the Gypsy beggars who go from door to door (almost all of my discussion partners mentioned this image to strike terror into children's hearts).[30] Serb children also learn to associate Gypsies with dirt, mud and other dirty things. When the eight-year-old daughter of an acquaintance sat down on the ground out of doors, she was told in no uncertain terms that she was not a Gypsy and had her ears boxed into the bargain. Children who arrive at home covered in mud are told off for being as black as a Gypsy.

Remarks and punishments like these teach Serb children at least two basic notions. First, they learn that the world is not an indivisible whole, but that there is another world where other people live other lives. Second, Serb children learn that they have Gypsy tendencies inside them which belong to that other world. 'Don't do that, or you're a Gypsy.' 'Don't do this, or you're a Gypsy.' Besides the explicit prohibitions, Serb children also receive an implicit message: something they did, something they produced was just like a Gypsy. Although this message is immediately followed by the instruction to banish the internalised Gypsy, bound and tied, to the deepest recesses of the unconscious, nevertheless the lack of control or the remark blurted out without thinking is something that Serbs and Gypsies have in common.

This internalised Gypsy whose origins go back to the childhood of the Serbs continues to operate when they are older. This can best be illustrated by the common use of the word *cigan* as a term of abuse among non-Gypsies. In Yugoslavia under Tito, it was mainly the Croatian football fans who never failed to welcome the Serb teams with loud cries of 'Gypsies! Gypsies!'.[31] Now, when the barracks of the federal army in Croatia were under siege, the Serb press carried frequent reports of crowds of Croats shouting '*Cigani! Cigani! Cigani!*' to emphasise the alleged wildness of the Serbs and of the Serb-dominated army. 'Instead of the well-mannered protest demonstration that had been announced, the ten thousand or so mothers, fathers and children from Rijeka who had gathered here shouted 'peace-loving' slogans like: 'To battle, to battle', 'Gypsies, Gypsies', and 'murderers', '*četniks, četniks*'.[32] And: 'Two barracks in Zadar were flooded with a crowd chanting "*četniks!* Gypsies!"'[33] And we can recall the anecdote from the previous chapter in which a Croatian accused his wife of being a 'Gypsy-like Serb' before abandoning her.

The use of the word Gypsy as a term of abuse – and this is certainly interesting in the present context – is also practised by Serbs among themselves. The untidy family with the dirty balcony a few storeys below the flat where I lived in Novi Sad was compared to a Gypsy family. Forms of action that meet with disapproval are disparagingly labelled as *ciganska posla* (Gypsy work). A mean trick is a *ciganija*. More general terms of abuse are *prljavi ciganin* (dirty Gypsy), *ciganski sin* (Gypsy child), or the suggestion that someone's mother is a Gypsy (*psovali su mu mater cigansku*).[34]

The effectiveness of this term of abuse is instructive for the way people deal with the internalised Gypsy in themselves in their everyday dealings with one another. A Serb who is called a Hungarian, Romanian or Icelander will disregard the term with a shrug of the shoulders. Unless there really is Hungarian, Romanian or Icelandic blood coursing through his veins, he will not even feel that he is being addressed. But being called a Gypsy is very different. Even if to the best of his knowledge he has no ancestors who were Gypsies, he will feel that he is being addressed and will react angrily. Why? Apparently binding and banishing the internalised Gypsy is not equivalent to its complete elimination: apparently there is still a Gypsy in every Serb who can be addressed, no matter how hidden or concealed he may be.

This form of address may take place in a heated exchange, but it can also be found in a friendlier setting: in a film, a poem, or – as we shall see in the next chapter – in an evening out with a Gypsy orchestra. An appeal is still made to the Gypsy in everyone. It is thus highly revealing when the reviewer of the collection of poems entitled *Pain, a Gypsy Rhapsody* notes that the reader of the poems 'is introduced by the pleasant strophes and pleasant language to the life of the Gypsies, a world that is essentially ours, even though we may not be aware of the fact. Poetry about Gypsies is not only that; it is poetry about everyone.'[35]

The association of Gypsies with the inner human instincts, with wildness, with the lack of control that lurks in every body, is a crucial factor in trying to understand the Gypsy as a figure of thought.[36] For the *fini ljudi*, there is hardly any scope for awareness of the fact that is so undeniable in these parts – that people are driven not only by reason, but just as much by irrational forces. In the discourse they use to transform the world they live in unambiguously into a civilised, European world, every memory of their own asocial impulses and the possibility of going off the rails evokes only fear and shame. But the insight into the irrational, wild human being – an insight that has to be preserved because people know that they simply cannot allow themselves to ignore it – is relocated in the fantastic imaginary world that is woven around the figure of the Gypsy. By taking a lively interest in the lives of Gypsies, the *fini ljudi* can enter the terra incognita of their own prohibited and hidden impulses – what Michael Taussig has called 'that great steaming morass of chaos that lies on the underside of order' -[37] indirectly and safely. The material I collected in Serbia on the image of the Gypsy teaches us that they use this opportunity extensively.

Disguising and revealing: the collective fantasies about the cigansko carstvo

Cigansko carstvo, the kingdom of the Gypsies, is a folk story that Serb ethnographers have recorded in numerous versions all over Serbia. This is how Serb villagers pictured the Gypsy's kingdom:

> Altogether the kingdom of the Gypsies lasted three days. The first day the king chased his mother through the city, the second day he strung up his father, and the third day he was thrown out by the Gypsies.[38]

It would be hard to imagine a more concise commentary on the human condition in a world which has to make shift without the regulatory and orderly effect of civilisation. The world of the *cigansko carstvo* is a barbarous world. People are driven by nothing but their impulse to strictly individual self-preservation and strictly individual satisfaction of their desires. The Ego demands full attention and energy and will not brook any rivals. Not even a God, as the folk story *kako je propalo cigansko carstvo* (how the kingdom of the Gypsies came to an end) shows:

> The Lord God passed through the land. And the people went there, ran behind Him and worshipped Him. And the king of the Gypsies was enraged that the people followed the Lord and shouted: 'I'm the King, you must look to me! Just wait, I shall kill Him!' And the Gypsy king chased the Lord, and the Lord prayed and dug a pit and hid there as if He was afraid that the king of the Gypsies was going to kill Him. But when the Gypsy king leapt into the pit, the Lord closed the earth in upon him. That is how the kingdom of the Gypsies came to an end.[39]

The *cigansko carstvo* is a world of constant strife, of each against each and all against all. The moral of these stories is that nothing lasts long in a world like that. In his discussion of this story, Tihomir Djordjević adds: 'That is why people say about something that does not last long: it lasts as long as the kingdom of the Gypsies'.

The stories about the *cigansko carstvo* can be read as an attempt by the Serbs to gain access to their own deep motives, desires, wishes and innermost feelings without having to deploy the normative and value-charged terms of the civilisation debate. Other sources offer the opportunity to explore and supplement the fantastic visions that are elaborated about the *cigansko carstvo* and its savage inhabitants in more detail.

Violence

The violence that rules this world is typical of life in the *cigansko carstvo*. This is not the noble, heroic strife we know from the Serb epics and partisan stories, nor the cold, calculating violence of the *ustaši* or other foes. Occasionally the violence among the Gypsies is the *crime passionnel* of a jealous lover, but usually the violence is simply there, lacking any use or purpose. The violent act itself – yielding to an impulse – is the most important motif. The ethnographer Miroslav Lutovac, who reports frequent brawls among the Gypsies in Montenegro, stresses this eruptive character of violence among Gypsies, its temporary quality:

> Mutual disagreements usually end in frenetic blows, insults and curses. Sometimes a brawl will leave a few dead. It is as if the dramatic settling of accounts among them is simply the consequence of the 'Gypsy temperament'. These arguments and commotions usually take place in full view of everyone in the Gypsy neighbourhood, and neighbours and passers-by act as if nothing is going on. Soon afterwards they can be found in one another's company again in high spirits. There is no calculation involved, it is just the way they are...[40]

To emphasise his view that Gypsies commit acts of violence because their nature prompts them to do so and because they are unable to control their impulses, Lutovac remarks that 'Gypsies will not be quick to physically mistreat somebody, especially not when that person is from a different ethnic group' and that 'a not insignificant number of Gypsies are opposed to fighting and war'.[41] He also notes that 'Gypsies are among the few peoples who do not display any tendency towards genocide against anyone whomsoever. In other words, they are the only non-barbaric people and their country is the whole world.'[42]

Another ethnographer, Jovan Jovanović from Leskovac, states that the Gypsies of this town in South Serbia regularly engage in fights with one another. The women are supposed to be particularly dangerous. They fight with stones, sticks and knives. There are often casualties, sometimes serious. 'To judge from the way in which they quarrel and fight with one another, Gypsies can be categorised as a temperamental people', Jovanić concludes.[43]

Sex

Jovanović is also one of the ethnographer who presents extensive material on the sex life of the Gypsies. The inhabitants of this world are not only unpredictable and violent, but they also live in a permanent state of sexual arousal:

> The sex life of the Gypsies begins early, as among all peoples from a warm climate. Although they have been here for six hundred years by now, where there is a continental climate, it is as if our climate has not essentially altered their physical development and maturation.[44]

Gypsy sexuality is thoroughly explored and exploited in more burlesque genres such as songs and jokes. Songs about (love) life in a Gypsy camp are full of 'fiery eyes', 'blazing glances' and 'wild nights'. Mutual relations are dominated by short-lived but passionate sexual relations, promiscuity and one-night stands. In a much coarser tone, these themes also dominate jokes about the sexual life of Gypsies. Hot, hotter, hottest is the punch-line to a joke about a number of men – rather half-heartedly called 'villains' in the story – who claim to have been with a Serb, a Bosnian and a Gypsy woman at the same time:

> When the women got excited, they decided to see which of them was the hottest. They claimed that the Serb woman was able to boil eggs; the Bosnian woman was able to turn uncooked dough into kifla; and the Gypsy woman stuck a lamp into herself and set it alight.[45]

In the shameless world of the Gypsy joke, sexuality is open, naked and omnipresent. Whole families lie together in a single bed in the small huts, incest is an everyday occurrence, and women are up for grabs. The Gypsy parents who make love, causing the bed to shake vigorously, provoke the laconic remark from one of the children who are playing under the bed: 'Say, stop it, or you'll start one and kill seven!'

Waste

Boundless waste is another recurrent theme in the images of the *cigansko carstvo*. Although Gypsies have a reputation for greed – with their itching fingers and their brazen methods to obtain money and possessions – that greed seems to be motivated by an even stronger urge to consume everything right away. Without any sense of responsibility towards any person or thing, entire fortunes are spent in a single riot of consumption. Everything is expended in one single magnificent gesture as if there were no future. Once again it is the film director Emir Kusturica who manages to render this figure – Ahmed, a rogue who buys children to get them to beg and steal in Italy – as a larger than life personality who embodies these potlatch-like celebrations of the Ego. Ahmed is cast as the *fini ljudi* characterise their fellow countrymen who work abroad as migrant labourers: men in white suits, brothel-creepers and a Humphrey Bogart-style hat. In the film he drives into the poor Gypsy neighbourhood in his big white Mercedes to attend a party in his honour. Like an oriental despot, he has a dirty young boy sitting on the hood to sing his praises to the accompaniment of the rapid beat of darabukka drums, and he dispenses banknotes through the open window here and there. Oriental music can be heard in the party tent. He dances like a belly dancer, turning with his hands in front of his face. Then he sticks a bottle of beer in his belt and juts his pelvis forwards. The beer pours out in foaming jets. In Italy Ahmed lives in a decrepit caravan, a dismal spot near an intersection, just behind a big billboard, somewhere in the middle of nowhere. But now Ahmed is home, waving his money, and dancing, and copulating and acting like the king of the neighbourhood.

Anomie

The story of the Gypsy king chasing his mother through town and stringing his father up suggests that family life in this world is not all it might be. The social fabric – or rather, the lack of it – in the *cigansko carstvo* is dominated by individuals who pursue nothing but the satisfaction of their own instincts and impulses. 'The girls marry early', reports ethnographer Jovanović, 'from the age of thirteen'. They do not marry officially, 'but it is all the same to a Gypsy whether the children are legitimate or not'. Often they also enter into 'wild' marriages with other women and 'there are even cases of polygamy'.[46] The married life of Gypsies is thus described as chaotic. Children deceive and menace their parents, but vice versa, parents' attitudes towards their children are anything but stable and caring. Mothers sell their children, fathers break their children's arms and legs to send them out begging. In one of the jokes about

Gypsies, a Gypsy phones a first aid centre in panic to say that his son has swallowed a nail. 'Help me! Help me!' The first aid team are already putting on their coats to go and get the boy when the phone rings again. 'False alarm', the Gypsy says, 'I've found another nail'. Or there is the one about the Gypsy woman doing the washing. Her children get in her way, so she calls her husband to keep them indoors. When she enters the hut soon afterwards, she finds her husband sleeping without his trousers on while the children play with his genitals. The Gypsy woman's anger – 'What are you letting the children play with!' – is answered by a pretty vague idea of parental responsibility: 'So what should I have given them, a pair of scissors to poke out one another's eyes?!'[47]

One more time: fusion
The most crucial insight that finds expression in the collective fantasies about Gypsies is perhaps the idea that the same pool of desires and instincts is drawn on for violence, partying, destruction, wasteful consumption and sexuality. This sketch of the individual impulses (violence, sex, waste, the urge to destroy) in the *cigansko carstvo* may therefore be concluded with two scenes expressing the insight that it is not an orderly arrangement but fusion that determines reality. Two scenes expressing the insight that it is not an orderly arrangement but fusion that determines reality may therefore conclude these sketches of the *cigansko carstvo*.

Kusturica opens his Gypsy epic in a masterly way with a scene showing the complete interchangeability of the pleasures of partying and the pleasures of violence. The scene shows a Gypsy bride, a fat and clumsy child, wearing a pathetic white veil, sobbing, sniffling and shuddering because she has realised that it is not her lot to enjoy the pleasures of the celebration: her bridegroom is already in a comatose state of inebriation before the wedding has begun, and has to be carried off in a sort of barrow. Without the slightest difficulty the young bride knows how to channel the flow of adrenalin in a different direction: mercilessly and with a bitter expression on her face, she hits her brand-new spouse with her shoe. A couple of older women make half-hearted attempts to keep the bride away from her husband-to-be. Other wedding guests seem to encourage her taunts and blows, laughing and screaming in their thirst for sensation. They may have missed a party, but the satisfaction of huffing and puffing is not so easily taken away.

Aleksandar Petrović's film *The world will be collapsing soon – Let it collapse, what difference does it make* also contains essential insights into the vague and problematic character of the boundaries we draw between different instincts and impulses. In a scene full of the inimitable bitter, black humour of Yugoslavia, six Gypsy musicians cycle aimlessly round an isolated church that has been shelled. Resting their instruments – including the large double bass – on their handlebars, they sing of the charm of the Srem district in the Vojvodina:

Divan je kićeni Srem,	It's wonderful in Srem
lepo je živet' u njem.	Beautiful to live there
Devojka zdrava k'o dren,	A girl blushing like a rosebud
sladak je poljubac njen.	Her kisses are sweet
Srem, Srem, Srem!	Srem, Srem, Srem!
Lepo je živet' u njem!	Beautiful to live there!
Kad Sremac podje na rad,	When the *Sremac* goes to work
da kopa vinograd.	To work in the vineyard
Ponese litru – dve,	He takes a litre or two with him
Sremice poljubi me!	Girl from Srem, kiss me.

A stupid text with a stupid tune, but in the film the song acquires an un-expected hidden meaning. The references to love-making and drink against the background of the damaged church, pointing into the sky like an admonitory finger, turn the scene into an extraordinary commentary on both the pleasures and pains that the life of the human instincts has in store.

All in all, the world that the Serbs have depicted in the *cigansko carstvo* is a nihilistic world as black as ink. Instinct, emotion, and uncontrolled impulse hold sway there. The only certainties one can be sure of in this world are failure, decay and decline. All the same, the vast majority of the people I talked to regarded films like Kusturica's *Dom za Vešanje* and Petrović's *Skupljači Perja* as nothing less than unshakeable truths. 'Look, now you can see what kind of people they are', were the comments when I watched these Gypsy dramas on the VCR in company. 'That's how it is'. The joy of recognition. It was nothing unusual for some people to have seen the film four or five times. In the land of idle talk, a world where people constantly undermine the correspondence to reality of their own and of other people's stories, Kusturica's film met with a strik-ing amount of credence. These stained illusions were no *prazne priče*; this was 'how it is'.

If this review of the fragmentary material seems to confirm my thesis that fantasies about the Gypsies serve to provide a place to accommodate the painful and disturbing truths about the beast in man and the irrational world, allowing people to 'approach the danger zone without actually entering it',[48] this should not be taken to mean that the Serbs are interested in the Gypsies themselves. When they shed a tear at the pitiful fate of the Gypsies in Kusturica's film, when they boisterously sing a strophe from a sentimental Gypsy song, when they reflect on a Gypsy poem by Glišić or Dretar, they find themselves in contact with the implicit social knowledge for which the figure of the Gypsy has become a repository.

But we have still not answered the question: why *Gypsies*? Two other striking characteristics of the collective fantasies about Gypsies may shed more light on why Gypsies have been singled out to be the guardians of this implicit knowledge.

Anti-structural tendencies in the fantasies about Gypsies

After you've seen blood in the snow and brains smashed against the wall, does the world still look the same as it did before? Is an unconditional belief in the modern, capitalist consumer society still possible when jeans, walkmans and a big red shopping bag with the logo *Glory!* have become the attributes of a sniper and a victim on snipers alley? The insights into implicit social knowledge, I have argued, are insights into the relativity of stories. They are rooted in experiences that essentially undermine the reality told in stories, like the sight of blood in the snow and brains smashed against the wall. They are reminders of what people and the world are when they have been expelled from the story and reduced to their most physical proportions.

The victims introduced in previous chapters remained silent because every story about people and the world in wartime fails to do justice to the knowledge derived from these experiences. It is therefore hardly surprising that it is difficult to incorporate the insights of this knowledge in the signifying structures of a story. After all, implicit social knowledge is not about an answer to the histories created by the historians or the epic poets, in the sense of a new conferral of meaning and significance, a new story, a new version of history in which claims are corrected, denied, hedged or replaced by other claims.

Articulation of implicit social knowledge calls for anti-structure, anti-language, anti-logic – the forms of expression devised, for example, by the Dadaists after World War I. For the Dadaists attacked not only the bourgeois and academic values of European civilisation, but their very forms of expression:

> The dadaist enterprise attacked the form of language, breaking words down to their phonetic components, films into the abstract play of light and shadow, sculptures into mere objects, paintings into arbitrary combinations of color and line. It generated, at the same time, a series of 'anti-forms' – anti-narratives in films and novels, anti-representation in art, anti-poems.[49]

Tristan Tzara wrote in his 1918 Dadaist manifesto: 'We must have strong, upright works, precise and forever unintelligible. Logic is a complication. Logic is always false. It draws the strings of ideas, words, along their formal exterior, towards illusory extremes and centres [...] Dada means nothing.'[50] In the manifesto of the Yugoslavian followers of Dadaism, the artists associated with *Zenitizam*, we read:

> cosmos is chaos – spirit rules over the chaos but is not its master – chaos is eternal – there must be chaos – spirit is not absolute – spirit is not absolute because it has not reached its final form – the final form of the spirit is the death of the earth – without chaos no creation – without creation no chaos – the new always elicits chaos – the spirit of *Zenitizam* is the ethics of chaos – man is continual chaos – man is chaos.[51]

The collective fantasies about Gypsies could be seen as a popular pendant to the obscurantist and intellectual legacy of movements like Dadaism and *Zenitizam*.[52] The imaginary Gypsies represent the same spirit of anti-structure, anti-language and anti-logic.

We can single out two remarkable anti-structural tendencies in the collective fantasies about Gypsies: 'nothing is what it seems', and – to borrow a formulation from Geertz[53] – 'everything is what it is and not another thing'.

Nothing is what it seems

'Nothing is what it seems' is the first, most striking anti-structural tendency in the collective fantasies about Gypsies. The imaginary Gypsy seems to exist merely to play the role of a trickster in demonstrating the relativity of what is told in stories: 'By his mere presence [he] dissolves events, evades issues, and throws doubt on the finality of fact'.[54] This already begins at the level of characterisation. It is absolutely impossible to characterise or designate without ambiguity the Gypsies who people

'Unlike our own folkdances, the dances of gypsies don't have a name', says painter Ivan Generalić in a discussion of his painting *Gypsy Wedding*. 'They dance in a very special way, jumping around in a strange fashion. At any rate, that is how I remember it!' (Quoted in Tomašević 1976:127)

the Serb imagination. The material I collected on the imaginary figure of the Gypsy and of Gypsy life offers no more than a confusion of images which is impossible to designate or organise in any way. Every Gypsy image has its anti-image, every statement about Gypsies has its counterstatement. The Gypsies who figure in the Serb imagination are strange and familiar, poor and rich, greedy and generous, self-centred and altruistic, selfish and outgoing, ugly and beautiful, attractive and repulsive, eternal victors over fate and eternal victims of fate. Sometimes image and anti-image are superimposed in the same representation, as in the popular Gypsy film *Cigani lete u nebo*, where the most beautiful and seductive Gypsy women smoke pipes. These pipe-smoking Gypsy beauties produce a completely impossible image that you can feel grating on your retina.[55]

It looks very much as if its unnameability is the very raison d'être of this imaginary figure. Take the following statements with a high level of absurdism that are presented as Serb home truths:

If you weigh a Gypsy you never arrive at a determinate and round figure. For example, the weight of a Gypsy can never be exactly 50, 51 or 52 kilos, but it is always slightly less or slightly more: you never arrive at a whole, round figure.[56]

There are seventy-seven-and-a-half religions in the world, the Gypsies are the half religion.[57]

But perhaps the best illustration of the connection of the Gypsies with a world where nothing can be designated unequivocally can be found in Petrović's film *The world will be collapsing soon – Let is collapse, what difference does it make*. The peasant village in the Vojvodina that is portrayed in this film in all its backwardness is visited by a travelling Gypsy who performs with a freak show. The scene in question opens with a shot of a fragile and hastily erected podium containing two empty chairs. Simple, primitive Serb peasants sit on rough wooden benches and expectantly stare at the Gypsy who is speaking. The Gypsy sports gold teeth and is well dressed like one of the city folk. To judge from his diction, he must have had difficulty in learning the text that he is rattling off by heart:

'Ladies and gentlemen! Thank you very much for coming to see our great attraction! When I open these curtains in a minute you will see Jolanda and Peter, who are very much in love with one another, sitting on these chairs which were empty a moment ago!'

Then he pulls the curtain open to reveal two lilliputians sitting on the chairs. It is an elderly couple, the man with an impressive grey moustache, the woman with a no less impressive one – hers is a black handlebar moustache. They both stare in front of them as they hear the waves of laughter from the audience. 'Ladies and gentlemen!' the gentleman shouts above the uproar,

'Ladies and gentlemen! Ladies and gentlemen! You can see Jolanda and Peter sitting here. I know that you don't know which one is the man and which one is the woman. Some of you may doubt that Jolanda is a woman at all. Come, come, Jolanda, show these ladies and gentlemen what you have under your skirt! That's right, Jolanda! Bravo, Jolanda! That's it, Jolanda!'

Scenes like these, in which the Gypsy functions literally as the supplier of impossible possibilities, refer unmistakably to the awareness that unam-

biguous stories are an impossibility.[58] I shall return to the litmus test that
the Gypsy carries out – obscenely raising the skirt – to determine what is
real.

The essentially arbitrary character of words, terms and concepts with
which reality is created in the stories is also a recurrent theme in the jokes
about Gypsies. The Gypsies do not leave a single truth intact. For instance, the symbol of Tito's new Yugoslavia, the red five-pointed star, is
explained in a highly novel way in the next Gypsy joke, which plays on
the fact that the same word is used for 'cross' and 'crotch':

> After the war people no longer dared to talk about religion. People were
> even afraid to utter the word 'cross', it's said. You could be punished for
> it. One day a Gypsy woman went to see the doctor, pointed to the spot be-
> tween her legs called the crotch, and said: 'Give me medicine, doctor, my
> five-pointed star is hurting and I want it cured!'[59]

Fear as a motive in human action; the constant exchange of stories and
symbols; and pain that does not stop: implicit social knowledge in a nutshell. The Gypsy jokes that circulate among the Serbs also provide the
clearest examples of the anti-logic to which the imaginary Gypsies resort:

> A young man was abroad for study purposes. One day his father sent him
> a Gypsy to give him a package. When he arrived, the young man asked
> him if he had news from home. The Gypsy replied:
> – No, sir, no news, except that your raven is dead.
> – What did he die of?
> – He was bound to die after eating all the meat on the four horses that
>   died.
> – Are the horses dead? And you said there's no news?
> – Well, how on earth could they have stayed alive? After they'd had to
>   haul so much water?
> – Why did they have to haul so much water?
> – But sir, if you please! What do you expect if the house burns down? They
>   had to haul water to put out the fire, of course...

The Gypsies who people the Serb imagination simply do not fit into any
category: neither the laws of language and text, nor the dominant classi-
ficatory systems, nor the systems of norms, religion and morals of any
kind at all. The Gypsies are permanently elusive in the structuring terms
that Serb everyday life offers for an understanding of people and the
world they live in. They continually refer to the existence of impossible

possibilities.[60] Commenting on the making of his popular Gypsy epic *Dom za Vešanje*, Emir Kusturica says that he deliberately opted for a non-narrative form. He alternates his representation of reality with dream scenes, fantasies and mirages:

> The film has the structure of life itself. I once saw an old Gypsy return from Italy with his family. His car crammed with furniture, with an ancient table and a modern fridge on top. The man was dressed like a clown, I suddenly thought: 'I can't use the normal way of telling a story here, the film will have to be wild and non-narrative'. So I opted for arbitrary moments that came from Gypsy life itself.[61]

Elsewhere he has written:

> The film recalls the typical clothing of the Gypsy. He wears three different coloured T-shirts beneath his shirt, his trousers look as if they're from another planet. It's a film in which everything is combined with everything else, simply because that's how it is in life too.[62]

A reality that refuses to be organised in any way. Everything is combined with everything else. Simply because that's how it is in life too. This is close to Taussig's 'great steaming morass of chaos that lies on the underside of order'.

Everything is what it is and not another thing

The second anti-structural tendency to emerge from the material I collected (and which, in full accordance with the anti-logic of the collective fantasy, is diametrically opposed to the dominant 'nothing is what it seems') has already cropped up briefly in the case of the woman with the handlebar moustache who had to pull up her skirt in the freak show to demonstrate her real gender: *Everything is what it is and nothing else.* The pictures of the *cigansko carstvo*, the kingdom of the Gypsies where life has no other purpose, no other point or meaning except itself, displayed the same tendency to reduce all the stories about the imaginary world of the Gypsies to their most banal, elementary and basic forms. The people of the *cigansko carstvo* take life as it comes. There is nothing else. They live from day to day, they do not think about tomorrow, they squander all they have. Aimlessly they wander over the earth, without purpose, except, that is, the purpose of wandering itself. 'We travel over the globe towards the left', as a presenter of a Gypsy folklore show summed up this vision on Serb television, 'and the earth turns to the right, so that we do not move anywhere in relation to the sun. That is why we are so sun-burnt.'

Obscenity in particular is used like a crowbar in jokes about Gypsies to break open the world of the stories of the *fini ljudi*. The embarrassment of having to go to a doctor or chemist for a sexually transmitted disease is the key element in a joke that clearly illustrates the effect of obscenity in the world of the stories:

> A Gypsy woman comes into a chemist's, walks up to the counter, and says to the chemist: 'I need some powder for my cunt because it itches so'. The chemist is shocked by the Gypsy's language. He says: 'Go outside and then come back in, but first knock politely on the door, say 'good afternoon, sir', and then you can ask for a remedy for crab louse'. The Gypsy woman sees nothing wrong in this. She goes outside, knocks politely on the door, says 'good afternoon, sir', and asks for a remedy for crab louse. The chemist is very pleased and politely asks her how much she needs. The Gypsy woman replies: 'Enough for two cunts'.

The man who told me this joke left no doubt as to who was its hero. He presented the chemist as a narrow-minded individual by speaking his words in a nasal tone. The Gypsy woman, who called a spade a spade, who faced up to the facts of life and did not pay much attention to the rules of the world of the stories, was the heroine of his story.

It is interesting to see that such foul-mouthed Gypsies feature particularly in those social institutions where the world in stories is produced: the law court, the political party, the classroom. In the following Gypsy joke, the anti-structural effect is heightened by the fact that the Gypsy is confronted with a doctor who, like the chemist, only wants to be addressed in polite language, but who is forced to use an increasingly obscene language by the Gypsy's failure to understand him:

> The Gypsy has stomach cramps and goes to the doctor. The doctor feels his belly and asks:
> – What about answering nature's call?
> – Plenty of it, brother, plenty of it! It's my nature to call out for poor relief, otherwise I wouldn't be here...
> – That's not what I meant. How are your stools?
> – Wooden, doctor, and very old and shaky, totally ruined you could say...
> – Ama! Man! Try to understand! How often do you go into the outhouse?
> – The outhouse? What do you mean? I live outside the house, don't I?

- Shit, Gypsy! what's your shit like?
– Er... well, doctor, I haven't tried it!

By telling obscene jokes about Gypsies and thereby flagrantly violating the rules of decency, the *fini ljudi* reduce the world to a place where everything is what it is and not another thing. Not only do the Gypsies in Serb fantasies unmask the world in stories as a system of *prazne priče*, idle stories, but by returning to the physical, to the body and its products, they replace it by a reality that is not interchangeable with something else. Cunt. Bitch. Shit. The limits of the world in stories.

This discussion of anti-structural tendencies in the collective fantasies about Gypsies brings us closer to understanding why *Gypsies* were selected to be the guardians of implicit social knowledge. As we saw in Chapter 3, implicit social knowledge is concerned with insights whose essence undermines the world in stories. It is a knowledge about a world in which physical laws, chance and arbitrariness show no regard for human will. It is a knowledge of the world which is simply there, the world out there in the rain and the mud, detached from what it is supposed to be according to the terms of the civilisation debate, detached from any other discursive mediation. Implicit social knowledge is a kind of knowledge which is recalcitrant to the signifying structures of language, of narrative, of a story.

The fantasy of images that has been woven around the figure of the Gypsy provides an anti-structure, an anti-language, an anti-logic which can get much closer to the essence of implicit social knowledge. Wherever the Gypsies appear, the façades of bourgeois, civilised society begin to crumble. Their entry initiates the decline of the world created in stories. Fantasies about Gypsies sow the seeds of doubt. They do not deny the paradoxes and ambiguities of existence; on the contrary, they emphasise them. That is why there is not a story about Gypsies – the only story is the lack of a story. There is no narrative, no coherent whole with a clear structure that can be brought to light from the complexity of diverse material. There are images and ideas about Gypsies. And there are images and ideas about Gypsies that are exactly the opposite. That is as far as structuring goes. And any further structuring is possible.[63]

Play frames

The lessons from the wartime reform school dislocate the world as created in stories. Its articulation can never take place just like that. Play frames have to ensure that implicit social knowledge is kept away from normality. That even applies to implicit social knowledge in the disguises that I have discussed above.

The jokes about Gypsies (though this is just as true of the films, songs, books and ethnographies) provide clear examples of how a play frame enables Serbs to enter the domain of the Gypsies for the duration of a joke. The joke has a clear beginning ('Do you know the one about the Gypsy who...?') and a clear end (the punch-line and the ensuing laughter). Within the confines of the joke, the stories that dominate everyday reality are temporarily suspended and a space is created in which to say the unsayable: it's only a joke, it's only a Gypsy talking. The embarrassing situation that arises when a joke falls flat, when no one gets the punch-line and no one laughs already says something about the necessity of play frames; a painful confusion and embarrassment arise when the unsayable insights that can be freely aired in a joke are not kept at bay by excluding them and are allowed to enter the world of normality unhindered.

While the disorderly consequences of a joke that fails can still be surmounted, this is less so in the case of other play frames. During my fieldwork I discovered how crucial it is to maintain the play frames connected with implicit social knowledge. I have already mentioned the reticence and reluctance of the people of Novi Sad to talk to me about Gypsies, and I have discussed a number of motives for this. I mentioned the annoyance of the *fini ljudi* at a Westerner who came to portray them as the wild men of the Balkans and at the inappropriateness of such a trivial research topic in wartime conditions. However, these remarks on the strict and necessary separation of implicit social knowledge by means of play frames reveal another dimension to their reluctance and reticence. By raising academic questions about the Gypsies, I was interfering with the boundaries between two knowledge systems that are supposed to be kept apart. In other words, the defensive reactions I met with all the time during my research were an expression of the need to maintain the play frames, the attempt to keep the knowledge and insights of one frame separate and distinct from another.

My research experiences with the colleagues in the ethnological museum in Novi Sad are the most telling in this respect. They also had difficulty in talking about the imaginary Gypsy. The only Gypsies one could talk about were the *salonfähige* Gypsies who appeared in the stories of specialists in the field of Gypsy ethnography. These ethnographic Gypsies had been domesticated through counting, classification, designation, description and analysis. They led a tame existence in the dusty filing cabinets in the museum attic. The Gypsies served up by ethnographers when they were drinking coffee together in the museum canteen were of a very different kind from the ones they told me about from behind their desks. The anecdotes and jokes at coffee time were peopled by the wild Gypsy, the trickster, the smelly, dirty-mouthed and artful Gypsy I have already described, a Gypsy who resists quantification, classification and designation. That was the Gypsy I was interested in. But it was also the Gypsy who proved to be impossible to find once the laughter had died down and the conversation took a serious turn.

To give a colleague from the museum a better idea of the purpose of my research, I presented her with a written outline of my research plans. She was furious at the idea of a hidden identification of Serbs with Gypsies. 'How could I imagine that?', she asked with a baleful look, when we met a few days after she had read the text. The passage where I suggested that Gypsies are strange and recognisable at the same time, that they are just like Serbs *and* not at all like Serbs,[64] particularly aroused her wrath. She had made written comments on my text, including the following:

> Where are the apostrophes when you claim that 'Gypsies are just like Serbs and vice versa?' I think that we are here dealing with two totally different cultures with totally different moral and other principles (one group consists of the old inhabitants of the Balkan peninsula, in contrast to the others, most of whom are nomads). Gypsies were allowed into the patriarchal micro-society of Serbia, but that did not go for their life-style, because that was where the boundary lay that could not be crossed. And if it has to be stated that Serbs and Gypsies live together, that is not because of the thesis that Gypsies are 'just like Serbs' and different at the same time.

This reaction of indignation and vigorous rebuttal of my claims about the hidden identification of Serbs with Gypsies becomes more understandable in the light of the above discussion of the concealed layers of meaning of the imaginary figure of the Gypsy. Within the story of the *fini ljudi*, the story that includes academic practice and within which our contacts as colleagues took place, my claims and ideas were impolite and insulting. It was as if I wanted to bolster the Croatian propaganda with its continual suggestions about the wild Serbs. Claims of this kind had to be denied within the frame of the appropriate forms of behaviour, the European ideal of civilisation and the intellectual world – in fact, the suggestion that trivialities like Gypsy jokes and visits to a Gypsy orchestra had any importance had to be denied.

However, the defensive reactions and pronounced reluctance to talk about Gypsies point in another direction too. The play frame works as a boundary in two directions: it protects the world of the stories from implicit social knowledge; and at the same time it protects the domain of the Gypsies from interrogation and designation.

Play frames create an imaginary space outside the stories that shape everyday life. They enable people to step out of their story (temporarily) in order to be able to take a look at that story. Play frames, according to Turner, are:

> the metaphorical borders within which the facts of experience can be viewed, reflected upon and evaluated [... and] within which members of a given group strive to see their own reality in new ways and to generate a language, verbal or non-verbal, which enables them to talk about what they normally talk about.[65]

As such, this society cherishes the imaginary space that is woven around the figure of the Gypsy. The knowledge and insights that are deposited there are too essential, too close to the collective experience of the peoples of this part of Europe. Where fusion, anti-structure, unnameability and meaninglessness constitute the essence and the raison d'être of fantasies about Gypsies, raising academic questions – and in fact any questions or attempts to include this knowledge within the world of the stories – is out of order. The Gypsy fantasy has to remain unquestioned, closed and protected from the reason that can do nothing but limit and order the chaos, the confusion, the flowing lines. Hands off our Gypsies.

Hands off. My Gypsy. That was the implicit warning of the fellow anthropologist from Novi Sad who had promised me every support but who did not want to read a research proposal. Embarrassed by the situation, he remarked that if he read the proposal, he would be forced to think about the subject, and then the evenings with the Gypsy orchestra might never be the same again.

Hands off. My Gypsy. That must have been the implicit message of the stony silence and beads of sweat on the upper lip of an informant whom I questioned too long in a desperate attempt to break the wall of silence. Hands off.

This 'hands off' must have also informed the responses of Bora, a former road construction expert, who had been thrown out of the house after he separated from his wife, and now lived the life of a bohemian bar musician. I had already heard enthusiastic stories about this colourful figure who, it was said, knew everything about Gypsies and was even like one himself. During a visit to a bar called *Boem* [Bohemian], I made desperate attempts to ask this Bora about the visits to Gypsies and to the Gypsy orchestra. He grabbed the sheet of paper with the questions I had prepared out of my hand and raced through the list. 'Question one: nonsense. Question two: nonsense. Nonsense, nonsense, nonsense, nonsense. More than 80% of those questions are nonsense.' I couldn't have got a clearer reply. My academic way of asking questions was out of place. Gypsies, and particularly the cult connected with the Gypsy orchestra, he seemed to be saying, should be left unquestioned, preserved from analysis and scientific approaches. Forbidden territory for academics. Hands off!

Creator protects his creation. Film director Emir Kusturica and actress Ljubica Adzović. (Photo: Thierry Rajić)

Hands off! is the message of Emir Kusturica, here photographed with the actress from his Gypsy film, Ljubica Adzović. I have always found it an enigmatic double portrait, this embrace that looks like a stranglehold. The photo only becomes meaningful when you stop reading it as a portrait of the director and the actress and start seeing it as a portrait of the creator and his creation. Hands off. My Gypsy. The Gypsies who don't want to be subjected to his creation are expelled from his inverted Garden of Eden. In answer to criticisms that his film confirms the prejudices about Gypsies, Kusturica replied:

> This is my third film and all that time I have been the target of various groups. Some Muslims claimed that *Do you know about Dolly Bell* was an anti-Islam film. Supporters of the Communist regime tried to get *When dad was on a business trip* banned. And now Gypsies in Paris have started legal proceedings against me. Who are they? The ones who want to make their way into the topmost layer of French society, who deny their origins and have money and possessions. They turn against those who live on the streets as they themselves once did.[66]

But the most telling example of the attempts to preserve the domain of the Gypsies from the meaning that language and reason impose came from the man who guided me around one of the many country houses that Tito had owned, not far from Novi Sad. The man laughed at my academic interest in Gypsies and claimed that I could only really get to know them by drinking with them or, better still, fucking them. That was the only way. He made graphic movements to make it clear what the word 'fuck' meant. Perhaps this pantomime was prompted by doubts about my linguistic skill, but I think that a more fundamental doubt lay behind his explicit illustration of the word 'fuck'. Westerners are regarded as cool and unemotional by the Serbs, and they have a poor reputation for sexual skills into the bargain. That, according to this informant, is why they lack the ability to get through to the essence of the Gypsy.

They thought up a world and they called it a living world

The Gypsies we have been looking at in this chapter, like the mud you find everywhere in their world, are a combination of elements. Dirty, down to earth and obscene, they crop up in the Serb imagination to soil stories about a cultivated and civilised world in the Balkans, to break open the world of the stories of the *fini ljudi*, with its rigid, petrified patterns.

The reaction to the appearance of Gypsies in the polished story of the *fini ljudi* is like the reaction to everything that is out of place: an attempt to eliminate it and restore order. All the same, as we have seen, Gypsies also evoke a spectrum of different reactions, ranging from curious interest and fascination, tension and excitement to seduction and direct glorification. These reactions should not be taken for reactions to Gypsies themselves, but to the wildness they represent; their alleged affinity with a precultural state, both cognitively and affectively. The Gypsies who figure in the Serb imagination are a compromise between the psychological and social need to forget how wild people and the world can be, and the impossibility (and perhaps also undesirability) of banishing that implicit social knowledge. They offer an escape from the story that my discussion partners inhabit, the story that says that Novi Sad is the Athens of Serbia, the birthplace of European Serbia, the seat of good taste, morality and forms of behaviour, the story in which a collective experience of recurrent neglect, destruction and decline (and the primitivism on which that is based) is not allowed to exist, the story in which the degeneration into an orgy of violence is always someone else's fault, someone else's Evil, someone else's primitive character. The Gypsies enable a different approach to that wildness and that lack of control.

Sometimes the world is just like the world of the Gypsies. Sometimes life becomes like the life of the Gypsies. That is the message that crops up time and again in the collective fantasies about Gypsies. In order to realise that it is all relative, these etiquette manuals and *biedermeier* bouquets, the daily round of the office, these framed Pierrots with a blue tear running down their whitened faces, these badly prepared and disgusting pig's heads, these tight asses, this talking about Serbia and what it is to be Serbian. Because once the days of the *cigansko carstvo* are upon us, the kingdom of the Gypsies, all that will turn out to have been nothing more than stage props, attributes, texts, scripts to bolster a life of illusion. In a veiling and revealing masquerade that recognises that experiences are unnamable, and within the safe boundaries of fiction, collective fantasies about Gypsies reveal not only the differences but also the points of contact between the civilised people of Novi Sad and their wild and primitive others.

5 Kafana

> Nowhere in the world does the imagination fly so high as among us. Especially in our bars. Whether it's a remote stop for travellers, a third-rate bar or a high-class restaurant, the principle is the same everywhere: everything is allowed and everyone dares everything in the *kafana*. Sadness leads to a flood of tears before you know it. Happiness is multiplied by fourteen. That's what counts in every *kafana*. All the rest is a question of emphasis. *Kafana*! An everyday human necessity! Whether we admit it or not.
>
> – Announcement of the Sarajevo Festival of the Bar Song, 1991[1]

In the same interview in which the Novi Sad writer Aleksandar Tišma refers to his early confrontation with blood in the snow and brains spattered against the wall as the essential experience of his life, he mentions an old school friend who makes no qualitative distinction between reading books and going to a bar:

> Recently I met an old school friend here, a simple man. He says: 'Why are you still bothering with those books, Tišma? You'll still die like the rest of us. Come and have a good time in the bar!' That man, a very kind man, simply can't understand that I see a qualitative distinction between writing books and sitting in a bar.

Perhaps Tišma is right in seeing this qualitative distinction between writing a book and sitting in a bar. But in the light of the preceding chapter, I think that Tišma has overlooked an interesting correspondence between his own literary reflections on the human condition in this country pockmarked by war and conflict and his old friend's sitting in a bar.

A number of cases are presented in this chapter to show how the lessons from the wartime reform school are continued in the Gypsy bar. No history lessons, no sociology. The syllabus of the Gypsy bar can best be described as philosophy, pondering on the basic forms of Being. Themes from the world as the South Slavs experience it which have cropped up repeatedly in the preceding chapters – the transitoriness of every story, the ephemeral nature of money and possessions, the pain and tears of disillusionment, the joys of friendship, the unpredictable dynamism of human instincts and impulses – are brought together in this space and can be combined in various ways to form Victor Turner's 'more apt or interesting "designs for living"'.[2]

Mimetic play

> In Benin, when people belonging to the Gun tribes are possessed by Yoruba divinities, they speak Yoruba and sing Yoruba songs. In South Africa, when the Thongha are possessed by spirits of Zulu or Ndau origin, then they sing Zulu or Ndau tunes. In Greece, in order to become possessed by Dionysus, one needed tunes originating in Phrygia.[3]
>
> – Gilbert Rouget, *Music and Trance*

Let me start the discussion of what goes on in the Gypsy bar with something already mentioned in the introductory chapter: the remarkable attempts at rapprochement between Serbs and Gypsies in the bars in Novi Sad and the environs. I have already described how the guests would shout 'great friend' and hand out cigarettes and drinks in an attempt to win the Gypsy musicians over to a less professional and more intimate attitude. The discussion of the collective fantasies about Gypsies sets these friendly approaches in a different light. After all, it has become clear that the interest in Gypsies is motivated not by considerations of a Gypsy-loving or philanthropic nature, but by a preoccupation of the Serbs with their own secret emotional life. It is therefore legitimate to ask with whom or what intimacy is being sought here.

Upon closer inspection, the attempts to establish contact between Serbs and Gypsies are just the opening moves in a complex game of mimicry and imitation on both sides. Taussig would call this mimesis, the creation of a situation 'in which it is far from easy to say who is the imitator and who is the imitated, which is copy and which is original'.[4] And that is exactly what seems to be going on in the Gypsy bars: a mimetic game in which the players create confusion around the question: 'Who is who and who is imitating whom?'

The game played in the Gypsy bars has two parties – Serbs and Gypsies. Each group has its own reasons for approaching the other and imitating it. As far as the reasons that motivate the Gypsies are concerned, much more can and should be said than what I am able to do within the confines of this study. I shall therefore concentrate on those elements that are relevant for the Serb perception of the events in the Gypsy bar, subjecting the motives of the Serb audience to a more extensive scrutiny.

When I asked Gypsy musicians their motives for performing in the bars, the answer was prosaic and realistic: 'To earn money'. Jovica, the bass player with the orchestra in *Dukat*, whose performances I followed closely for a year, always replied: 'To earn some bread'. But that answer is already a part of the mimetic game – 'I say I'm a poor and hungry Gypsy because that's what you want me to be'. Once he had made sure I had written down his reply in my notebook ('What are you writing now? What's that?'), he resumed his conversation with his colleagues: about how the roof of his house badly needed repairing, about the threat of war, about a Rolex he had managed to get second-hand, about the expensive medicines his wife needed, about the new BMW that Milan, the tamburica player from *Champagne*, had recently brought back from Germany. Clearly, the Gypsy musicians chase their own dreams in the Gypsy bar. For the Serb perception of the dramas that are given form in relation to the Gypsy orchestra, the fact that these musicians are making desperate attempts to escape from the ghetto is only relevant in so far as the Gypsies who perform in the bars hardly remind them of the uncivilised wild men of Serb fantasy. The Gypsy musicians often appear in pin-striped suits with immaculate white shirts, polished shoes, brilliantined hair and chic trilbies. They are full of smiles, affability and decency until they start on the *bećarci* songs and delight everyone by filling the bar with a flood of obscenities and double entendres, in spite of their posh clothes and bourgeois manners.[5]

Mi cigani, soćermani,	We Gypsies, *soćermani* [a nonsense word]
Mi smo pravi garagani!	We're real darkies!
He! Haj! Mi cigani!	Hey! Hah! We Gypsies!
Uvek smo raspevani!	We always sing lustily!
Faraonska naša sorta,	We're descended from the Pharaoh
gleda šta da smota!	And always see what we can pinch!
Jedan peva, drugi svira,	One sings, another plays,
treći šlajpik visitira!	And the third man empties someone's purse!
Bilo krava, ili ždrebe,	Whether it's a cow or a foal,
Ciga mora da gu jebe!	The Gypsy has to fuck it!

The Serb audience join in exuberantly and follow the rules of the mimetic game as they sing 'We Gypsies...'.

The motives adduced by the Serbs for playing the mimetic game are more diffuse and unclear, lacking as they do the unambiguous economic motive. Like questions about their notions of Gypsies, direct questions about the motives of my discussion partners for visiting a Gypsy bar did not yield much. 'To enjoy listening to Gypsy music.' 'Because they play music with soul.' 'To have a good time.' 'Cheerfulness.' 'To let it all hang out.' Fair enough, but these answers don't get us very far in trying to understand what goes on in the Gypsy bars.

The more guarded research attitude that I had to assume for a number of reasons already mentioned did not get me much further either. Knowing the right place for real Gypsies was discussed a lot among Gypsy music fans, but in the same way that my informants talked about cars or women: stating fixed certainties in the most general (and empty) terms but with an air that rules out any contradiction. 'Those from Temerin are the real thing! What a night I had there!' Or: 'Ha! When my daughter got married I spent a month going to all the villages in the Vojvodina to find the best Gypsy orchestra for her wedding. What a month that was...' And then, once again, the meaningful silence, as if to make room for 'the infinity of the unsaid'.[6] What I have already described in relation to the fantasies about Gypsies applied with even greater force when it came to what went on in the Gypsy bars. My discussion partners tried to shield them off from questioning, discussion, analysis or academic approaches. The Gypsy bar had to be protected against linguistic signifying and discursive thought. 'You have to realise that there are people here who can't live without the Gypsy orchestras' were the words of the chairperson of the city council when he heard what I intended to do, staring at the ice-cubes whirling around in his whisky glass. He said it in an almost conspiratorial tone, like an enigma that can only be answered by silence. Any further questions (Why? What is your view of the matter? What's the matter with them?) were out of the question. Well, perhaps not, but it would only have been painful and inappropriate. Above all, in this situation it would have been signal proof of my inability and incomprehension.

A more useful way to obtain insight into what prompts Serbs to go to the Gypsy bars to play the mimetic game is to describe what they do there, in combination with the insights into their collective fantasies about the world of the Gypsies.

CASE I

Hajde, Milane, hajde, da nam nešto lepo sviraš, za dušu. I can still hear her saying it, with a lingering, plaintive voice. Come on, Milan, play us something beautiful, something for the soul.

She's a Serb beauty. Her dark hair pinned up, a few strands hanging loose. Big gold ear-rings. A floral scarf with long fringes. A tambourine on the table in front of her. The name of the bar is *Gypsy Night*. Ties hang from every wall as decoration. The place for the Gypsy music with the most soul in Novi Sad. This is where Gypsy musicians from all over Novi Sad meet after closing time. Sometimes they play for their own enjoyment. I had offered to give Milan, one of the musicians from *Dukat*, a lift home after work to drop in at *Gypsy Night*. He laps up the Serb beauty's flattery.

The scenario: she wants to be a Gypsy woman for one night. That's why she's sitting there dressed like that in a Gypsy bar at three o'clock in the morning. Although she's pretty drunk and the Gypsy orchestra has been playing for hours, she hasn't got completely into the mood yet. She's invited Milan to her table and asks him to play something for her soul. He has to do it voluntarily. Even if she had the money, she could not pay for this, because it's one of the rules of Serb bar folklore that the real soul of Gypsy music is only released when the musicians play for themselves and not as professional musicians. So she tries to seduce Milan, she plays up to his confidence. She tries to get intimate with him. Milan can feel the power, doesn't move a muscle, no, no, no, but orders another whisky – just enough to keep her hope alive and to hang on to her enjoyable company.

Milan doesn't play. Back in the car, he asks if I'd noticed how the woman had asked and begged for a song with soul. 'What does she expect? Look, if she'd offered me a thousand marks, I'd have played for her soul'.

Who is who and who is imitating whom? This woman is not just trying to build up an intimate relationship with the Gypsy musician. To judge from her Carmen-esque dress and her tambourine, she has gone a step further: she has come here to be a Gypsy. But masquerades are not enough to taste the life of a Gypsy (nothing is as lifeless as a tambourine lying idle on a table). Someone has to touch her, someone has to bring to life the Gypsy that she wants to become. According to the conventions of the Gypsy bar, Milan is capable of doing that. He can give her back what she has had to lose to become a civilised citizen of Novi Sad: her soul. In the last resort, that is what these curious nocturnal negotiations about the soul – 'play something for your own soul so that I can get my soul back' – is all about. In other words, it is the task of the Gypsy musician to bring the internalised Gypsy of the Serbs to life. Both parties know this, as can be seen from the comments of Janoš, a violin player, about his work in one of the establishments in Novi Sad:

> The ideal is to give the customer the feeling that he's understood. Didn't I tell you that we Gypsies have a great understanding of people, we are great psychologists? If a visitor comes in, say a large group of fifteen, twenty people come in and sit down, then you start to play... [whispers] ... and then you can tell by a visitor's face, by his facial expression, whether he's taking in the music, whether it interests him at all...
> – How can you see that?
> You can feel it, it's a feeling. But from the expression on his face as well. Anyway, you adjust your programme immediately... Aha! ...There! Look... now I must not play something sentimental. If I do, I've lost him. Something to show off your skill, or the opposite, something entertaining. I mean, it depends on people's mentality, you know, and you have to find a way of reaching it. If you can't, I think they don't even notice you're there, that you're playing. They might look at you for a moment because they hear something. You have to strike the right chord with people, like touching the string of a violin, you understand, that's how you have to touch people's strings. It's a purely psychological affair, and we Gypsies learn that from when we're children...

Although it would not be correct to minimise the mastery of the Gypsy musicians, I would suggest, despite the claims of this violin player and in line with Gilbert Rouget's thesis on the relation between music and possession, that the ecstatic experiencing of Gypsy music is in the first and last resort stimulated by the Serb fantasy. The main task of the Gypsy musician is to supply a musical product that can be recognised as 'Gypsy' and that enables the audience to identify with the 'Gypsy spirit'.[7] The simple fact that a Gypsy produces the music facilitates that identification, but he does not have to be present, as the following case shows.

CASE 2

Restaurant *Play Off*, in a suburb of Novi Sad, is lacking in just about everything that goes to create a Gypsy setting. This is no remote inn or fisher's hut at the end of the world. It lacks even the quasi authenticity of the Gypsy bars in the city with their wagon wheels, copper pots and harnesses on the wall. *Play Off* is what my discussion partners would label as *fin*: white bistro chairs with pastel-coloured floral cushions, tables with artificial flowers in reed baskets, a view of a terrace with illuminated floor tiles here and there, and waiters who only know how to interpret the order 'behave correctly to our customers' by being extremely ill-tempered and formal. The drinks are served in glasses which seem predestined to prevent any enjoyment: hexagonal, greenish, with a heavy glass bottom with air bubbles encased in it.

Play Off also has a tamburica orchestra that goes from table to table to entertain the clientèle and play requests in exchange for payment. There are no Gypsy musicians in *Play Off*, only Serb musicians.

A couple is seated one table away from where I am sitting with a few friends. The man is grey-haired and indeterminate, the woman is in her mid-forties, wearing a white and navy blue striped cardigan, white trousers, a blouse with a shawl, carefully made up and wearing a large pair of glasses. What I remember above all are the mondaine cigarette holder with which she smoked one cigarette after another, and her hair dyed red – and by red I mean red.

She has just worked her way through a large plate of grilled meat – *rostilj* is regarded as the speciality of the house in *Play Off*, just like in any other Yugoslavian restaurant – and she has downed innumerable glasses of white wine. When the orchestra approaches her table, she asks for Gypsy songs. First she asks for a few Russian Gypsy songs, the genre within the Gypsy repertoire that is considered the most refined and tasteful. However, after a couple of songs she switches to songs in Romany, the language of the Gypsies. The musicians comply without any difficulty, even though it is a foreign language and they probably have little or no idea of what the words mean. Then something snaps inside her. She pushes her chair back, grips the edge of the table, and starts to sing. SING! She sings at the top of her voice. Everyone in the room turns to look at the vocal eruption coming so unexpectedly from behind the empty plate with the crumpled floral paper serviettes, rind and bones. HA-HA-HA-YOOHOO she screams between couplets. AY! AY! AY! CHORORO! She flings her hands in the air in what looks like a reflex action. Clapping. Beating on the table. Jingling jewellery. Then she makes turning movements with her hands and shakes her shoulders and breasts as if she is doing a seductive oriental belly dance. She waves her head about as if she had a wild mass of black hair instead of trimmed hair dyed red. Her mimicry is noteworthy as well. 'I own the world', she says by pursing her lips during the musical intermezzi and assuming an expression which (my notes taken that evening remind me, though I was probably not completely sober by this time either) 'unmistakably recalled the way US porno starlets simulate an orgasm'.[8]

The bass player gives me a wink – 'crazy bitch', he seems to be saying. You aren't supposed to behave like that in a place like *Play Off*. People go there to talk, to engage in never ending Vojvodinian philosophising, but now every discussion has been suspended and everyone is watching. Her husband also seems to be somewhat embarrassed by her performance. It is not just his hair that is grey as he sits fidgeting with the bridge of his spectacles and sings quietly as he stares at his empty plate, not looking up or around him. He has no choice: joining in is the only way to prevent his wife's singing from looking like the public performance of a cheap chanteuse. That would have been terribly inappropriate. His half-hearted humming makes his wife's performance at least acceptable as part of the scenario 'couple dine out and round off the evening with a bit of music'. My companions – who later turn out to know this woman vaguely – look rather sheepishly in my direction. They share my enthusiastic remarks that it's nice to see people letting themselves go. Yes, yes... nice, yes. Later, when the woman rather nervously sits puffing away at her cigarette holder – she is embarrassed too – they compliment her on her beautiful voice. She is getting over it. She shakes the incident off with a laugh. 'Oh, yes, I can sing all right, yes, I used to sing in a church choir, you know, but this, oh, this was nothing...'

There was not a single Gypsy to be seen in the *Play Off*. All the same, the woman in this case not only sang Gypsy songs, but was transformed completely into a Gypsy when she sang. The ethnographer of a so-called primitive society would very probably have used the term 'possession' to describe a scene like this. The term opens an interesting perspective in this case. 'Possession is essentially identification with another', says Gilbert Rouget in an attempt to formulate the general logic of possession. People who are possessed behave like the spirit that has taken them over. Rouget refers to examples from Africa, where 'people who ordinarily speak a given African language talk in Arabic if the spirit possessing them is thought to be of Arab origin', and to Jeanne des Agnes, a nun from eighteenth-century Loudun who spoke Hebrew when she was possessed by Beelzebub. 'What in fact is possession other than an invasion of the field of consciousness by the *other*, that is, by someone who has come from elsewhere?'[9]

The same can be said of this Serb woman. When she is possessed by their spirit, she sings incomprehensible songs in the language of the Gypsies and becomes a Gypsy in other ways too.[10] Screaming, 'oriental belly dancing', seductively twisting with her hands in front of her face, beating and clapping, jingling golden chains and shaking her hair: this is all part of the repertoire of expressions that she has learnt and known as

'Gypsy'. That is how Koštana sings and dances, the Gypsy in the regularly performed play of the same name by Borisav Stanković. That is how the Gypsies dance the *čoček* in the TV folklore shows. That is how the seductive Gypsy singer shakes her hair out of her face in Aleksandar Petrović's film *Skupljači Perja*. For a brief moment, between a meal and the next cigarette, the Gypsy had surged up from the deepest recesses of her soul and taken possession of her, revealing itself above all in the impudent, proud and undisguisedly physical attitude with which she claimed the world as her own.

In the previous chapter the Serbs were confronted with their own ideas and fantastic representations as if in a mirror, or rather, a reflecting shop window in which their own image coincided with the forms and shapes that can be discerned in the semi-darkness on the other side of the glass. In the dramatic incidents associated with the Gypsy orchestra that distance disappears. The scenes described above show that, during the mimetic game, the bar clientèle are no longer spectators of their own fantastic imaginary world. They smash the shop windows to smithereens and enter the world of their imagination. Fantasy turns into experience, fiction into fact.

It is that merging of a fantastic world of representations with the physical, non-negotiable reality of the acting and feeling body, the unfettered emotion and irrational impulse, which gives the events in the Gypsy bar their special significance. Agreed, the jokes, texts, images and films that the Serbs make about Gypsies explore the outer limits of the stories they inhabit. But no matter how much these forms of expression may go against the grain, destroy forms and undermine stories, in the end they cannot escape the conclusions that they themselves generate: they continue to form a part of the worded reality that they unmasked. When we turn to the insights that emerge from this mimetic game, on the other hand, it is no longer a question of perception but of *reali*sation in the fullest sense of the word – a rare item in this land of idle stories.

The following story about a situation that got out of hand was told me by Goran Stajić, a journalist for the local, pro-government paper in Novi Sad and as such, perhaps more than the others, entangled in a net of lies and half-truths. It shows how *reali*sation can lead to new, unshakeable insights.

CASE 3

'I lose control. I can't keep thingts together.' One of the first things he says as he sits down on the terrace. Goran Stajić is much too late and a bit tipsy. It is a warm, sultry August evening and we're talking about the war again. I note what a bizarre gulf there is between, on the one hand, the world of a terrace in Novi Sad, full of *fini ljudi* dressed according to the latest dictates of fashion and engaging in polite conversation and, on the other, the actual situation fifty kilometres away, where people are being killed in a horrifying way at the very same moment. My discussion partner shakes his head grimly, gazing silently in front of him. 'There isn't any difference at all between the people here on the terrace and the people shooting one another to bits out there', he says. The civilisation I think I can see is just a 'thin layer of varnish, a very thin layer of varnish' and 'in the last resort we Serbs are all the same'.

These were certainly dramatic words. Until shortly before this conversation, Stajić, like many others of my discussion partners, had put all the blame for the violence on the 'colonists', the hot-headed Balkan Serbs from south of the rivers. This distinction had become blurred by now. 'I feel so threatened, so cornered. If they give me a rifle tomorrow and send me off to defend my country, I'll do it. I'll be ready.' My reaction was one of incredulity. I knew Stajić as a person who was anything but violent. But to convince me of the changes in his frame of mind, Stajić illustrated his point with an anecdote.

There were four of them: Stajić, a female colleague from Novi Sad, and two politicians from Belgrade. They had reserved a back room in a restaurant in town for lunch in order to discuss various matters by themselves, out of reach of curious glances. They must have been talking about the war, as the story made clear, because during the lunch two members of a volunteer force who were active on the East Slavonic front suddenly turned up. 'Big guys', Stajić commented. 'They'd been in the foreign legion. The kind of men who only drink fruit juice, you know they're killers. They were looking for silencers.' (It was August 1991, the war had only just begun, people were still looking for silencers.)

When they had gone, Stajić and his colleagues paid a large sum to get a Gypsy musician, the old tamburica player from the orchestra, to play for them. He joined them at the table and sat down a little to one side of the woman in the company so that he could 'play into her ears' from behind. They drank wine and sang songs. The Gypsy sang only 'old songs, our songs, the songs of the Vojvodina'. There was also a song that he recognised as a poem by Miroslav Antić, *Molitva* (Prayer), a song about longing for security, for permanence – above all, a protest against being uprooted:

MOLITVA	PRAYER
Poslušaj me, bože,	Hear my prayer, God,
veliki gospodine!	Mighty Lord.
Ako me još nekad	If you were
ponovo budeš pravio	to recreate me
molim ti se,	Then I ask you,
udesi mi da ne budem	Make sure that I'm not
ni milicajac,	A militia man,
ni car,	An emperor
ni Ciganin.	Or a Gypsy.
Pretvori me	Change me
u jedno veliko drvo.	Into a big tree
Sto godina	So I can grow
tako da rastem	For a hundred years
i da me onda poseku	Then they can cut me down
Naće od mene da naprave.	And turn me into
Sto godina	A kneading bowl.
u meni testo da mese.	Then they can knead dough in me
Od leba	For a hundred years.
sav da se raspadnem.	Until, full of bread, I burst apart.

Then he told me how they got drunk. They had ordered one bottle of wine after another and drunk the wine from empty dessert coupes. Stajić himself had smashed three or four glasses. They had crashed to the floor. He had never done that in his life – 'perhaps once, but more for the fun of it'. He described the feeling as 'wonderful'.

One of the men from Belgrade had a gun on him, loaded and ready. At a certain point he took it out and put it demonstratively on the table. They made jokes about which direction the barrel should be pointing. In turn, each of them turned the gun to point to someone different. Later they bullied the Gypsy musician with it. They forced him to play 'beautifully and sensitively'. They shouted at him that he must sing the couplets to the end and not try to shorten the songs stealthily. Performing at gunpoint, he did not try any such tricks. The old Gypsy was shaking with fear.

Goran Stajić told his anecdote coolly, without the showing off that usually goes along with stories like this, but without any shame either. It was as if it was about someone else, or rather, with an expression on his face that seemed to ask 'I was a part of that, can you understand it?' Later we came back to the subject again. I asked whether he had felt like trying to get something out of the Gypsy with that gun. 'Yes, it was very tempting.' Thinking aloud, I tried to imagine it: you have power in the most direct way. He agreed.

What I would like to emphasise in this story is the fact that Stajić illustrates the new insights that he mentioned earlier on in our conversation ('I lose control. I start to drop things' – 'There's no difference between Vojvodina Serbs and *Balkanci*' – 'We Serbs are all primitive' – 'I'm prepared to kill if necessary' – 'I'm ready for the fight') with the story about the blow-out in the back room of the restaurant. It is there that Stajić seems to have first acquired the insights that he now utters with such conviction. Ideas and feelings that he had attributed to others – to Gypsies, to *primitivci*, to the people in the Balkans – until recently and that he had probably not even suspected in himself. Under the threat of war, they started to wander around in his mind, and they were dramatically acted out in the back room. They passed from the mental world of representations and fantasies to the concrete and physical world of action and experience, and thereby became real. Stajić, a *fin čovek* from Novi Sad, appropriated the world of primitive others. This was not because the world he had always wanted to shut out suddenly seemed attractive to him. Stajić simply realised that the world had changed and that, as a result of the rapidly escalating war, he had to relate to the Balkans now. Now Stajić says that civilisation in Serbia is just a thin layer of varnish, that in the last resort we Serbs are all the same. It is no longer an idle story for him. He knows it now. He has experienced it.

In the Gypsy's skin

These examples show that within the Gypsy bar the door is opened to all those forbidden and hidden things which were deposited in the figure of the Gypsy. By becoming Gypsies, as it were, the visitors to the Gypsy bar gain access to the insights and knowledge about people and the world that I have called implicit social knowledge. As would-be Gypsies, the visitors gain access to what is labelled as primitive and Balkan in the civilisation debate, while at the same time being Serb and part of their own culture. The shame, insecurity, anxiety and fear of being taken for a primitive disappear in the Gypsy bar. Everyone there is unmasked as a trickster.

It is important to realise that what is going on in the Gypsy bars is not a ritual of reversal. It is not a case where the laws of civilisation apply outside the bar, while the laws of the wilderness – or no laws at all – apply inside the bars. The *kafana* does not make things that clear-cut. Of course, as a whole the Gypsy bar is a space that is wilder than the public arena in Novi Sad, but that should not blind us to the fact that, as was the case in the collective fantasies about Gypsies, it is once again the fusion, the sharp juxtaposition of incompatible categories, that dominates the area. Urbanites of both sexes misbehave 'like Gypsies'. The Gypsies look like well-dressed urbanites. There are ties on the walls. Floral serviettes beside the bones and rind. And with a single meaningful gesture, Goran Stajić, who forces the Gypsy musician at gunpoint to produce beautiful and sensitive music, comments on both the civilisation offensive in Novi Sad and the wildness in the Balkans.

The crux of the Gypsy bar is the border between wildness and civilisation. The clientèle of the Gypsy bar have access to both. They are both who they are and who they should not be. They are Europeans and inhabitants of the Balkans, wild men and *fini ljudi*, self and other, human and animal. The dichotomies that structure everyday life and which often force people to make impossible choices for one thing and against another are suspended here. Gone. Disappeared. Everything merges with everything. The world lies open.

And then? Do the clientèle of the Gypsy bar let their hair down with a smile to enjoy this blissful situation of union and harmony?

Sometimes. There are moments of bliss in the Gypsy bars. The Montenegran, for example, who had to wait a long time for the orchestra to come to his table, too long, because he was already worked up and had roughly tugged on the Gypsy musicians' coats a couple of times. But the first notes from the violin were enough to turn his expression of deep dissatisfaction and frustration into that of an intensely contented baby at the breast. There were scenes of fraternisation, scenes of men who threw their arms around one another's shoulders, threw their heads back and gently swayed from side to side in time to the music. Or in *At the End of the World*, where Western visitors were called Vikings (*vikinzi*) to give more relief to the drunken fraternisation with the peoples of the Balkans. And there were situations in which Turner's notion of *communitas*, that 'egalitarian "sentiment for humanity" [...] representing the desire for a total, unmediated relationship between person and person' dominated the scene.[11]

CASE 4

Hotel Vojvodina, right in the centre of Novi Sad, in the late summer of 1991. Refugees from neighbouring East Slavonia are here as well, Serbs fleeing from the violence of the war, fearfully awaiting what lies in store for them. They sit together in small groups beneath the big chestnut trees in the hotel patio. The Gypsy orchestra goes from table to table, playing requests. The repeated calls for Bosnian *sevdalinke* make the audience realise that the vast majority of them are Bosnian Serbs. That unsuspected link among the fleeing individuals and broken families who have been brought together in this patio 'by fate', as they put it, soon enables the Gypsies with their Bosnian Serb repertoire to turn the whole patio into a single sobbing and singing community. The atmosphere is bewitching; everyone stays at their own table, but they talk to one another. They address one another as brother and sister. '*Brate moj, to što sam ja doživeo, tu nema reči*' (Brother, there are no words to describe what I've been through). A woman noisily and lengthily explains that she is not from Bosnia herself, but that she can claim to be regarded as Bosnian because of her connections. Everyone wants to be part of this. The waiter has tears in his eyes when he hears the song about the mother who does not like to see her son leaving for the army. He throws down his purse and notebook and stamps up and down the patio to calm himself. With their inimitable sense of drama, the Gypsies follow up the song about a soldier's departure with the song 'We are the *Srbijanci* (southern Serbs) with our *opanci* (peasant sandals)'. A man shouts that he would like it to continue into the early morning. They sing songs from the Vojvodina, Serbia, Montenegro. And Vranje. A man sitting near me explains: 'You'll always hear a song from Vranje if the soul's hurting'. The cry goes up: 'Now something from Macedonia'. Songs from every part of Yugoslavia can be heard in the patio – except for songs from Croatia and Slovenia: it's a party for southerners. A platinum blond calls that it is here, in this patio, that she really feels *Bratstvo i Jedinstvo*, Brotherhood and Unity. She folds her hands and presses them to her heart. It is her friend's birthday, so she sings her an 'old song', *Vino Piju Age Sarajlije* (The Lords of Sarajevo drink wine), a maid's lament:

Ako moram, nane,	Mother, if I,
Ako moram, nane,	Mother, if I
svakom sluga biti.	Must be everyone's servant.
Ja ne moram, nane,	I needn't, mother,
ja ne moram, nane,	I needn't, mother,
svakom ljubav biti.	Be everyone's darling.

Her friend pulls at her hair, throws her hands in the air, gestures as if she is cutting her wrists with a knife, and smashes a glass. The sobbing waiter joins them at their table for a moment to listen. The other waiters and cooks, with their white coats and chef's hats, are all ears too. People are leaning from the open windows that look down on the patio. Everyone wants to share in this euphoria. Just as I am leaving, the waiter comes to excuse himself and the behaviour of the rest. As a foreigner, it must be strange to me...

'Heavenly harmony', I discover in the Gypsy bar, is certainly not the only dream that is fulfilled when self and other coincide, when the human and the bestial intermingle. Dark, regressive desires and wishes have their place here too. In fact, the only thing you can be sure of in the Gypsy bars is the unpredictability of the scripts and scenarios. When you enter, you don't know what you will be like when you leave. There could just as easily have been a big fight between the people assembled in the patio of Hotel Vojvodina. Or they might just have listened to the Gypsies, bored and yawning.

The explicit lack of a single narrative, a meta-narrative, in the Gypsy bars means that a number of pregnant and recurrent scenarios which can still be identified – a fuzzy set of recurrent ritual actions and elements[12] – can best be described as basic forms of Being. Transitoriness, waste, power and dependence, resolution, the urge to destroy, physicality: the list is not exhaustive, but these are the most striking elements with which the clientèle of the Gypsy bars build their stories. I shall conclude this chapter with a discussion of this symbolic vocabulary on the basis of my own observations, (tall) stories, films, novels and the scanty literature that exists on this subject.

Transitoriness

> 'The Hungarian celebrates in tears', in the words of a melancholic song that comes from these plains, and it is true of every people that lives there.
>
> – Aleksandar Tišma, *Suspicion and Trust*

The awareness of transitoriness is omnipresent in the Gypsy bars of Novi Sad. There could be no clearer indication of those sombre undertones to the drama of the bar than the paintings that Stevan Aleksić (1876-1923) produced in Novi Sad. They are self-portraits, a number of which are set in the bar, showing the artist among a laughing public, food and drink. There is always a stuffed money pouch prominently in the picture, a sign of overabundance, but in this context also a symbol of waste and loss. There is nothing cheerful about these paintings. The colours are dead,

Celebrating transitoriness in the gypsy bar. Painting by the Novi Sad artist Stevan Aleksić (1906).

the smiles verge on insanity, and the violin player who plays to the ears of the revellers is regularly replaced in these paintings by a grinning skull.

The deep-seated awareness that the only certainty is death, that fortunes are ephemeral, and that it is best to take advantage of success while there is still an opportunity to do so, can be heard in innumerable songs from the bar repertoire. A good example is the song 'She came walking from the hill', with a beautiful mild and calm melody in the minor key. The first three lines sketch an attractive rustic scene. And then in the fourth line – boom! – it takes a completely different turn:

Dolinom se šetala	She came walking from the hill
devojčica mlada	The young girl
Razno cveće birala	Plucking flowers here and there
plakala od jada.	Crying wretchedly.
A šta će mi život taj	What's the good of this life
na ovome svetu	On this earth

kad ja moram umreti	If I'm to die
u najlepšem cvetlu?	In the flower of my youth?

Vesel'te se, drugovi	Enjoy yourselves, comrades,
pored čaše vina	With a glass of wine
ovaj život ne traje	This life won't last
hiljadu godina.	A thousand years.

This awareness of transitoriness can also be seen in the practice known as *pratiti*: the reveller hires a number of Gypsy musicians to accompany him from bar to bar and later, early in the morning, take him home. Film director Emir Kusturica did something similar at the Cannes film festival:

> Almost surrealist and entirely in the spirit of his film was the scene that Kusturica himself created when *Time of the Gypsies* was screened at the Cannes festival last year, where it won the director's prize. He had brought a group of Gypsies along and he strolled along the boulevard with them now and then. While they played, he walked dreamily along. That is how he and his band went to the beach...[13]

This scene embodies the spirit of the Gypsy bar: a baroque celebration of success – financial or otherwise – accompanied by Gypsies, the symbols par excellence, as we have seen, of how relative and futile success and fortune are. The successful, victorious Ego with the rumour of decline already in the background.

Wastefulness

Čija frula našim šorom svira?	Who's playing the flute in our street?
To je frula sirotinjskog sina	It's the flute of a poor child.
Bogatome ni svirati neće	The rich won't play like that.
Bogat plati, pa ga svirac prati.	The rich pay for a musician to accompany them!

The enormous extravagance of the clientèle in the Gypsy bars is one of their most striking characteristics. While it is the Gypsy rogue Ahmed who embodies this unfettered profligacy in Kusturica's Gypsy film *Dom za Vešanje*, in the Gypsy bars it is the Serbs themselves who indulge in waste (*potrošiti*) or squandering their money (*razbaciti pare*).

This extravagance is deliberate and explicit. With demonstrative gestures, banknotes are tucked under the strings of the violin, between the strings of the tamburica, into the violin player's bow, or stuck to the sweating forehead of the Gypsy musician. In those bars where the orchestra does not go from table to table but performs on stage, time and again you can see a drunken customer teetering to the front waving a bundle of banknotes to consume his fortune in public. The theme of waste is prominent in the stories about wild nights in the Gypsy bars, sometimes blown up, sometimes accompanied by a remark like 'that was in the golden era of Tito'. A fervent Gypsy orchestra fan told me the following:

> I started doing it, I began going to the Gypsies when I earned my own money. I didn't go while I was still living with my parents, of course, but once I started to earn my keep, yes, I often went. I lived here in Novi Sad, but I went everywhere within a radius of, say, a hundred kilometres. If I heard there was good music somewhere, I just went. It was possible then, because life was a lot better then. You could do anything... there was no inflation and, I don't know, so that I could just let myself go, you know, I was earning good money, of course I didn't spend it all on the Gypsies, but... still... yes, I spent a lot because I didn't care.

Goran Plavšić told me how he was in a bar one evening when a number of customers ('I think they were migrant labourers') were literally throwing away their money – there were banknotes everywhere: on the floor, on the table, in the pockets of the Gypsy musicians, in the brims of their trilbies. The musicians didn't even have the time to pick it all up. Somebody shouted: 'Let's smear jam on the soles of their shoes, then they won't have to bend down to pick up the money!' Another of Plavšić's stories was about a friend – typically, these half-mythological stories about uncontrolled behaviour were always about someone else – who had hired a whole restaurant, complete with Gypsy orchestra, for one evening. More or less by accident, he found this friend all by himself in a large room. 'He was sitting there like a mogul', he explained. He was holding a whole beaker of wine, which he later smashed to the floor, and was surrounded by the Gypsies. What they did was more like beating (*tući*) than playing (*svirati*). One of them was dancing on the table in his underpants. And money was strewn everywhere. He had scattered it all around. He just pulled it out of his breast pocket and tossed it carelessly into the bar.

'The pockets of the *bećar* are always full of money', as Ante Kovač concisely puts it, 'the poor don't throw their money away'. Despite their impressionism, my own observations in the Gypsy bars in and around Novi Sad confirm this remark: these people aren't flush, they have something to lose. They have a taste of it now. The squandering clearly has points of contact with the awareness of transitoriness. All the same, there are other, more cheerful undertones to the extravagance. 'Is it *Weltschmertz*? Dissatisfaction?' Ante Kovač asks in an attempt to explain the wasteful consumption associated with the Gypsy orchestra:

> Is it bottled up worries, an unfortunate love affair, or some kind of mental collapse? Is it perhaps simple high spirits at finding a girl friend? Or is it to show off, to show the world who he is, what he is capable of? And then there are also the art for art's sake *bećari*. They throw their money away for the sake of throwing it away. They simply love this atmosphere of extravagance, the ritual which sets the musicians at their beck and call.[14]

A clearer motive for the extravagance can be found in a passage from *Djuka Begović*, a romantic story by Ivo Kozarac situated in and around Vinkoci, East Slavonia:

> Everything indicated that the song would be interrupted, that the game would stop, now... Djuka was crazed... At every song that was sung for him he had smashed glasses, he had tremors, his lips were twisted, and his whole body brought him closer and closer to the musicians. Pain was written on his face. He didn't make a sound. Glisha, the Gypsy musician, took him further and further... he walked backwards step by step, and Djuka's head followed him... It was as if Djuka was in a trance... he could hear his lost happiness in the sound of these strings. It was as if his heart would stop beating, his breath would be cut off, his life would be broken for ever. When Glisha goes too far Djuka clasps his hand – 'Don't go'. Glisha plays more and more loudly. He puts a piece of glass beneath the bridge of his violin. The strings produce a wailing sound. Djuka scatters banknotes, fivers and tenners, and with a trembling voice he whispers 'Quiet... quiet... I beg you...!' Glisha retreats again, step by step, and then suddenly starts to play the song more loudly again. Once again Djuka grips Glisha's hand and stuffs a banknote into it – 'Softer!... Softly!... Dear mother!... Gypsy!... Glisha!' Djuka now loses himself completely in the gigantic feeling that the potent, quiet song has created in him. He does not know it, but tears are running down his cheeks. 'What's the point of all those banknotes, that land, that house, the children, the family, the whole world? What is it all worth compared with this gigantic feeling?'

The lessons of implicit social knowledge – the awareness of the futility of possessions, the possibility of losing everything in one go – are here driven home in a remarkable guise. Waste also teaches the *nouveaux riches* of Serb society to scrutinise the frugality and moderation they exercise in the daytime to secure a prosperous future in the light of the implicit social knowledge that successive generations have learned: nothing is permanent, you can lose it all from one moment to the next. But here, in the loss, there lurks a desire to shake off money, possessions and other earthly ambitions that are obstacles to the celebration of the here and now.

Power and dependence

Once a customer is under the spell of the music, his satisfaction is strictly dependent on the musician. He can take the customer to the dry cleaner's – the expression popular among Gypsy musicians in Novi Sad for stripping a customer of his last dinar. But the customer also disposes of the resources of power (money, violence) that can be deployed. There are more cases like that of Goran Stajić (our *case 3*). Kovač lists the gymnastic exercises that were carried out with the Gypsy musicians in an unspecified past: customers who forced the Gypsies to play on their knees, lying on their back, to climb up a tree and play there, to jump up onto the bar or to dance on the table. Coins were tossed into a muddy pool and the Gypsy was ordered to fish them out.[15]

> Or this phenomenon: one of the musician's ears was pulled and perforated with a revolver. He received his due remuneration of two hundred krones. A number of Gypsies were immediately ready to have their ear perforated too.[16]

Kovač even notes that the readiness of Gypsies to be mistreated contributes to their popularity as musicians. 'Gypsies are easier to order around. You can curse and beat them', scenarios that would not be tolerated by other musicians.[17] Take the following case.

CASE 5

The owner of *Stari Fijaker* (The Old Carriage) got the Gypsy orchestra to play for him and three of his friends. Mirko, the Gypsy musician in the Novi Sad Radio and Television company's orchestra, took me along and suggested that I could pick something up there. I saw these men getting drunk from the corners of my eyes: they grew more and more physical after consuming vast quantities of beer. They threw their arms around one another's shoulders, slouched even deeper in their chairs and leaned against one another. The orchestra had been playing requests all evening:

clumsy and dishevelled versions of *Novakomponovana Narodna Muzika*-type songs that were usually performed lifelessly with a synthesizer, songs from Emir Kusturica's Gypsy film, and Serb nationalist songs that had been banned under Tito and were now extremely popular such as 'Serbia isn't small, it's waged three wars', 'Serbs keep quiet until they get mad', and the current hit 'We are the *Srbijanci* with our *opanci*'. This was followed by the *bećarci*, ten-syllabic poems full of obscenities and allusions to illicit sexuality. The gimmick of the musicians in this orchestra was a background chorus singing the words '*SIDA, SIDA*' (AIDS, AIDS) to songs about adultery. A song in praise of Yugoslavia – clearly intended as a cynical joke in these days of decay – did not go down well, and it petered out.

At two o'clock in the morning the musicians were still playing, dead tired by now, but unstoppable. 'So much money, so much music', was Mirko's reply when I asked him why there was no interval, and there was indeed a non-stop flow of banknotes from breast and trouser pockets. By this time most of the musicians were seated at tables as guests. The bass player was leaning wearily on his instrument. One of the men shared a wooden bench with the harmonica player and was completely fixated on the musicians. He stared at them, deeply moved, his eyes sometimes filled with tears. He joined in the singing for all he was worth until they started singing songs in Romany and he didn't know the words. Then an angry and frustrated expression suddenly appeared on his face. He started banging on the harmonica player's shoulder, pushing him and threatening him. The customer did not subside until the harmonica player, after catching the eye of the other musicians, started to play a new song, *Kreće se ladja francuska* (The French ship is leaving), a well-known Serb hymn on a sad episode from the First World War. Large sums of money were transferred to the musicians, and he embraced the accordion player whom he had just been mistreating and covered him with kisses out of pure gratitude. Idolatry.

Later a similar scene was repeated. The violin player got a pain in his neck and wanted to stop for a moment. He sat down next to the proprietor, but the latter would not hear of it. 'Play!' he shouted at him angrily, 'Play!' Hatred. Passionately dissatisfied. You could read it on his face. This was not a joke, it was an order, a merciless act of exercising his power. The accordion player and the violin player exchanged glances; go on, go on... Mirko had to smile at my indignation. 'It goes with the job', he said.

The last song died out at around three-thirty. The violin player was obviously at the end of his tether and the musicians had concluded their session with a final explosive, galloping *kolo* to make it clear that this was the end. Then, taking everyone by surprise, the harmonica player started another song. The message was clear: there is always, always, always more.

This case is not so much a matter of power and dependence. Rather, it raises the question: 'What is a person's price?' That too is one of the basic forms of Being that is at stake in the Gypsy bars.

Destructiveness

We have already come across countless examples of glasses and dishes being smashed – simple and meaningful illustrations of the theme of destruction. *Napraviti lom*, creating havoc somewhere, is a metaphor both in ordinary language and in the lyrics of the songs for everything that goes on in the Gypsy bar. Literally it means 'breaking into pieces'; *lom* comes from the verb *lomiti*, to break into pieces. It may be an empty glass, smashed dramatically at the moment when an instrumentalist concludes a prolonged, melismatic prelude, or when a song reaches catharsis. It may be the bar furniture. Or, figuratively, it may be a person, as in the phrase 'Gypsies smash my soul to pieces' from the drinking song 'I've had enough of you, bar!' or the female singer who 'smashes to pieces' everyone she kisses in the song *Poljupci će moji da naprave lom*. And *napraviti lom* refers more abstractly to collapse, to collapse in itself. For instance, Kovač mentions an estate owner in the Vojvodina who preferred the Gypsies to play for him 'in the Serb, collapsing style' (*preferirao [je] srpski upropastiteljski način*).[18]

But no one put this destructiveness into words better than the man who told me about the time when he threw a heavy glass ash-tray to the floor in a moment of catharsis, but instead of breaking it rolled around the *kafana*. He compared his feeling to that of coitus interruptus.

Physicality

Another of the basic forms of Being that is given a prominent role in the Gypsy bars is the body, or rather, the feeling body. The body of the Novi Sad bourgeoisie, denied and domesticated, stripped of smells, secretions and so on, is restored to full glory in this exuberant celebration. Above all in dance. 'Jump! Jump! Let them hear the earth shaking under your feet!' goes *Neven Kolo*, a dance song. 'Dance! Dance! Until the early morning! Until your feet can't go on any more!' goes another. Of course, the folklore of the theatres is not to be found in the bars. There are rudiments of the *kolo* round dance, there is dancing cheek to cheek, and although I have never witnessed it myself there is dancing on the table – a metaphor for the ultimate festivity.

Eruptions of violence in the *kafana*. A painting by the Serbian painter Janko Bra-
sić (1960).

CASE 6

The Gypsy musician in *Petlov Salaš* had made a deal with a prostitute.
The agreement was that the musicians would warm the men up a bit and
encourage them to dance. At least, that was the scenario that I saw repeated in the patio of this Gypsy bar on the dyke of the Danube, between
Novi Sad and Futog.

The prostitute has a *coupe soleil* and a white, sleeveless dress with a regular pattern of green wavy stripes and black kittens petting. And mules
with high heels. 'A Russian', my companion Jasna tells me. 'They do it
for peanuts', she adds, with the air of a notorious haunter of brothels. The
Russian whores who 'do it for peanuts' are a much discussed novelty in
Novi Sad, one of the stories the people of Novi Sad use to add lustre to
the poor image they have of themselves. It's even worse further east.
People there still regard this as a country flowing with milk and honey.

The trick seems to be working with two men who are sitting at a table. One of them requests only 'authentic' Gypsy music, songs by the popular Ivanović brothers and Esma Redjepova, the Gypsy from Skopje. He sings along with the words in Romany as if it's his own language. He is completely fixated on the violin player, and to a lesser extent on the accordionist. He keeps raising his hands to the musicians, as if he can add something to the music by moving his hands. He is concentrating completely on the musicians. The world outside him, including the man sharing his table, does not seem to exist.

The prostitute waits her turn. She drinks beer, smokes and talks a little with a shy young man who is sitting at her table. If he's the pimp – Jasna thinks he is – he doesn't have much say in the matter. She's the one pulling the strings. She keeps a sharp eye on the table with the man, and the musicians keep a sharp eye on her. Then she gets up and saunters over to the two men at the table. 'Sa-sa!', she cries with a piercing voice, 'Sa-sa!' This is the call of a wild Gypsy dance from the south of Serbia. 'How is a Russian supposed to know that?', I ask Jasna, who assumes a wronged expression. And a wild dance is exactly what the woman has in mind for this man. At first he does not look very enthusiastic, but his companion pushes him onto the dance floor. The musicians are enjoying themselves.

Now the man dances. He rolls up his shirt to his arm-pits and rolls his bare white stomach like a belly-dancer. The whore shakes her shoulders, bosom and buttocks. Dancing, she approaches the man and rubs her crotch against his. The man performs a few obligatory erotic moves, but she's the one who has the initiative. Then it all stops fairly suddenly and clumsily. Not everyone has the role of the wild man in him.

Jasna watches this scene, obsessed. Softly and distantly she sings along with the songs. She can't help laughing now and then, but she also looks apologetically in my direction from time to time.

The celebration of the feeling body can also take the form of a fight, whether it comes to blows or blades, or self-castigation. I saw plenty of bar brawls. Sudden changes of mood: people are sitting chatting together, then suddenly the chairs are overturned, people run up to see what is going on, and there is a lot of shouting and waving of broken bottles until someone leaves the room with his shirt half out of his trousers and his face bleeding. Self-castigation, like dancing on the table, is something I only know from hearsay. One man proudly showed me a scar on the palm of his hand – he had smashed a glass during a binge soon after the death of his wife.

Two Gypsy musicians, Jovan and Bane, told me why they had given up their long-cherished dream of making music like the Beatles and adapted their repertoire to life in the Gypsy bar:

CASE 7

Bane: We had the bad experience that the rock 'n roll that kicked off our performances wasn't the real thing. There's no place for our love of the Beatles and rock 'n roll in these parts. What helped us enormously at that time was that we'd learnt a couple of local folk songs. Every band did that, you know, just in case. When you're playing, once the public has got drunk, they start shouting 'Come on, bring us another two barrels of beer' and then they say 'Just keep playing until early morning'. And then you know it's time to watch out, because some of them have a gun with them. We tried to avoid gigs like that, but you could never know what it was going to be like, so it was better to learn a bit of that folk music repertoire [...].

There were situations where there wasn't a stage, for example, and you had to play among the public. Well, somebody with an empty bottle in his hand might come up to you and ask: 'What are you going to play next?' Then you said: 'Something by Tomas Draškovic' [a singer of Serb sentimental ballads] and he would reply 'OK, that's fine'. Situations like that. They were in jeans, you know, with long hair and hippy signs...
Jovan: Give peace a chance!
Bane: Right! Those people... Uh!... You know, they were a good rock 'n roll public until eleven. But after eleven-thirty their peasant mentality started to play up. That's when they came up to you and started smashing bottles and glasses. During a song by Tomas Draškovic they smashed bottles on their own heads!
Mattijs: On their own heads?
Bane: Yes, on their own heads! You know, they behaved just like hippies with a Janis Joplin song...
Jovan: Hippies!
Bane: And then, once they'd got drunk...
Jovan: After Midnight!
Bane: Right, after midnight they didn't even realise how much their true nature lies in their peasant sandals (*istina im izašla iz opanaka*)!
Jovan: Authentic!
Bane: Right, and when we saw them smashing those bottles we realised that that is much closer to the truth of this world, just as the Beatles or rock 'n roll are the truth of the English world...

Finally, there are the dramatic scenes in feature films that centre on self-castigation. In Kusturica's *Dom za Vešanje*, the protagonist heightens his experience of the sentimental Gypsy trumpets playing for him by stubbing out a burning cigarette on his arm. In Petrović's *Skupljači Perja* a Gypsy drives the main character ecstatic with the song 'I go, I go, over endless roads...'. Without betraying a trace of emotion, he smashes two glasses on the edge of the table, places the broken bottoms of the glasses on the table, raises his hands, and brings them down with a loud crash on the two glasses. 'I go, I go, over endless roads...', the Gypsy chanteuse continues. As he watches the blood flowing from the wound, he laughs and cries at the same time.

The unspeakable character of reality

A final basic form of Being that finds expression in the Gypsy bar that I would like to mention here is the awareness of the unspeakable character of reality. This deep-rooted awareness that stories are duplicitous and that the essence of things is unspeakable is, in my opinion, the most essential insight that can find expression here. Strictly speaking, it is problematic to label this under the same category of basic forms of Being, as this is rather the mental bedrock on which all of the basic forms of Being discussed so far are founded.

The Gypsy bars are about losing control of oneself. In the last resort, everything is aimed at stopping all conversation. In their attempts to bypass language as a dominant source of knowledge and insight, the bar clientèle behave like the devotees of Dadaism and *Zenitizam*, or like the trickster Gypsy figures of their own fantasies. The world has to be surrendered to the fluid and confused perceptions of the drunkard's euphoria. Priority is given to the perceptions that are conveyed in the music, the emotional transport, and the physical feeling. For it is only by keeping language and reason – the instruments of appearances, lies and alienation – out of the bar that people are able to enter those realities that lie 'on the left bank of the heart', as a contemporary Serb bar song puts it, 'there where there is no treachery, there deep in myself'.

The most direct expression of this attempt to ban the Word is the 'prohibition' on speaking about what goes on in the Gypsy bar, or worse still, on entering into (serious) conversations in the bar itself. I soon learned that anyone who wants to bring something up in conversation is soon put right. But just being silent was not enough. 'Don't look around so inquisitive!' my friends kept on saying to me when I sat with them in the Gypsy bar and looked around. 'Don't look so serious!' they said when I wasn't looking around and joined in the singing as best I could. Simply the idea that someone was looking, taking note and analysing, that there was someone who, if not now then later, would formulate ideas about what was going on there, was unbearable for some of them. 'What are you going to write about next?'

Then there is the music, which – in Wagner's words – 'silences all while it speaks the unthinkable'. And there is the silence.

Ovamo dodji	Come here
kraj meni stani	Come and stand behind me
Ciganski sine, garave puti,	Black-skinned Gypsy boy
strune nategni	And tighten
četiri svoje	Your four strings
i čekaj, Cigo	And wait, Gypsy,
čekaj – i šuti	Wait – and be silent

Come and stand behind me, tighten your strings and wait. Don't play. The tension sought here is the tension of the moment preceding the choice. The excitement when anything is still possible – a sentimental song, a love song, an obscene song. The experience of totality is still in-tact in that silence, before it is shattered into a choice of songs.

Finally, a key role is assigned to the eloquence of direct experience. The power games played out between musician and customer enable the latter to experience power in every one of its guises. The pain experienced when glasses are smashed with bare hands or when a cigarette butt is stubbed out on the bare skin is unmediated by language, meaning or signification. It has no purpose, it has no use, it simply *is*. A glass smashed on the floor and shattered into pieces. Broken. Irreparably destroyed. And when someone spends a month's salary in one night on Gypsy musicians and drink, 'suffering loss' is something real; no longer a story or a memory, but the return of an experience.

In their conviction that the basic forms of Being can only be found outside language, the clientèle of the Gypsy bars belong to the category of people whom Georges Bataille once called 'persistent truth-seekers'. They do not belong to the thinkers who desperately cling to a rigid world that is divided up into fixed units. But they are not discouraged by the fact that reality constantly eludes thought. In moments of losing control, of ecstasy, of inebriation, of sexual excitement, and, ultimately, in the moment of death they try to get closer to undifferentiated Being and reach for Truths that lie outside the world of the spoken word.

Why are you still bothering with those books, Tišma? You'll still die like the rest of us. Come and have a good time in the bar!

A fundamental mistrust of every story, and the hope that the Truth lies at the end of the muddy road over land where the Gypsies entertain the world. That is what Tišma's friend is getting at when he recommends the writer to abandon his literary reflections on the human condition in this war-ridden country, to leave the books for what they are, and to go off to the bar.

Opting for the unreason of the Gypsy bar

Idem kući, a već zora	I'm going home, day is already dawning
žena viče sa prozora	The woman shouts from behind the window
ćuti, ženo, ne blebeći!	Shut up, woman, stop chattering!
Jezik ću ti ja odseći!	I'll cut out your tongue one of these days!

This song presents the return home as the return to a world of words, the world of language, the world of screaming and chattering women who have holed themselves up in their homes as guardians of morality and decency. That return to the world of the stories is inevitable (except for the man who was said to have killed himself in the *Gypsy Night*).[19] But it brings no joy. The Ego in this song makes no bones about that.

This society tolerates a platform for unreason in the *kafana*. Amid the modern world they have built, the people of Novi Sad have erected platforms in back streets, back rooms and isolated taverns where they stash wilder versions of themselves, where they do not lose sight of the irrationality and the mud that are such an essential part of their history.

This is not to say that there are no forces at work trying to domesticate these platforms. They do exist. The peripheral location of the bars speaks volumes, as well as the fact that it is often a question of *imitating* pulling the hairs out of one's head, slashing one's wrists and smashing glasses. And there is the phenomenon of the *fini cigani*, the refined Gypsies who have trained at the music academies. Following their colleagues in Budapest, they slick back their hair and play Brahms' Hungarian Dances or skilfully imitate the song of a bird on their violin strings. And there is the sign on the wall in the Slovakian restaurant in Novi Sad stating that every glass that gets broken has to be paid for. However, these attempts cannot stop the Gypsy bar from pulling in new generations. Even *Bon-Ton*, the manual of etiquette discussed in an earlier chapter, makes an exception for the *kafana*: 'If a man goes alone to the *kafana*, he does not need to follow many rules'.[20] Another manual, *Lepo Ponašanje*, admits: 'We are bound to recognise that there are times when people have to swear and should be allowed to do so, but those are exceptional occasions and exceptional places! In one's own at home, for example, or on one's own land, in intimate company. And when the company is in high spirits and a little tipsy – "then everything is forgiven".'

This concern for the preservation of the Gypsy bars is remarkable. Here too the warning towards the strict inspector from the West is loud and clear: 'Hands off!' The arguments advanced in the present study enable us to understand that concern better.

In this chapter I have tried to show that the *fini ljudi* are not content with just fantasising about Gypsies. They want to turn those fantasies into fact, to *realise* them, and the Gypsy bars provide them with a platform for doing precisely that. The mimetic game that is played there enables them to become real Gypsies.

We have also seen how the figure of the Gypsy functioned as a repository for all kinds of other shapes and guises which have been expelled from the story of the *fini ljudi* and are normally located in the obscure recesses of the image that the Serbs have of themselves. The warm-blooded Serb, Czar Lazar (the Czar who chose defeat), the Habsburg wild man, the *homo balcanicus*, the primitive peasant, the migrant labourer; once the customer in the Gypsy bar has become a Gypsy, once he has set aside the fear of asocial impulses and misbehaviour, once he is far out of reach of the embarrassing civilisation debate, they all loom up. It is in the Gypsy bar that the *fini ljudi* can openly engage with these figures: they can become reconciled with them, resist them, or allow themselves to be seduced or repelled by them.

This shows that there is more to the Gypsy bars than just a safety valve in a rapidly urbanising society where large sectors of the population subject themselves and one another to a strict civilising regime and where one is constantly enjoined 'If it doesn't come to you naturally, just pretend'. What takes place in connection with the Gypsy orchestra is not just a passive letting off steam, taking a breather, or getting one's breath back from the tensions that confront the *fini ljudi* in urban society. To confine the events in the Gypsy bar to this interpretation alone would be to deny the subversive and creative character of these gatherings. The Gypsy bar is there to re-create the world. It gives the imagination enough rein to sketch designs for living which, if not more interesting, are at any rate more apt.

It is obvious that we are not talking about no-strings-attached recreation. Serious undertones can clearly be heard. The discussion of the symbolic vocabulary of the Gypsy bar – the fuzzy sets of poses and scenarios – indicates that the metamorphosis into a Gypsy is above all an attempt not to become alienated from the basic forms of Being that are seen as inevitable aspects of fate in this part of the world: flight, transitoriness, loss, pain, separation.

Nothing is as it seems. The Yugoslavs learnt that lesson in the war. And: Everything is exactly what it is and nothing else. Nothing is what it seems, said the Gypsies who figured in their collective fantasies. And: Everything is exactly what it is and nothing else. In other words, there are constant messages in this society about the feeble and unreliable nature of the stories which give meaning and significance to life. And there are also constant messages about the firm, crystal-clear and inevitable Truths which lurk outside reason in violence, sex, obscenity, consumption, desire, destruction, ecstasy. The alienation that is created by this flow of messages can be suspended in the Gypsy bar.

'Come on, let's go where life is', was one of the ways my discussion partners announced their plans to undertake a trip to the Gypsy bar. *Hajde, idemo u život*. No *prazne priče*, no idle stories, but life. The choice of the Serbs to join the Gypsies and to throw themselves into an irrational world seems to be inspired by this promise.

Conclusions: The Embrace of Unreason

In Euripides' tragedy *The Bacchae*, the women possessed by Dionysian madness put on branches, leaves and animal skins and retreat to an idyllic, paradisiac wilderness, where they put fawns and wolf cubs to the breast. When their mood changes, however, they become frenzied and tear anyone who crosses their path to pieces. A messenger who comes to inform the Theban ruler Pentheus about the women reports what he has seen in the hills near Thebes:

> You could see one take a full-uddered bellowing young heifer
> And hold it by the legs with her two arms stretched wide;
> Others seized some ribs, or a cleft hoof, tossed high and low;
> And rags of flesh hung from pine-branches, dripping blood.
> Bulls, which one moment felt proud rage hot in their horns,
> The next were thrown bodily to the ground, dragged down
> By the hands of girls in thousands; and they stripped the flesh
> From the bodies faster than you could wink your royal eyes.

These women are depicted on Greek vases: with their heads thrown back in ecstasy, they almost nonchalantly swing two halves of a fawn in the air. *Sparagmos*, tearing, was the Greek word for this part of the cult of Dionysus.

Perhaps irrational and destructive acts have to be thousands of years old before one can detect a philosophical content in them. At least, that is what the young Nietzsche saw in the ecstatic tearing of the bacchae: an inquiry into the basic forms of Being, an attempt to get to the reality concealed behind the Apollonian world of beautiful ideals and lofty endeavours. In his *The Birth of Tragedy* (1872), Nietzsche refers to the Dionysian euphoria as the moment at which it was revealed to the Greek that his whole existence with all its beauty and moderation was based on a foundation of suffering and knowledge. The philosophical issue on which Nietzsche is focusing here is that 'the world, as we experience it as knowing subjects, is only a world of *appearances*, a totality of representations, at its most profound an illusory world. Behind those representations lies another world, which we cannot reach with our representations [...] All our knowledge and rational thinking is only connected with the phenomenal world. The inner essence of things is inconceivable for us. As long as we try to discover ourselves by means of representations, we shall never get beyond the outside. However, once we return to ourselves by means of a different, an inner path, the path of the body, we can establish contact with the inner world.'[1]

That is how Nietzsche understood the earthly, bloody and physical violence of the Dionysian ecstasy: as a tearing of the veils of illusion, for it is only when these 'hung in rags before the mysterious primal Oneness',[2] he claimed, that the great festivity could commence in which alienated, hostile or subjected nature reconciled herself with her lost son, humanity.

It was in my quest for the origins of the notion of the bacchanal that I came across these philosophical reflections on the cult of Dionysus via the Bacchae.[3] It is a pity that I only came across it at the end of my research, because the relevance of this complex philosophical material for the arguments advanced in this study seems evident. In the preceding chapters I have interpreted the celebration of irrationality that takes place in the Gypsy bars of Novi Sad as an attempt to break away from the alienation of the world of stories, as an attempt to get a glimpse of that underpainting which always lends a mildly absurd tone to bourgeois behaviour in Novi Sad. Nietzsche's interpretation of the ecstasy of the Bacchae as an ontological investigation, a quest for the basic forms of Being, offers enough points of contact with my findings to follow the path indicated by the philosopher a little further.

The idea that a regressive movement, entering relatively wild and disorderly fields of experience – 'to the mountains, to the mountains', sings the chorus in the Euripidean tragedy – generates truths that lie outside the reach of reason has been suggested in different formulations and with different emphases by many people. Walter F. Otto, author of the classic *Dionysus, Myth and Cult* (1933), understood bacchic ecstasy as follows:

> The familiar world, which people had occupied so securely and comfortably, no longer exists! The thunderous arrival of Dionysus has wiped it away. Everything has changed. But not into a charming fairy story, a paradise of childlike simplicity. The primitive world has appeared, the depths of Being have opened up, and the primeval figures of all that is creative and destructive, infinitely blissful and infinitely horrendous, have risen up and destroyed the innocent image of an orderly and familiar world. They bring neither Deceit nor Dream, they bring Truth – a Truth that drives people crazy.

Ruth Benedict talks about 'the illuminations of frenzy' in the cult of Dionysus, and E.R. Dodds calls it 'the blessings of madness'.[4] Georges Bataille, whose notion of euphoria cropped up at the end of the last chapter, sees a reflection of his repeatedly expressed notion of the 'tragic position of thought' in the Dionysian cult. In *The Tears of Eros* (1961) he discusses the cult as a celebration of irrationality:

> Of all the gods, Dionysus is the most essentially linked to the celebration. Dionysus is the god of the celebration, the god of the religious violation. Dionysus is usually portrayed as the god of wine and drunkenness. Dionysus is a drunken god, the god whose divine essence is madness. But in the last resort the madness itself is something essentially divine. Divine here in the sense of what pays no heed to the rules of reason.

Historians and anthropologists have shown that this Dionysian road to insight can be found in every time and every place. Norman Cohn's fascinating book on medieval religious fraternities like the Beghars, the Brethren of the Free Spirit and the Flagellants, for example, describes people who hoped to acquire knowledge about the eternal divine essence of things in an unorthodox manner. They flatly spurned theological dogmas and religious writings. Some of them delighted in disrupting ecclesiastical rituals. In their quest for the divine, adherents of these movements would brook no authority other than their own individual experiences, which they acquired through total abstinence, self-castigation and self-mutilation, nudity, or the cultivation of a completely amoral, indifferent attitude towards social regulations and moral commandments.[5]

In his book on the figure of the wild man, Bernheimer refers to the knights of the medieval romances like Yvain, Lancelot and Tristan who fled to the wilderness as soon as there was the slightest hint that the objects of their affections did not appreciate their passionate declarations. This assault on their courtly ideals was the pretext for scenes like the following:

> These warriors have a way of breaking all bonds, sometimes stripping themselves naked, and invariably repairing to the woods, expressing their sadness and degradation by leading the life of a wild man. Having lost the tie that bound them most strongly to courtly society they find the wilderness the only environment congenial to their sense of disorientation. There they wander aimlessly through the glades, subsisting on the raw flesh of wild animals or on the alms handed to them by pious hermits, until a miracle or the soothing touch of femininity restores them to reason.[6]

The ethnographic literature also contains many examples of people wandering in the wilderness in order to acquire special wisdom or occult powers.[7] For example, the members of the antinomic religious movement, the Na Ogii cult, that Thoden van Velzen and Van Wetering found among the Bush Negroes in the interior of Surinam glorified the wilderness in their myths as a source of pure, unsullied powers. As these anthropologists note:

> Many elements in the 'message' of Na Ogii sound familiar to a student of romantic ideas: the looking for inner, uncorrupted, and untapped powers; the idealistic notion that the present derelict world should make way for a better and purer one, though as yet undefined. And certainly the conviction that the existing order was not worth saving but should be trampled upon belongs to the same category of ideas.[8]

Rudi Laermans' reflections on the self-inflicted pain suffered by bodybuilders in contemporary fitness centres, or Noël Carroll's study of the horror film, provide present-day but essentially no less exotic examples of this search for essential, non-negotiable truths: 'A good many post-modernists deny the existence of such a thing as an absolute truth', comments Laermans, 'but I would like to hear them saying that when they're screaming with pain'.[9] Carroll associates the popularity of the splatter film or butcher-shop horror ('extreme gross fury visited upon the human body as it is burst, blown up, broken, and ripped apart; as it is dismembered and dissected; as it is devoured from the inside out') with the postmodern anxieties and insecurities connected with cultural categories:

> In the contemporary horror genre, the person is so often literally reduced to mere meat; indeed, the 'person-as-meat' could serve as the label for this tendency. And, in turn, this reduction of the person correlates in certain respects with what postmoderns herald as the 'death of man'. Within the horror fiction of the present, a person is not a member of some privileged ontological category but rather always a potential grist for the genre's satanic mills.[10]

In spite of the differences between a Greek bacchant, a medieval flagellant, or a present-day bodybuilder, we can distil at least two points in common: (1) they all share the idea that a movement back to the wilderness, away from cultural arrangements and back to relatively disorderly fields of experience, can be a valuable, positive and meaningful experience; and (2) this positive evaluation of wildness and disorder can almost always be connected with a crisis in what I have referred to in this study as the world in stories. Thus Dodds points to a genuine upsurge of foreign cults, mostly of a highly emotional orgiastic kind in Athens during the Peloponnesian War and its aftermath.[11] Cohn likewise sees a connection between the rise of flagellant movements and the situation in Italy in the thirteenth century, when it was plagued by famine, plague epidemics and heavy and cruel fighting: 'It was in a world which seemed poised on the brink of the abyss that these penitents cried out, as they beat themselves and threw themselves upon their faces'.[12] A single crack in the courtly dream of Bernheimer's knights is enough to send them to the forest and make them wander there as naked wild men, the only environment congenial to their sense of disorientation. And Laermans suggests a link between the hunger for pain of the fitness adepts and the advanced disintegration and fragmentation of stories that confer meaning and signification in postmodern society.

But what, we may wonder, do bloody tearing, wandering through the confusing world of ecstasy, returning to the physical experiences of the body, or listening to what is revealed in a cacophonic noise or in silence have to offer when the world of the stories is undermined by the real world?

In this study, based on my findings in the Gypsy bars in Novi Sad, I have argued that the cult of unreason offers *reali*sation. Like the people in the examples listed above, the clientèle of the *kafana* consider that truth has to be sought outside the world of the stories. They look for sources of knowledge in the pre-story world, a nameless, formless, precultural world. In the words of the popular bar song: 'I have cheated you, I have cheated everyone, but I couldn't cheat this here in my breast!'

We have seen a number of reasons why the clientèle of the Gypsy bars seek reality outside the world of the stories. They can be summarised as follows.

Reasons for the irrationality in Novi Sad

The people of Novi Sad (of the Vojvodina, of Serbia, of the South Slavic countries) live in a border zone. This circumstance plays a crucial role in undermining their belief and trust in the world of the stories because of two specificities of border zones which have both come up in this study: (1) the specific relation of the periphery to the political and cultural centre; and (2) the persistently recurring and large-scale disruptions of the peripheral society by violent conflict.

The first of these points undermines the world of the stories because of the fact that peripheries are always contact zones. They are zones where – as Ulf Hannerz optimistically puts it – 'a conversation between cultures goes on'.[13] The South Slavic countries are a textbook example of fusion on the periphery. This is even more the case in a territory like the Vojvodina, where so many different rulers and different states have tried to leave their mark on public life and where, as a result of the successive colonisation projects, different peoples, large and small, religious communities and ethnic groups have settled over the centuries. These groups interacted and intermingled. Marriages across ethnic barriers were particularly prominent in the urban centres. These people usually spoke two or even three languages, and their children of mixed ancestry went to school in the most diverse places. Aleksandar Tišma commented on the difficulty of arriving at unambiguous and uncontaminated stories in regions like the Vojvodina:

> This mixture of people is a very good thing of course, but it's a fact that when you have so many nationalities you cannot have one centre; you are always aware that there is another and a third and a fourth. If I offer an opinion, then I know that a Hungarian or Slovak or Romanian may think differently, for whatever reason. This is also a motive to be more discreet, not so open, so sure of one's opinion – that's the 'serenity' you mention. It's the Pannonian way of thinking, not outspoken or vehement, more relativistic.[14]

Tragically enough, however, it has to be admitted that the phenomenon of fusion and heterogeneity in the border zone is unable to temper the puritanical thirst for a clear-cut, simple and unambiguous world. I did not meet many of Tišma's relativistic, reticent, discreet Pannonians in Novi Sad. Perhaps there were some, but their voice was virtually inaudible amid the vast majority who were pushing their story, the story about a Serb, preferably purely Serb Vojvodina. When I was in the company of nationalistically minded discussion partners and tried to ventilate my views on how the plurality of peoples, religions and cultures in Yugoslavia could be seen as a factor of enrichment, I was roundly told that people had had more than enough of talk like that. Cosmopolitanism, Tito's Brotherhood and Unity, the Movement of Non-Aligned Countries, and the role of Yugoslavia as the pioneer in the Third World were all cast on the rubbish heap of idle stories.

While the fusion that is so characteristic of the border zones may make it difficult to arrive at stories in which everyone puts their trust, this is perhaps even more so for a second aspect of the periphery that tends towards the undermining of stories: the fact that border zones are generally war zones too. The people who live on the periphery are familiar with violence, flight, loss and other life-disrupting crises as recurrent phenomena. I have noted that the South Slavic countries have been plagued by five wars in this century alone. This is inconceivable now that we are so insistently reminded of what the word 'war' means, since we have been able to see day in, day out what havoc war can cause in human lives. The meaning of having to turn one's back on stories that justify existence and which are required to be unquestioned and free from doubt has perhaps been brought out the most clearly by the writer Dubravka Ugrešić. When she 'just' had to seek refuge in a shelter in Zagreb, she lost her concept of 'home' for good.

And yet, it also has to be stated that the impossibility of ever being able to believe in stories unconditionally cannot temper the urge to do so.

One of the ways in which the dilemma – wanting to believe in a story that confers meaning and significance and at the same time not being able to do so – was manifested on the part of my discussion partners in Novi Sad was in the civilisation debate. In the vigorous and vociferous defence of a cluster of stories about Novi Sad as a modern, urban, European society could be heard the echo of the wish and hope that things will turn out alright in the end. The permanently violated capacity to accept any story as true could be heard in the constant stream of resigned remarks about Novi Sad as now having become an inextricable part of the wild and savage Balkans. This debate was conducted at various levels. Among the different (ethnic, socio-economic) groups in urban society; among members of the groups themselves (in the hunt for so-called *šminkers*); and in the form of an interior dialogue, an intra-psychic debate between different images of self: at each of these levels the inhabitants of Novi Sad kept alive the awareness of the fictional dimension of their world. This is of essential importance if one is to understand why my discussion partners had to seek 'real truth' (*prava istina*), as they called it, *outside* the truth as it was told in the stories.

All those who are unable to deny the awareness of the role that stories play in constituting their world, all those who permanently regard the principles of their life as artificial and doubt their defensibility, easily fall prey to feelings of alienation. 'We act, and have to act as if mischief were not afoot in the kingdom of the real and that all around the ground lay firm. That is what the public secret, the facticity of the social fact, being a social being, is all about', Taussig remarks on the astounding ability of people to make up stories which they then refuse to see as such. Alienation was omnipresent in the Novi Sad that I came to know. Tito's dream of progress was denounced as yet another idle story. The years of plenty, the years of the weekend cottages, the parquet floors and the trips abroad with shopping arrangements turned out to be based on loans and credits that had not been paid off. While for a time it had been possible to feel as cosmopolitan as the Titoist propaganda led one to believe, the borders were now shrinking more and more. That was painfully obvious in the Chinese restaurant in Novi Sad, once the pride of the cosmopolitan *fini ljudi*. The Chinese who used to run the restaurant had already left; now there was a Serb waitress who had given herself slit-eyes with an eye-liner, and the various items on the large menu came more and more to resemble a soy sauce version of the cabbage, potatoes and onions that were served everywhere else as well. My discussion partners still referred to Novi Sad as the Athens of Serbia. They still called upon one another to just let everyone get on with his work. But without the hope of progress or a better future, stories like that sounded more and more false and deceitful. The war, with its barbarities, drove the *fini ljudi* even further out of the story that they had made up about themselves and their world.

Although the war aroused feelings of alienation and made the fictional dimension of life clearly visible, my discussion of the collective fantasies about Gypsies showed that this awareness existed a long time before the war broke out. Those fantasies betrayed a genuine preoccupation with questions about what is fact and what is fiction, what is true and what is false, what is reality and what is appearance. They indicate that the South Slavs were looking for a form to express their awareness of the fact that the postwar order was an artificial creation. However, that discussion makes something else clear as well. The creators of fantasies about Gypsies (writers and film directors, singers, comedians and bar clientèle) also knew how to use this imaginary space to suspend the alienation.

The Gypsies of the Serb imagination open the attack on fictional reality in every conceivable way. They destroy existing cultural arrangements, they transgress rules of decency and moral prescriptions, they deny the laws of language and logic, and they present the truth at one moment as an evanescent figment of the imagination and at another as a crude obscenity. After that total demolition of fictional reality, after which not much is left except the basic forms of Being, the space is created for paradox, for images and counterimages, for impossible possibilities. The dilemmas facing the inhabitants of this border zone that undermine the stories no longer exist in the imaginary world of the Gypsies. The theme of hybridisation, as we have seen, is conspicuously present in the fantasies about the Gypsies, but it is no longer a problem. The Gypsies are chameleon-like characters that exist outside every story as well as inside it, characters that are exempt from having to make an un-ambiguous choice for one thing or against another. They do not feel torn by a life on the edge of different stories. In this sense, they appear as the real border people that the South Slavs themselves cannot be.

The theme of the recurrent war (and the corresponding disruption of fictional reality) also features prominently in the Serb fantasies about Gypsy life. Here too, we could ascertain that fantasies about Gypsies of-fer a haven for untold histories from a world that, in the vision of the *fini ljudi*, does not and must not be allowed to exist.

By recognising what is excluded from fictional reality, by bringing the blind spots into focus, and by giving untold histories a right to exist, the collective fantasies about Gypsies oppose the alienation. These repeated attempts to reconcile the world of the stories with the world that people experience and that cannot be denied also leave their mark on the cult of the irrational connected with the Gypsy orchestras.

Like the Gypsies of their imagination, like the followers of Dionysus, the bar clientèle choose the path of destruction and ecstasy. They try to suspend every structure that confers meaning so that the fluid, disorder-ly, formless essence of Being can be revealed to them. Sometimes they opt for a return to bodily realisation when Being reveals itself in stabs of pain, spasms and other sensorial experiences, which – and this is what it is all about – penetrate consciousness unmediated by any kind of lan-guage or symbolic structure. Usually we find combinations of both ap-proaches. The constant in the symbolic vocabulary of the Gypsy bar, however, is clear: the Serbs who come to listen to a Gypsy orchestra are trying to reach a state that precedes designation and knowledge, because they believe that it is only there they can attain the essential, non-nego-tiable realities that lie behind the world of the stories. Only there, they believe, can they find an escape from the world that constantly appears to them as one huge labyrinth of semblance, fiction and untruth.

The idea that knowledge acquired outside language and reason is truer than knowledge produced by reason echoes once again the lesson that the recurrence of war has taught the people here time and again: 'I am reality, I am the end of all stories'. But a new – and extremely dis-turbing – line has been added: 'I am the escape from the confusion, from the labyrinth of lies and fictions'.

Beyond the stories

> To kill and die on the battlefield, to mutilate and bleed, brings one before
> the dicing table of the gods, where luck and skill and courage combine to
> name the players definitely. Some will be chosen to play again tomorrow,
> some will be wounded and scarred, and some will be mutilated beyond
> recognition; but all have been gathered in the presence of the most real
> thing.
>
> – Dudley Young, *Origins of the Sacred. The Ecstasies of Love and War*

What are people seduced by when they overthrow everything that we, and
they, regard as reasonable, civilised and humane? Less abstractly: what
prompts the sniper to kill complete strangers? What prompts the militia-
man to fire mortars at a hospital, a queue at the baker's, a bus full of children? What prompts the soldier to rape old women? What prompts the
commandant to order the destruction of universally acclaimed and loved
cultural objects? What prompts the women and children to stop food convoys destined for their former neighbours, or to stone refugees?

Questions like these, which constantly hovered in the background as I
explored the choice of irrationality in the Gypsy bar, cannot be answered
with the material that I collected during my stay in Novi Sad. It is impossible to simply extrapolate findings from one arena to another. In this
sense, I agree with the remarks that Clifford Geertz made in a footnote
to his classic study of the Balinese cockfight. Writing about how a study
of cockfighting can help to understand the massacre on the island during
the 1965 coup, he notes that the cockfight was not the cause of the
killings, that the killings could not have been predicted on the basis of the
cockfight, and that the killings were not an enlarged version of the cockfight with people taking the place of cocks. 'But', he goes on, 'if one looks
at Bali not just through the medium of its dances, its shadow-plays, its
sculpture, and its girls, but – as the Balinese themselves do – also through
the medium of its cockfight, the fact that the massacre occurred seems,
if no less appalling, less like a contradiction to the laws of nature'.[15]
Joseba Zulaika developed this idea of an analogy in his study of the underlying motives in the violence of the Basque separatist movement
ETA. This anthropologist argues that an understanding of terrorist violence might greatly benefit from an analysis of apparently irrelevant matters such as Basque games, hunting, and the traditional song improvisa-
tions in bars: 'Games, hunting and troubadourial improvisation are not
only fictional constructions to talk about violence; they are also, so to
speak, descriptions of violence "as it is", they are explanations [...]
through and by means of an underlying analogy'.[16]

I would like to adopt this idea that the relation between war and festivities is not a mechanical one of cause and effect but an analogy that elaborates on underlying similarities. As such, the insights that I have advanced in this study of the Gypsy bar yield a number of suggestions; considerations and focal points that must be taken into account in the further study of conflict, destruction and violent warfare.

> *These people are fully aware of what they are doing when they reject reason (civilisation, humanity); they opt for unreason; and they deliberately choose unreason as such.*

It is often said that they don't know what they're doing, that they are barbarians, drunkards, people of the Balkans. Take the exposé about what-kind-of-people-the-Yugoslavs-are that Lord David Owen, peace negotiator for the European Union, presented in an interview. He began generously enough: 'They are just like everyone else. They are certainly good fathers. And in certain respects they have the same feelings as we do.' But then he went on: 'But it is still the Balkans. And this part in particular has a certain rudeness. Perhaps because of the extreme climate. The people are characterised by a certain cruelty. They attach a different value to life than we do. A certain roughness. Uncouthness, you might almost call it. And yet they have their writers, their culture. Important generalisations, but still everyone says: this is Europe, this is around the corner. As if Yugoslavia is the same as the Netherlands! It isn't.'[17]

Remarks in a similar vein can be found among social scientists like Fred E. Katz, who claims that people who engage in irrational actions are temporarily in a different frame of mind. They are therefore not aware of the irrationality of their actions ('they aren't themselves').[18] However, such qualifications are in fact an expression of our inability (or reluctance) to see the temptations of unreason and that they say something about why these people act the way they do. The events in the Gypsy bars teach us that people know what they are doing when they deliberately adopt unreason instead of reason, civilisation and humanity.

The soldiers mentioned in the introduction provide a clear example of this – the Montenegran youths and men who fired their bombs and mortars from high in a mountain above Dubrovnik down on the old city. Here and there they were described as ignorant barbarians who had no awareness of the value that the city of Dubrovnik represented. However, I believe that these soldiers were well aware of that fact. On the basis of my findings in the Serb Gypsy bars, I would argue that the point is precisely that a lot of people in this war wanted to challenge and expel such respect for traditional European culture.

The choice of unreason has its reasons. Unreason is the dynamite used to blow up old, threadbare stories.

The idea I find plausible for the Gypsy bars is that people have been led into a total destruction of the threadbare stories they lived in. As for the war, it can also be said that the fighters, militia and snipers are settling accounts with stories that say that a human being is more than a target, that the sick need assistance, that the hungry should be fed, that children are innocent, that pensioners deserve respect, that historic monuments are valuable, that different groups can live together. Perhaps not so much because, if asked, they would disagree with these stories (in an interview, the sniper Pipo who killed 325 total strangers said he was avenging his mother), but because these stories are a part of a view of civilisation that they find strange, false and deceitful.

This suggestion is not only in line with what goes on in the Gypsy bars. Bataille talks about the violation of religious and moral laws as a road that gives access to the sacral. Cohn mentioned cultivating a completely amoral, indifferent attitude towards social regulations and commandments as one of the ways in which flagellants and other late medieval sects tried to acquire knowledge about the divine essence. Thoden van Velzen and Van Wetering described how the followers of an antinomic cult of Danger (*Na Ogii*) in East Surinam completely overthrew the Gaan Gadu cult which had been dominant until then: 'The followers of Na Ogii were willing to defy this 'Ndjuka' deity (as Gaan Gadu was often called) by flouting its taboos, 'mocking' its moral claims, and parading as confident aggressors. The corruption and hypocrisy of the first cult served as an excuse for the cruelty of the second.'[19]

In a different connection – the nihilistic motifs in Nietzsche – Joop Goudsblom has also pointed to the motif of 'doing no', which he describes as '...taking a stand against all values and meanings which the nihilist regards without exception as false and shallow'. Deeds follow judgements: 'Active nihilism can unleash an enormous resource of productive energy; it destroys the existing goals, convictions, articles of faith, and it creates scope for a new mode of existence which will be free of false assumptions and values; for this reason it could be a "divine way of thinking"'. But this negative praxis also includes 'those who have lost their faith in morality and religion, who therefore lack any form of comfort in their humble and pitiable condition and who, in their own way, are now "doing no". Destruction is their only aim and they force the powerful to lead them in this...'[20]

Serb irregular, Croatia 1991. (Photo Paul Jenks/Camera Press London).

The choice of Unreason has its reasons. Unreason is a meaningful concept in itself.

'To characterise violence as pointless or irrational is to abandon research at the point where it should start. [...] Violence as a cultural category or construction should be understood in the first place as a symbolic activity – not as meaningless, but as meaningful behaviour.'[21] This seems to offer a useful starting-point for further research on the irrational dimension of the war in former Yugoslavia. Just as the wild poses and savage scenarios of lack of control adopted in the Gypsy bars can be understood as an appropriation of the forbidden and disgraceful self-images of the Serbs, so the militia seem to adopt the pose of the barbarian. In the terms of the civilisation debate that dominated until recently, Unreason was an attribute of the Balkan Serbs. In the dress of the militia who grow beards and wear their hair long, wear tall black fur caps, adorn themselves with daggers, bandoleers and other emblems of the Serb martial traditions (or have they seen too many Sylvester Stallone films?), and sit around the camp fire in the evening singing of the centuries-old struggle against Turkish domination to the tune of the one-stringed fiddle (with a pack of Camel or Marlboro close at hand if possible), Unreason is an attractive attribute which they hope will make them feel unambiguously Serbian.

   Bitterness against those who have depicted them as primitives and inhabitants of the Balkans for so long certainly plays a part in all this. By behaving as barbarians, they challenge those from whose views they now want to free themselves.

The choice of Unreason has its reasons. Unreason can play a role in the construction of new stories.

The fancy dressing – including the appropriation of unreason – also plays an important role in the creation of a new story. Anyone who has been reading the papers will need no convincing that the Serb militia men were engaged in creating a new story for themselves and the world they live in. The story they were creating was one of an ethnically purified Great Serbia. A simple, uncomplicated world without confusion, without foreign elements. A world where all knowledge is one, 'a Serbia without cities, those breeding grounds of all kinds of evil', as one militia commander put it in the weekly *Vreme*, the world as it was 'when there was no electricity, no computers, when the Serbs were still happy'. Phenomena such as ethnic cleansing, forcing Muslims and Croats who are left behind to change their names, the total destruction of mosques, Catholic churches and convents,[22] the destruction of the Institute for Oriental Studies and its library in Sarajevo, and reports that the first victims in ethnic cleansing actions were people with glasses, notables and local intellectuals,[23] all form a part of this striving for a clear, intelligible and unambiguous story about the world. In *The City and Death*, Bogdanović comments on his war-hungry fellow patriots:

> It seems that in the panicky soul of the sackers of cities I can perceive an angry opposition to everything urban and to a complex semantic structure of spirit, morality, language, taste, style... I would like to recall that, from the 14th century to the present day, the word urbanity has always meant the same in the main European languages: refinement, articulation, correspondence of idea and word, word and emotion, emotion and motion... and so on. And if someone cannot submit to the laws of urbanity, it is easiest for him simply to destroy that urbanity.[24]

In the creation of that new story about a 'Serbian Serbia', the overthrow of rationality, civilisation and the humanistic ideal also plays a military and strategic role. Terror is sown with irrational acts. People are hunted and traumatised so that the idea of living together with these barbarians in the future becomes virtually inconceivable.

The temptation might lie in the irrational actions themselves.

Where stories that confer meaning and signification have lost their force, so-called meaningless and irrational actions gain meaning. The attackers of Dubrovnik were clear about this too. 'Then we'll just build a new ancient Dubrovnik again', one of them said. An answer like that makes you realise that someone is being asked to put something into words that cannot be put into words. Imagine sitting on a mountain, drinking, and firing one mortar after another at the ancient city; in all its horror, it is a way of obtaining knowledge that essentially bypasses language and rational thought. Confronted with a journalist, with someone who forces him to return to the world of words, who uses question and answer in an attempt to understand what reason there can be for the senseless shelling of the city, the young soldier tries to sound rational. But, of course, he fails.

Another revealing comment in this direction was made by the director of a commercial firm in Novi Sad who told me that he was very unhappy. When I asked him why, he told me that he had been drinking in a bar with a few friends, and that they suddenly hit upon the idea of driving to the East Slavonian front nearby 'to shoot about ten *ustaši*'. But reason had triumphed. Instead of going to the front, the director had gone home, back to the city, back to the world of words and stories. He realised he had made a sensible choice, but he still felt very unhappy. Živojin Pavlović, a Serb film director, claims to understand why people like this director feel so unhappy:

> This civil war is the product of internal turbulence which is bound to lead to catastrophe when it takes on collective forms. In our time the most elementary biological instincts, hunting an animal, hunting a woman, have been ideologised, rationalised. If you can't hunt, you eventually end up killing people.

The film director considers that the Yugoslav civil war is a simultaneous explosion of natural instincts and absolute freedom. He is surprised that the war is regarded with such 'hysterical' horror in the West, 'in countries with a high level of culture':

> High culture pays so much attention to prolonging human lives. People take pills and injections to keep death at a distance. But somewhere all those people know that here, in the Balkans, a dream of theirs is coming true: to step outside one's own cave, to step into the world of the wild animals, the world of unlimited risk, of absolute freedom.[25]

The most outspoken and explicitly formulated desire for some kind of purifying blood-letting, in which all the confusion caused by language, reason, stories and lies would be washed away, was in the comments of Jasna Kuzmanov: 'Let the war come in God's name, at least then we will be able to start with a clean slate afterwards'. This was in the period just before the war actually broke out, the period in which everyone was panicking and wondering aloud whether the war had started or not. Jasna called me, she sounded worried, and asked if I could come and see her. She was watching television, looking at a crowd of shouting and screaming parents of conscripts who had occupied the Serb parliament. We watched the programme together. The cameras of the Serb state broadcasting company filmed non-stop for hours. The parents called for their children to be freed from the barracks that had been surrounded in Croatia, but it was what they did rather than their specific demands which displayed a world of words that had gone completely mad: hysterical people were pushing to get at the microphones everywhere to voice their ideas, thoughts, fearful suspicions, conspiracy theories and thinly disguised propaganda slogans. They were interrupted by others who snatched the microphones from under their noses to cast other stories, other theories, other claims, other slogans into the parliament building. There was a lot of shouting and screaming and people fainting. 'Let the war come, in God's name' said Jasna, completely flabbergasted by this endless theatre of madness.

Unreason harbours clarity, the end of all stories. Blood in the snow, brains spattered against the wall. That was the lesson the South Slavs had to learn time and again in wartime, that was the syllabus that they perpetuated in the obscene anti-structures of their fantasies about Gypsies, and in the 'get down, get down' of the incidents connected with the Gypsy orchestra. In 1991, when the world bandied nothing but crazed masses of words around, a person like Jasna Kuzmanov fell back on the same motif. Let the war come, in God's name.

The contours of a tragic cycle loom up here...

The war taught the South Slavs that in war there is clarity; it is only in war that true can be separated from false. They were terrible lessons, and for a long time those appalling and banal truths about people and the world that are generated in wartime served to accommodate people in any kind of story. Any castle in the air that offers protection against the naked truth is better than nothing. But it seems that a change occurs after a while. As the stories become increasingly hollow, as the façades grow more and more transparent, as the alienation grows, and as confusion increases about what is true and what is untrue, those terrible and banal truths become an increasingly tempting option. Let the war come, in God's name.

Final remarks

> My mother said, I never should
> Play with the Gypsies, in the Wood
>
> – English nursery rhyme

In the course of writing this book I was seized now and then by panic. As I reread texts that I hadn't looked at for a few weeks, the informants in my text seemed to be grappling with conflicts and dilemmas that were clearly my own personal ones. The alarming thing was that this had all taken place without my being aware of it; that it was only in the second instance that I discovered my presence in what others were saying. Confrontations like these raised perpetual doubts about the scientific value of this study, presented as it is as an empirical study of others. It became hard to resist the idea that my interpretations were simply attempts to project my own personal conflicts and doubts – partly the result of what was in many respects a shocking fieldwork experience – onto my discussion partners in order to be able to reflect on them in that objectified setting.

It is therefore unavoidable that the people who figure in this book (have come to) resemble me closely. For instance, when I point to alienation as a crucial factor in the lives of the people of Novi Sad, I cannot deny that this view is partly determined by the alienation that the war in former Yugoslavia has caused in my own stories about people and the world. Again, the insight that obscenities can perform a useful job in suspending alienation is partly the product of the enjoyment I took in using crude language (in the chapter on the fantasies about Gypsies) as a way of sullying the alienating vehicle of the academic text. As for what I personally find convincing and credible in claims about fictional reality (a reality that can exist as something unquestioned and 'natural' until something expels you from it and makes you realise its fictional character) is due as much to autobiographical factors – particularly my homosexuality, the realisation that life before coming out was someone else's story – than to any of my findings in Novi Sad. Similarly, my claims about 'the lessons' that the Serbs have learnt in the war are unmistakably influenced by the fact that I have spent almost all my life in educational institutions. The notion that Serbs frequent the Gypsy bars to obtain 'knowledge' about people and the world is interesting in this context as well, for I seem to be turning my informants into fellow anthropologists, engaged, as I am, in trying to understand representations of people and the world. By going into the field, to savage Serbia, I can learn something about people and the world; and I understand the Serbs' quest for wild Gypsies outside the city in the same way. My accusations that the Serbs suffered from spy paranoia are a cunning strategy to transfer my guilt feelings – in many ways I felt like a spy. Finally, the family culture in which I grew up – perhaps best characterised by the expression my late grandmother always used to avert any threat of lack of control or display of emotions: 'child, no scenes please' – has unmistakably coloured both my fascination with wild and undomesticated areas like the Gypsy bars of Novi Sad (platforms for pure scenes) and my understanding of them. When I see three Serb men throwing their arms around one another, resting their drunken heads in their neck and softly swaying from side to side to the tune of the orchestra playing for them, I can empathise.

Every time I made one of these discoveries, I was left in a state of perplexity. I felt that this projective identification, this hidden presence of myself in a text that describes others, heavily undermined the value of my claims about those others. 'Help!' was my panic-stricken reaction, 'this book isn't about Serbs at all, it's just about me!'

It was during one of these attacks of panic that I grabbed the dictionary, just to get grips on the term 'empiricism'. According to the New Shorter Oxford English Dictionary, empirical means: '1. Based on, guided by, or employing observation and experiment rather than theory (of a remedy, rule, etc.) used because it works, or is believed to. 2. Derived from or verifiable by experience, esp. sense-experience'. (I leave aside the uncomfortable meanings such as 'That practises medicine without scientific knowledge' and the association with a quack or a charlatan...). At any rate, the importance attached to (sense-) experience in the OED definitions accords with one of the lessons of the present study: the need to take account of the world of experience in which anthropological knowledge is produced.

In this respect, there *are* plenty of correspondences between anthropologists and the series of seekers after truth who have chosen the murky, Dionysian road.[26] Anthropologists too claim that the wilderness is a place where knowledge about people and the world can be acquired. Even when their fieldwork is carried out in less exotic places, a scrambling of meaning is still the preliminary to every piece of fieldwork. No matter how orderly, coherent and systematic the anthropologist's final account may be, it started as a leap in the dark when the anthropologist arrived in the research location – in most cases, s/he did not know anyone; s/he was overwhelmed by strange phenomena and incomprehensible impressions of an unknown society every minute of the day; s/he did not understand the forms of speaking and expression, the implicit allusions contained in figurative speech and metaphors; s/he was obliged to supplement a shaky linguistic skill with everything that helped to learn: imagination, intuition, empathy, and the senses. Isn't fieldwork almost always an experience of collapsing presuppositions, of impossible demands for representative research populations, a coherent corpus of data, and a panicky urge to systematise? Doesn't it almost always begin with a series of 'events which lack not just interpretations but interpretability', as Geertz calls these highly disorientating circumstances?[27] In the terms of the present study, then, all anthropologists who carry out field work, whether they like it or not, are engaged in driving themselves out of their story.

Strangely enough, after you have returned from the field, you are supposed to deny, cover up or conceal that knowledge derived from experience. Not in the corridors, at informal gatherings or private dinner parties where anthropologists discuss their fieldwork as if it were some kind of mystical experience. But apart from this, most of their energy is spent on articles, research proposals, and the public platforms for the reconstruction of the academic story – ways of conferring academic respectability on fieldwork, an essentially non-academic form of collecting information.

There is no need for this. The energy spent on maintaining the academic status of the story would be better spent on trying to find different, better forms of expression for the knowledge acquired in the field. My plea for a genuinely empirical anthropology based on (sense-) experience suggests tracking down the points of contact between researcher and researched and exploiting them in order to arrive at a better understanding. Still, this is only a suggestion, because if there is anything that I have wanted to achieve with this study, it is the recognition that there are many ways of telling how it is.

Notes

INTRODUCTION

[1] Euripides 1973, *The Bacchae*, strophe 3 (tr. Philip Vellacott).

[2] Turner 1988, p. 24.

[3] Van de Port 1990.

[4] For studies of the arrival of the gypsies in the Balkans and the historical developments that led to their marginalisation, see Ćirić 1979, Dalbello 1989, Lutovac 1987, Matasović 1928, Petrović 1976, Vukanović 1983, and Zirojević 1976. As for research on the current socio-economic position of gypsies in Serbia (or Yugoslavia), the study by Aleksandra Mitrović (1990) may be singled out as especially significant. For Vojvodina, see Bećin 1977, for Novi Sad, Batistić 1990. The social distance between Serbs and gypsies has been studied by Krkeljić (1977) and Vukajlović (1986).

[5] See Krkeljić 1977, Mitrović 1990, Kuzmanović 1992.

[6] Djordjević 1911, p. 187.

[7] D.H. Lawrence 1982, p. 499. The episode 'Maggie Tries to Run Away from Her Shadow' in George Eliot's novel *The Mill on the Floss* (1860) contains a fine example of the mixture of fear and fascination with which the Victorians viewed the gypsy camp.

[8] Schopf 1980, p. 52.

[9] See Seigel 1986.

[10] For general discussions of images of gypsies, see Clébert (1967), Kenrick & Puxon (1972) and the bibliography compiled by Gmelch (1986). The problem of marginalisation and stigmatisation is discussed in connection with images of gypsies in the work of Pitt-Rivers (1971) and Brandes (1980) on Andalusia; Bell (1986) and Steward (1993) on Hungary; Guy (1975) on Czechoslovakia; Beck (1989) on Romania; Hohman (1980), Schopf (1980) and Rakelman (1980a, b) on Germany; Mayerhofer (1987) on Austria; Okely (1983) on Great Britain; Andersen (1976) on Finland; and on the Netherlands, see Egmond (1994) and several of the articles in a special edition of the journal *O-Drom*, vol. 6 (2), June 1991. I should also like to mention here studies of the wider-ranging theme of images of so-called primitive or wild peoples, though not all of these books are mentioned in the text: White 1972, Sheehan 1980, Elias 1983, Price 1989, Torgovnick 1990, Bartra 1991, 1997, Sinclair 1991, Verrips 1989, 1991, 1993, and Zulaika 1993.

[11] In an exhibition called *Stijl vormt Functie* in the Stedelijk Museum Amsterdam, 21 December - 2 February 1991, the industrial designer Boris Šipek tried to impart vitality to his beautiful, aesthetic but above all lifeless objects by photographing them in the context of the grimy, muddy squalor of a gypsy camp.

[12] *Dajte vina, hoću lom.* Music, lyrics and performance: Haris Džinović (*Haris Džinović*, 1991). The narrator in this song is disappointed in love, and is drowning his sorrows in the bar. Love, nostalgia and parting are some of the popular causes of lyrical despair in these drinking songs, but the lyrics sometimes allude to other, less clearly defined sources of sadness. See Chapter VI below.

[13] The word has the same root as the German *lumperei*, 'shambles'. It is conceivable that it was originally used pejoratively by the German-oriented bourgeoisie of Novi Sad, only acquiring its current, positive connotations at a later stage. Živko Marković (n.d.), who employs the term *lumpovati* to describe the wild behaviour of the Bohemians of Novi Sad in the nineteenth century, uses it in combination with another revealing term, *srbovati*, a verb deriving from *Srbin*, Serb, and which means 'to behave like a Serb'.

[14] *I tebe sam sit, kafano!* Music and lyrics: Ž. Subotić, H. Džinović and A. Radulović. Performed by Haris Džinovic (*Haris*, 1989).

[15] *Nema lepše devojke.* Music and lyrics: traditional. Performed by Zvonko Bogdan (*Zvonko Bogdan i Orkestar Šandora Lakatoša*).

[16] *Ovo u grudima.* Music and lyrics: D. Dervišhalidović and Z. Radetić. Performed by Vesna Zmijanac (*Svatovi*, 1990).

[17] Glenny 1992.

[18] For general studies of the civil war in former Yugoslavia, see Furkes & Schlarp (eds.) 1991, Libal 1991, Glenny 1992, Gelhard 1992, Thompson 1992, Banac (ed.) 1993, Djurić 1993, Nahoum-Grappé 1993, Kaplan 1993, Magraš 1993, Grmek, Gjidara & Simac 1993, Blagojević & Demirović 1994, and Vulliamy 1994. Mart Bax's anthropological study of heavenly peace and earthly war in *Medjugorje: Religion, Politics, and Violence in Rural Bosnia* (1995) goes beyond the usual explanations by showing how, at grassroots level, wartime atrocities are in fact a continuum of peacetime blood vengeance. Anthropologist Tone Bringa (1993, 1995) returned to the Bosnian village that she had studied some years before the war to film the growing, and seemingly inevitable eruption of hatred and violence between Croat and Muslim neighbours and friends. Many publications have appeared recording personal impressions of, and reflections on, the war: Bogdanović 1993, Dizdarević 1993, Drakulić 1993, Ugrešić 1993, Karahasan 1994, Mertus, Tesanović, Metikos et al. 1997.

[19] Bogdanović 1993, p. 33.

[20] Taken from Radovan Tadić's documentary, *Life and death in the ruins of Sarajevo*, 1993.

21 Van den Boogaard 1993, p. 134.
22 Reported in the Dutch daily *De Volkskrant*, 13 November 1992.
23 Annet Bleich in *De Volkskrant*, 20 November 1993.
24 Bowman 1997, emphasis added.
25 Čolović 1993.
26 Žižek 1995.
27 *Time Magazine*, 14 March 1994.
28 Verrips 1993, p. 11.
29 Taussig 1987, Fernandez 1986, Zulaika 1988.
30 Taussig 1987, p. 370.
31 Pp. 229-230 and 214.
32 Zulaika 1993, p. 28.
33 Bataille 1993, Caillois 1959. On striking similarities between festivity and war, see also Tatar 1992, p. 169, Mosse 1990, pp. 55ff., Stevens 1989, p. 82, Katz 1993, p. 106, and Buford 1991. With specific reference to Serbia, see Čolović 1993.
34 *Vreme*, 4 November 1991.
35 A more detailed introduction to the people who became my informants follows in Chapter I.
36 Geertz 1973, p. 452.
37 Thomas 1991, p. 315. See also Fabian 1983 and 1991; Ortner 1984; Clifford 1986; Messick 1987; Hannerz 1987.
38 Pool (1991) has commented that, in contrast to the many theoretical reflections on postmodern ethnography, there are hardly any postmodern ethnographies (a similar point is made in Tyler 1986).
39 Vladimir Macura 1992.
40 Cohen 1989, p. 10.
41 Duerr 1985, p. 115.
42 Okely 1989, pp. 20ff.
43 Taussig 1987, p. 443.
44 Ibid., pp. 10-11.
45 I suppose this term was invented by others, perhaps by the very ones who complain about an excess of fancy writing.
46 Clifford 1986, p. 4.
47 Geertz 1988. For other discussions of the relationship between the social sciences and literature, see also Lepenies 1986 and Bruner 1993.
48 Thoden van Velzen & Van Wetering 1988.
49 Good 1989, p. 16.
50 I'm thinking about Colin Turnbull's *The Mountain People* (1972) and Nancy Scheper-Hughes' *Death Without Weeping. The Violence of Everyday Life in Brazil* (1993): both are truly disturbing accounts of hunger and poverty in the sense

that they don't try to sanitise or aestheticise the lived experience of hunger in their texts and interpretations, nor subordinate it to larger academic concerns. Parts of Michael Taussig's *Shamanism, Colonialism and the Wildman. A Study in Terror and Healing* (1987) on terror; and Christopher Brownings's *Ordinary Men: Reserve Police Battalion 101 and the Final Solution in Poland* (1992) come to mind as well.

[51] Verrips (1989, p. 45) has already commented on the myth-making task of the social sciences.

[52] Although I have only recently been introduced to the work of Jacques Lacan, and therefore cautious to refer to his thinking, it seems that his notion of the Real as a lack, something that resists symbolization, comes close to what I'm trying to say here (and throughout this book).

[53] Geertz 1973, p. 100.

[54] Ibid., p. 108.

[55] Rushdie 1992, p. 378, emphasis added.

[56] The photograph (Reuter) was published in the Dutch daily *NRC-Handelsblad* on 21 January 1993.

[57] Aleksandar Tišma in an interview (conducted by Raymond van den Boogaard) in *NRC Handelsblad*, 15 June 1991.

[58] Šosberger 1988, p. 40.

[59] Drakulić 1993, p. 101.

[60] For a more thorough exploration of this theme and its implications for the practice of anthropology, see the articles in Okely & Callaway (1992).

CHAPTER ONE

[1] In Bakić-Hayden and Hayden 1992.

[2] Magris 1988, p. 323.

[3] Masculine singular: *fin čovek*; feminine singular: *fina žena*.

[4] Grabovac and Knor 1991; Bojičić 1990.

[5] Grabovac and Knor 1991, pp. 9-10.

[6] Ibid., p. 10. Emphasis added.

[7] Bojičić 1990, p. 5.

[8] Spangler 1984; Veselinov 1987; Zarkov 1992.

[9] Simić 1973, p. 145.

[10] Spangler 1984, p. 85; see also Halpern 1967, pp. 34-35.

[11] Simić 1984, p. 207.

[12] Terms like 'primitive', 'backward' and so on that recur in this and subsequent chapters are the labels applied by my informants, and should in no way be taken to reflect any judgement on the part of the author. Although they are

not presented between inverted commas every time they occur, this is how they should be read.

[13] Simić 1973, p. 81.
[14] Van de Port 1990.
[15] Denitch 1969.
[16] Simić 1973.
[17] Halpern 1967.
[18] Denitch 1969; Simić 1973, 1984; Spangler 1984.
[19] Simić 1973, pp. 149-150.
[20] Pešić 1977.
[21] Dragičević-Šešić 1985.
[22] Prica 1991.
[23] Doder 1978, p. 196.
[24] Doder 1978 p. 196.
[25] Pešić 1977, p. 170.
[26] Idem, p. 170.
[27] The sociologist Vesna Pešić notes in this connection: 'The largest social distance is that between the intellectuals, on the one hand, and all other social groups, on the others.' (1977: 168)
[28] Drakulić 1992, p. 60.
[29] On stereotypes, see Popovič, Janča and Petovar 1990, p. 135.
[30] Bukurov 1957; Filipovič 1958; Gačeša 1984.
[31] For a critical account of Yugoslav (and especially Croatian) ethnography, see Dunja Rihtman-Auguštin 1988.
[32] The works of Van Gennep, Lévi-Strauss and Leach – who have been translated into Serbocroat – are popular among the new generation of anthropologists.
[33] Prica 1988, p. 85.
[34] Čolović 1988, p. 114.
[35] Prica 1988, p. 86.
[36] Cited in Prica 1988, p. 86.
[37] Cited in Prica 1988, p. 47.
[38] *Kakav narod, takva i pesma*, cited in Prica 1988, p. 85.
[39] Prica 1988; Čolović 1984, 1988; Dragičević-Čečič 1988.
[40] For an extended discussion of the significance and importance of *Novakomponovana Narodna Muzika* see Čolović 1984 and 1988.
[41] Kršič 1989.
[42] Kršič 1989, p. 604.
[43] For a discussion of the cilivisation debate as it is employed today in the political rhetoric of the former Yugoslavian leaders, see Bakić-Hayden and Hayden 1992. Gal (1992, p. 443), referring to Hungary, speaks of 'debates

about affinities with Europe as against indigenous distinctiveness'. Similar discussions about national character versus European character are reported from Romania (Verdery 1991) and Greece (Herzfeld 1985). For a more general study concerning the relation between Europe and the Balkans, see Todorova (1997).

[44] Douglas 1996 [1966], p. 163.

[45] Tišma 1983, pp. 238-239.

[46] In *Vreme*, 2 December 1991.

[47] Thoden van Velzen 1991, pp. 35ff.

CHAPTER TWO

[1] Slobodan Momčilović, 'Razum je Pobednik'. (letter to the editor). *Borba* 6/09/1991.

[2] 'Stop huškanju rat', letter to the editor. *Borba* 19/11/1991.

[3] *Borba* 05/09/1991.

[4] *Borba* 24/06/1991.

[5] Vlado Teslić, 'Od Haga ka Njujorku. Nedelja u Svetu'. *Borba* 15/11/1991.

[6] Svetomir Spasić, 'Hoću da budem Bušman'. *Borba* 09/01/1992.

[7] Vava, *Borba* 01/09/1991.

[8] Jara Ribnikar, 'Karta viće za partizane', *Borba* 11/11/1991.

[9] Velikić, in *Vreme* 16/11/1991.

[10] *Nedeljina Borba*, 11-12/01/1992.

[11] Mirko Klarin, 'Vidi šta su nam uradili od zemlje', *Borba* 16-17/11/1991.

[12] Davidčo, *Vreme* October 1991.

[13] This survey is not intended as a general survey, let alone an exhaustive historical one. It is strictly limited to the problem under discussion here: the ambiguous values attached to Serb identity.

[14] For a splendid and detailed analysis of this pattern in other parts of the Balkans, see Todorova 1997.

[15] Hadžić 1891, p. 625.

[16] See Popović 1957a, p. 49.

[17] Spangler 1984, p. 85.

[18] The Srem and Bačka districts came under Turkish rule in 1526 and 1689, the Bannat from 1552 to 1716.

[19] Szentklavan 1891, p. 550.

[20] Szentklavan 1891, p. 554.

[21] Hadžić 1891, p. 627.

[22] For documentation on the earliest movements to the north, see Hadžić 1891, p. 629.

[23] Idem, p. 322.

[24] Popović 1957b, pp. 28-29.

[25] Popović 1957b, p. 113.

[26] Jelavich 1991a, p. 147.

[27] Popović 1957b, p. 153.

[28] Popović 1957b, p. 31.

[29] Idem.

[30] Idem, p. 35.

[31] Idem.

[32] Cited in Popović 1957c, pp. 134-135 (italics added).

[33] The Croatian officer Matija Antun Reljković (1732-1798), who worked in the *Militärgrenze*, was one of the first South Slavs to portray his fellow Serbs in Slavonia. The title of his book *Satir, iliti Divji Čovik* (Sater, or the Wild Man) (1762) speaks volumes about the content. Without further ado Reljković classifies his fellow countrymen as backward primitives whose ignorance is matched only by their shamelessness.

[34] Popović 1957b, p. 95; Jelavich 1992a, p. 185.

[35] Popović 1957c, p. 114.

[36] Tomandl 1953, 1954.

[37] Popović 1957c, p. 153.

[38] Djurić-Klajn 1971, p. 40.

[39] Jelavich 1991a, p. 149; see further Babić 1891, p. 590; Ramet 1988.

[40] Jelavich 1992a, p. 149.

[41] For a short, clear summary of the rise and success of the nationalist movements in the Habsburg Empire, see Jelavich 1991a.

[42] See Sundhaussen 1973.

[43] Burke 1978, p. 11.

[44] Burke 1978.

[45] Jelavich 1992a, p. 173.

[46] Burke 1978, p. 9.

[47] Forry 1990, pp. 47-48.

[48] Burke 1978, p. 13.

[49] Idem, p. 13.

[50] Forry (1990, p. 109) remarks: 'It is [...] one of the many ironies of contemporary South Slavic society that the sense of "tradition", the development of which eventually led to political liberation and self-determination, was brought to South Slavic lands through the ideology and institutions of 19th century central European civilization'.

[51] Popović 1985a, p. 22.

[52] Compare the remarks in Jelavich 1991b, p. 152.

[53] West 1982, p. 90.

[54] Idem, p. 87.
[55] Idem, pp. 84-85.
[56] Idem, p. 77.
[57] Popović 1984, p. 41.
[58] 'Evropa je stara žena, Balkan je mlado muško', and 'Naša je prednost što nemamo "kulturne tradicije"', cited in Golubović & Subotić 1991, p. 20.
[59] Drakulić 1992, p. 82.
[60] Doder 1974, pp. 42ff.
[61] Cited in Ramet 1992, pp. 99-100.
[62] Blagojević & Demirović 1994, pp. 28-29.
[63] Idem.
[64] Djurić 1989, p. 41.
[65] Ortner 1986, p. 153.

CHAPTER THREE

[1] Taussig 1987, p. 367.
[2] Popović 1957a, p. 322.
[3] Taussig 1987, p. 366. For a similar notion, see Messick 1987.
[4] Geertz 1983, pp. 76-84.
[5] Duerr 1985; Fernandez 1986.
[6] Thoden van Velzen and Van Wetering 1988, p. 8.
[7] Turner 1988, p. 24.
[8] Langer 1942, p. 287.
[9] Geertz 1973, p. 99.
[10] Douglas 1966; Leach 1976 and 1982; Babcock 1975, 1978 and 1984.
[11] Leach 1982, p. 115.
[12] Douglas 1966, p. 54.
[13] Taussig 1993, p. xv.
[14] Idem, xvii-xviii, emphasis added.
[15] Cited in the Dutch daily newspaper *Trouw* 21/07/93.
[16] Misha Glenny in the Dutch daily newspaper *NRC-Handelsblad* 14/08/1993.
[17] Dizdarević 1993, p. 40.
[18] For an in-depth analysis of War-time everyday life in Croatia 1991-92, see Povrzanović 1993, 1997.
[19] Amnesty International, *Yugoslavia. Further Reports of Torture and Deliberate and Arbitrary Killings in War Zones*, 1992.
[20] Benard & Schlaffer 1994, p. 106.
[21] Steiner 1984, p. 230
[22] Van Spaendonck 1977, p. 203.

[23] In the Dutch daily newspaper *De Volkskrant*, 05/08/1993.

[24] Popović 1957c, p. 297.

[25] Kennan 1993, p. 10.

[26] Kennan 1993, p. 10.

[27] Doder 1975, pp. 24-25.

[28] *NOS-Nova.*

[29] Dubravka Ugrešić, *Vreme* 22/11/93.

[30] Tišma 1990, p. 115.

[31] Bulatović 1970.

[32] *Vreme*, 16/08/1993.

[33] Bosnian refugees, *Nieuwslijn* 12/01/93.

[34] Mirsada Z. on her rape by Serb soldiers, *Nova*, January 1993.

[35] These interviews are taken from a programme 'Ingrijpen of niet?' [Intervene or not?] broadcast by the Dutch KRO station.

[36] Huston 1982, p. 272.

[37] Thompson 1992, p. 106.

[38] Speech by President Josip Broz Tito in Titovo Užice on 4 July 1961.

[39] Mosse 1990, p. 6.

[40] Glenny 1992, p. 23.

[41] Drakulić 1991, p. 10.

[42] Compare Duško Doder's remark that 'Yugoslavia is a country without a past. A real understanding of the past means free inquiry, which the regime thinks it cannot afford, and so history books are rewritten', Doder 1978, p. 238.

[43] Cited in Čavovški 1991, p. 72, emphasis added.

[44] Drakulić, 'My father's pistol', in *Balkan Express*, p. 35.

[45] Rade Mihaljčić (1989, pp. 230-231) claims that the first explicit reference to *Serb* armies and combatants is in the First Serbian Revolt. Earlier versions of the myths, recorded in the second half of the eighteenth century, do not specify the ethnicity of the Christian armies.

[46] Bandić 1990, p. 39.

[47] Ibid, pp. 41-42.

[48] The reaction to the fact that Croatians and Slovenes had sided with the Germans and Austrians in their quest for independence met with almost universal disgust, astonishment or amazement. 'They were no more than the feeders of the horses of the Austrians', I was told, 'they had everything in Yugoslavia'. My informant continued with a well-known story: how ungrateful everyone was to the Serbs. Even though they had fought on behalf of the Macedonians against the Bulgarians and Turks, had made the greatest sacrifices for the independence of the country, had always tried to accommodate with the Croatians and Slovenes, had protected Europe from the Turkish menace for centuries and were doing the same now, in Bosnia, all they got

for their pains was ingratitude.

[49] The nationalist euphoria that predominated during my fieldwork in Serbia had breathed new life into these ideas. The poet Matija Bećković, one of the mouthpieces of the Serb rebirth ideology, was a great success with texts like: 'The battle of Kosovo was never finished. It was as if the Serbian people have waged only one battle – by widening the Kosovo charnel-house, by adding wailing upon wailing, by counting new martyrs to the martyrs of Kosovo [...] Kosovo is the costliest Serbian word. It was paid by the blood of the whole people [...] Kosovo is the equator of the Serbian planet' (Bećković 1989, cited in Banac 1992, p. 172).

[50] *Osmica* 08/04/91.

[51] In an interview in *Hervormd Nederland*, 24 April 1993.

[52] Thompson 1991, p. 191.

[53] In *Het Parool*, 27/07/93.

[54] Doder 1978, p. 112.

[55] War correspondent Micha Glenny, cited in the Beograd weekly *Vreme* 08/02/1993.

CHAPTER FOUR

[1] Glišić 1990, p. 18.

[2] In Djurić 1985.

[3] Dretar 1991. The following quotation is from page 8.

[4] Dijak 1989, p. 12.

[5] Vujković 1991, p. 71.

[6] In: Stjepan Dokušec, 1935.

[7] In Djurić & Nikolić (s.d.) p. 86, and Vaša Petrović, 1894.

[8] Diogenes, VPRO Television.

[9] For an interview with a gypsy fortune-teller in a village near Beograd, see Tomašević & Djurić, 1988. See further Vukanović 1983, pp. 284-285 and Brozović 1938.

[10] Bandić 1991, pp. 142-143.

[11] Djordjević 1911, p. 175.

[12] Idem, p. 188.

[13] Katsahnias 1989, p. 34.

[14] Djordjević 1984d, p. 7.

[15] Djordjević 1984e, p. 13.

[16] Djordjević 1984a, p. 293.

[17] Maluckov 1979, p. 19.

[18] Vukanović 1983, p. 220.

19 Djordjević 1984c, p. 38.
20 Gojković 1964, p. 724.
21 Djordjević 1904, p. 52.
22 Barjaktarović 1970, p. 747.
23 Idem.
24 It is interesting to note that the informants who gave Stanley Brandes information about the class relations in a small Andalusian town were all agreed on one thing – the unconscious exclusion of gypsies from any part in the scheme (Brandes 1980, p. 55).
25 In his article on gypsies in Leskovac, Jovan Jovanović mentions the large percentage of illiterates among the gypsies there. 'They do not have a language, and they do not make any effort to learn it either. So there is no need for us to go into foreign languages.' (Jovanović 1970, p. 185)
26 Turner 1988, p. 125.
27 Thoden van Velzen 1991, pp. 35-36.
28 Obeyesekere 1990, p. 283; De Swaan 1993.
29 Kristeva 1988, p. 201.
30 On this see also Halpern 1967, p. 289; Djordjević 1984c, p. 134; Kuzmanović 1992, p. 120; Savić 1991, p. 33.
31 Doder 1974; see too Gračaković 1985, p. 7.
32 *Borba*, 30/08/1991.
33 *Borba*, 05/05/1991. Serbs, in turn, often refer to Romania as a *ciganska zemlja* or gypsy country without any culture or civilisation, implying that they themselves are superior.
34 One might compare English usage of the term 'gypsy' to denote 'a cunning, deceitful, or fickle woman' (*Oxford English Dictionary*).
35 Dretar 1991, p. 74.
36 This identification is dealt with in more detail in the next chapter to indicate that Serbs associated with the gypsy orchestra undergo a genuine transformation and become gypsies.
37 Taussig 1987, p. 4.
38 Djordjević 1911, p. 188.
39 Djordjević & Milošević-Djordjević 1988, p. 483.
40 Lutovac 1987, p. 209.
41 Idem, pp. 213-215.
42 Idem, p. 220.
43 Jovanović 1970, p. 187. Simonović (1924, p. 117) detects correspondences between the unpredictable outbursts of violence on the part of gypsies and their general mental state: 'By comparison with their feelings, their intellect is feebly developed; their feelings are eruptive, volatile and capricious'. On eruptive violence in the gypsy community of Apatin, one of the largest gypsy

communities in the Vojvodina, see Barjaktarović 1964, p. 203.

[44] Jovanović also detected other striking sexual curiosities in the world of the gypsies: prostitution, for example, and 'even a case of a lesbian affair'. (1970, p. 186)

[45] Djurić & Nikolić, s.d., p. 6.

[46] Jovanović 1970, p. 186.

[47] Djurić & Nikolić, s.d., p. 21.

[48] Thoden van Velzen 1990, p. 81.

[49] Hedges 1983, p. xii.

[50] Cited in Hedges 1983, pp. xiii-xv.

[51] Micić 1991, p. 21.

[52] In this connection it is worth noting that here and there in *Zenitizam* texts the gypsies are used as ammunition against the establishment. 'At the moment when he gives primarily and spontaneously of himself, the piper, the gypsy or the guest in a bar with music is a greater artist than all the chamber choirs or virtuosi on the violin, cello or keyboard together', Micić claims in his *Zenitizam* manifesto (1991, p. 107). It is also interesting that both Mirjana Ilić and Tatomir Vukanović have pointed out that, when gypsies perform as entertainers for non-gypsies, they more than live up to their reputation as destroyers of language. During the *klocalica* rituals in the Bannat, in which gypsies go through the villages with a figure disguised as a goat, they sing songs that they have made up from lines and strophes taken from different songs (Ilić 1964, p. 55). Vukanović refers to comic misinterpretations of well-known songs, and attributes this phenomenon to the overweening self-esteem and greed of the musicians who will do anything to please the customer: 'A considerable number of Gypsy singers in Yugoslav countries pronounce the words of a song quite incorrectly, paying no heed at all to whether what they say has or has not any sense [...]. For the famous song '*Zujte, strune!*' (Sound, ye chords!) the Gypsies sing: '*Zujte, strine!*' (Sound, ye aunts! – the word *strina* being used also scornfully for an unmanly person). There are also whole songs, patched up from lines of various others' (Vukanović 1962, p. 61).

[53] Geertz 1983, pp. 79-80.

[54] Babcock 1975, p. 154.

[55] For social scientific research on prejudices about gypsies in Serbia, see Krkeljić 1977, Vukaljlović 1986, Pantić 1987, Kuzmanović 1992.

[56] Djordjević 1911.

[57] Djordjević 1984c, p. 41.

[58] Compare the comments of Kaprow (1991) on a gypsy neighbourhood in the Spanish city of Zaragoza.

[59] Djurić & Nikolić, s.d., p. 36.

[60] The Serb discourse on gypsies underlines the relevance of what Taussig has

called 'the savage episteme' in connection with the travellers' stories from the interior of South America that he has studied: 'A wild episteme so raw, so nakedly empiricist, untheoretical, unabstract, and non-cultured that it amounted to no more than the trembling phenomenology of being, each head a world, each world alone and wavering.' (1987, p. 91)

[61] Interview in the Dutch daily *De Volkskrant* 14/06/1990, emphasis added.

[62] Kusturica 1989, p. 38, emphasis added.

[63] Compare Babcock: 'The joke [...] affords an opportunity for realizing that an accepted pattern has no necessity. Its excitement lies in the suggestion that any particular ordering of experience may be arbitrary and subjective. It is frivolous in that it produces no real alternative, only an exhilarated sense of freedom from form in general, though it may well provoke thought of real alternatives and prompt action towards their realization.' (1984, p. 184).

[64] See also Van de Port 1991.

[65] Turner 1988, p. 103.

[66] *De Volkskrant*, 14/06/1990.

Chapter Five

[1] *Sarajevski Svijet* 03/05/1991

[2] Turner 1988, p. 24.

[3] Rouget 1985.

[4] Taussig 1993, p. 78.

[5] The *bećarac* is a ten-syllabic poem with a comic, usually scabrous content, in which life is commented on in a no-nonsense way. For discussions and (censored) collections, see Veselinović 1954, Mandić 1971, Kovač 1971, Prćić 1971, Kolarov 1981, Leskovac 1979.

[6] Tyler 1978, p. 459.

[7] Gypsy musicians mainly resort to the musical idioms of their audience. This has led ethnomusicologists to discuss what gives gypsy music its special gypsy character. For an extensive treatment of these discussions, see Van de Port 1997. On gypsy music in the country formerly known as Yugoslavia, see Djordjević 1910, Vukanović 1962, Gojković 1964, 1977, 1983, 1985, 1989, Petrović 1974. Balint 1970 is a full-length study of Hungarian gypsy music in the Vojvodina. Forry 1990 discusses the role of gypsy musicians in the tamburica music of the Vojvodina. Burić 1990 goes into the musical forms of gypsies in the Vojvodina when they make music with one another, i.e. in a non-professional setting.

[8] This association is prompted by the fact that the Serb state broadcasting company transmitted adult porn late on Saturday night.

[9] Rouget 1985, p. 93. For a full-length study of trance and possession in South-East Europe, see Antonijević 1990.

[10] Kovač uses the term *trans* (trance) to describe the state into which the customer for whom the gypsy orchestra is playing falls: 'The *bećarac* is not played all the time and everywhere. The musicians know exactly when they should start the *bećarac*. They start to play it when they are working towards the climax of the *lumpovanje*. Then it is followed by an explosion, tables are overturned, glasses are broken, and the *bećar* falls into a trance.' (1971, pp. 81-82)

[11] Turner 1974, p. 274.

[12] Blok 1989, p. 267.

[13] *De Volkskrant*, 21/06/1990.

[14] Kovač 1971, p. 81.

[15] Idem, p. 85.

[16] Ibidem.

[17] Idem, p. 82.

[18] Idem, p. 84.

[19] 'Have you heard the news?' Stajić called me immediately to tell me about the suicide in *Ciganski Noć*. Later other people told me it had been a shoot-out, but it was still noteworthy how acceptable the suicide scenario was.

[20] Grabovac & Knor, 1991, p. 23.

CONCLUSIONS

[1] Vuyk 1987, pp. 9-10.

[2] Nietzsche 1993 [1872], p. 17.

[3] To be precise, via V. Ilić's poem 'Gypsy child', which explicitly compares the gypsies with the bacchic hordes. See Ilić 1953.

[4] Benedict 1934, p. 72; Dodds 1951, pp. 64ff.

[5] Cohn 1970, p. 150.

[6] Bernheimer 1952, p. 14.

[7] For a survey see Webster 1948.

[8] Thoden van Velzen & Van Wetering 1988, p. 396.

[9] Laermans s.d., p. 37.

[10] Carroll 1990, pp. 211-214.

[11] Dodds 1951, p. 193.

[12] Cohn 1970, pp. 128-129.

[13] Hannerz 1987, p. 553; see also Meyer 1994.

[14] Cited in Thompson 1992, p. 240.

[15] Geertz 1973, p. 452, n. 43.

[16] Zulaika 1988, p. 166.

[17] Diogenes, VPRO broadcasting company, 07/02/1994.

[18] Katz 1993.

[19] Thoden van Velzen & Van Wetering 1988, pp. 397-398.

[20] Goudsblom 1980, pp. 12-13.

[21] Blok 1991, p. 203.

[22] Mohammed Curac, mayor of the Bosnian city of Travnik, described the war against the Muslims as follows: 'Look at the way this war is being conducted: it has become city-cidal, culture-cidal, history-cidal, memory-cidal, dignity-cidal, economy-cidal – in short, genocidal'. (Vuliamy 1994, p. 352).

[23] Idem, p. 93.

[24] Bogdanović 1993, pp. 36-37.

[25] *NRC-Handelsblad*, 28/01/1993.

[26] Gouldner already pointed out this correspondence in 1973.

[27] Geertz 1973, p. 100.

Bibliography

Andersen, David M.

1976   Finnish Folk-Accounts for the Origins of the Gypsies. *Journal of the Gypsy-Lore Society* 4th series 1(2):73-79.

Amnesty International

1992   *Yugoslavia. Further Reports of Torture and Deliberate and Arbitrary Killings in War Zones*, March 1992. AI Index: Eur.48/13/92.

Antić, Miroslav

1986   *Garavi Sokak. Veselo Cigansko Vašarište sa Nekoliko Suza i Kapi Kiše*. Zagreb: Jugoart.

Antonietto, Alain

1986   La Musique Tsigane. Mythe ou Préjugés?... *Études Tsiganes* 1:21-27.

Antonijević, Dragoslav

1990   *Ritualni Trans*. Beograd: SANU.

Babcock, Barbara

1975   'A Tolerated Margin of Mess'. The Trickster and his Tales Reconsidered. *Journal of the Folklore Institute* 11(1/2):145-86.

1978   Introduction. In: Idem (ed.), *The Reversible World. Symbolic Inversion in Art and Society*. Ithaca: Cornell University Press. Pp. 13-36.

1984   Arrange me into Disorder. Fragments and Reflections on Ritual Clowning. In: John McAloon (ed.), *Rite, Drama, Festival, Spectacle. Rehearsals Toward a Theory of Cultural Performance*. Philadelphia: Institute for the Study of Human Issues. Pp. 102-128.

Babić, Franz

1891   Der Backa. *Die össterreichisch-ungarische Monarchie im Wort und Bild. Ungarn, Band II*. Wien: Druck und Verlag der Kaiserlich-Königlichen Hof- und Staatsdruckerei.

Bakić-Hayden, Milica & Robert M. Hayden

1992   Orientalist Variations on the Theme 'Balkans': Symbolic Geography in Recent Yugoslav Cultural Politics. *Slavic Review* 51(1):1-16.

Balint, Sarosi

1970   *Zigeunermusik*. Budapest: Corvina.

Banac, Ivo

1992   Post-Communism as Post-Yugoslavism. The Yugoslav Non-Revolutions of 1989-1990. In: Idem (ed.), *Eastern Europe in Revolution*. Ithaca: Cornell University Press. Pp. 168-188.

Bandić, Dušan
1990   *Carstvo Zemaljsko i Carstvo Nebesko*. Beograd: Biblioteka XX Vek.
1991   *Narodna Religija Srba u 100 Pojmova*. Beograd: Nolit.

Barjaktarović, Mirko
1964   Oaza Apatinskih Cigana. *Rad Vojvodjanskih Muzeja* 12-13:191-204.
1970   Cigani u Jugoslaviji Danas. *Zbornik Filozofskog Fakulteta u Beogradu* 11(1): 743-748.

Bartra, R.
1991   Identity and Wilderness. Ethnography and the History of an Imaginary Primitive Group. *Etnologia Europaea* 21(2):103-25.
1997   *The Artificial Savage. Modern Myths of the Wild Man*. Ann Arbor: The University of Michigan Press.

Bataille, Georges
1993   [1957] *De Erotiek*. Amsterdam: Arena.
1993   [1961] *De Tranen van Eros*. Nijmegen: Sun.

Batistić, Željko
1990   Romi u Novom Sadu. *Romologija* 1(1):88-108.

Bax, Mart
1995   *Medjugorje. Religion, Politics, and Violence in Rural Bosnia*. Amsterdam: VU Uitgeverij.

Bečin, Alexandar
1977   *Socijalni Problemi Roma u Vojvodini*. Novi Sad: Pokrajinska Zavod za Socijalna Istraživanja.

Beck, Sam
1989   The Origins of Gypsy Slavery in Romania. *Dialectical Anthropology* 14:53-61.

Bell, Peter D.
1984   The 'New Magyars'. In: Idem, *Peasants in a Collectivized Hungarian Village*. Berkeley: University of California Press. Pp. 283-296.

Benard, Cheryl & Edit Schlaffer
1994   *Dicht bij ons Bed. De Gruwelijke Oorlog in Bosnië en de Apathie van het Westen*. Baarn: Ambo.

Benedict, Ruth
1953   [1934] *Patterns of Culture*. New York: A Mentor Book.

Bernheimer, R.
1952   *Wild Men in the Middle Ages. A Study in Art, Sentiment, and Demonology*. Cambridge: Harvard University Press.

Blagojević, Slobodan & Hamdija Demirović
1994   *Bloedverwanten. De Joegoslavische Oorlog en de Europese Vrede*. Amsterdam: van Oorschot.

Blok, Anton
1989   Charivari's als purificatie-ritueel. *Volkskundig Bulletin* 15(3):266-281.
1991   Zinloos en Zinvol Geweld. *Amsterdams Sociologisch Tijdschrift* 18(3):189-207.

Bogdanović, Bogdan
1993   *Die Stadt und der Tod*. Klagenfurt: Wieser Verlag.

Bojičić Dušanka
1990   *Lepo Ponašanje*. Beograd: Pronalazaštvo.

Boogaard, Raymond van den
1993   De vele gedaanten van een burenmoord. In: Robert van de Roer & Hans Steketee (eds.), *De Verwoesting van Joegoslavië. Geschiedenis, Achtergronden, Reportages*. Rotterdam: NRC Handelsblad. Pp.133-135.

Bowman, Glenn
1994   Xenophobia, phantasy and the nation: the logic of ethnic violence in Former Yugoslavia. In: V. Goddard, J. Llobera and C. Shore (eds.), *Anthropology of Europe: Identity and Boundaries in Conflict*. London: Berg. Pp. 143-171.

Brandes, Stanley
1980   Gypsy Jokes and the Andalusian Self-Image. In: Idem, *Metaphors of Masculinity. Sex and Status in Andalusian Folklore*. University of Pennsylvania Press. Pp. 53-73.

Bringa, Tone
1995   *Being Muslim the Bosnian Way. Identity and Community in a Central Bosnian Village*. New Jersey: Princeton University Press.

Bringa, Tone & Debbie Christie
1993   *We Are All Neighbours* (film). Granada Television.

Brozović, L.
1938   Zigeuner als Aftertierartze (Tierkurpfuscher). *Medicinski Pregled*, 7,8 en 9:139-142.

Bruner, Edward M.
1993   Introduction: The Ethnographic Self and the Personal Self. In: Paul Benson (ed.), *Anthropology and Literature*. Urbana: University of Illinois Press.

Browning, Christopher
1992   *Ordinary Men: Reserve Police Battalion 101 and the Final solution in Poland*. New York: Harper Collins.

Buford, Bill
1993   *Among the Thugs*. London: Vintage Books

Bukurov, Branislav
1957   *Poreklo Stanovništva Vojvodine*. Novi Sad: Matica Srpska.

Bulatović, Miodrag
1970   *Rat je bio bolji* [Geef mij maar Oorlog]. Amsterdam: Meulenhoff.
Burić, Vesna
1990   *Vokalna Muzika Roma iz Vojvodine*. Diplomski Rad. Beograd: FMU u Beogradu, Etnomusikološki Odsek.
Burke, Peter
1978   *Popular Culture in Early Modern Europe*. New York: Harper.

Caillois, Roger
1959   *Man and the Sacred*. Illinois: The Free Press of Glencoe.
Carroll, Noël
1990   *The Philosophy of Horror or Paradoxes of the Heart*. New York: Routledge.
Čavoski, Kosta
1991   *Slobodan Protiv Slobode*. Beograd: Dosije.
Ćirić, Jovan V.
1979   Naselja Roma kao Obeleže Gradske Periferije. Na Primeru Gradovi Jugoistočne Srbije. *Leskovački Zbornik* 19:219-224.
Clébert, Jean-Paul
1967   *The Gypsies*. Harmondsworth: Penguin.
Clifford, James
1986   Introduction. Partial Truths. In: James Clifford & George E. Marcus (eds.), *Writing Culture. The Poetics and Politics of Ethnography*. Berkeley: University of California Press. Pp. 1-26.
1988   *The Predicament of Culture. Twentieth-Century Ethnography, Literature, and Art*. Cambridge, Mass.: Harvard University Press.
Cohen, Anthony P.
1989   Presentation. In: Tim Ingold (ed.), *Social Anthropology is a Generalizing Science or it is Nothing. A Debate held in the Muriel Stott Centre, John Rylands University Library of Manchester, on 29th October 1988*. Manchester: Group for Debates in Anthropological Theory.
Cohn, Norman
1970   *The Pursuit of the Millenium. Revolutionairy Millenarians and Mystical Anarchists of the Middle Ages*. London: Paladin.
Čolović, Ivan
1984   *Divlja Književnost. Etnolingvističko Proučavanje Paraliterature*. Beograd: Nolit.
1988   *Vreme Znakova*. Novi Sad: Književna Zajednica.
1993   *Bordel Ratnika. Folklor, Politika i Rat*. Beograd: Biblioteka XX Vek.

Dalbello, Marija
1989   Prilog bibliografiji o Romima (Ciganima) u SFR Jugoslaviji, s posebnim obzirom na etnolos:ku i folklorističku gradju u periodici. In: Sait Balić,

Milka Jauk-Pinhak, Čedo Kisić e.a. (eds.), *Medjunarodni Naučni Skup Jezik i Kultura Roma. Sarajevo, 9-11. VI 1986.* Sarajevo: Institut za Proučavanje Nacionalnih Odnosa. Pp. 429-441.

Denitch, Bette S.
1969   *Social Mobility and Industrialization in a Yugoslav Town.* PhD. dissertation, Berkeley: University of California.

Dijak, Vlado
1989   Ciganski Slavuj. In: *Čitanka za IV razred Osnovne Škole.* Novi Sad.

Dizdarević, Zlatko
1993   *Het laatste Nieuws uit Sarajevo.* Amsterdam: Arena.

Djordjević, Tihomir R.
1904   Fiziške i Duševne Osobine Cigana Kraljevine Srbije. *Srpski Književni Glasnik,* September 1904: 43-53.
1911   Cigani u Srpskom Narodnom Verovanju i Pripovedanju. *Nova Iskra. Ilustrovani List:* 187-189.
1984a   [1904] Ko su to Cigani. In: *Naš Narodni Život* (6):293-296. Beograd: Prosveta.
1984b   [1908] Vera u Cigana. In: *Naš Narodni Život* (7):41-45. Beograd: Prosveta.
1984c   [1910] Cigani i muzika u Srbiji. In: *Naš Narodni Život* (7):32-41. Beograd: Prosveta.
1984d   [1914] Čime se Cigani drže kao narod. In: *Naš Narodni Život* (7):7-13. Beograd: Prosveta.
1984e   [1932] Cigani kao nosioci kulture. In: *Naš Narodni Život* (7):13-17. Beograd: Prosveta.

Djordjević, Dragutin M. & Nada Milošević-Djordjević
1988   *Srpske Narodne Pripovetke i Predanja iz Leskovačke Oblasti.* Beograd: Srpska Akademija Nauka i Umetnost.

Djurić, Rajko
1985   *Ciganske Priče.* Beograd: RAD/ Bibliotheka Dom i Škola.

Djurić Rajko & Jovan Nikolić (eds.)
z.j.   *Ciganski Vic.* Beograd: Novinska Radna Organizacija 'JEŽ'

Djurić Rajko & Bertolt Bengsch
1993   *Der Zerfall Jugoslawiens.* Berlin: Morgenbuch Verlag.

Djurić, Vojislav
1989   *Antologija Narodnih Pripovedaka.* Beograd: Srpska Knjizevna Zadruga.

Djurić-Klajn, Stana
1971   *Istorijski Razvoj Muzičke Kulture u Srbiji.* Beograd: Pro Musica.

Dodds, E.R.
1985   [1951] *The Greeks and the Irrational.* Berkeley: University of California Press.

Doder, Duško
1978   *The Yugoslavs.* London: George Allen & Unwin.

Dokušec, Stjepan
1935   Tisuću i Jedna Noć Našega Naroda. Kajkavske Priće i Anegdote iz Lupoglava, srez Dugo Selo. *Vjesnik Etnografskog Muzeja u Zagrebu* 1(1/2):111-182.

Douglas, Mary
1970   *Purity and Danger. An Analysis of Concepts of Polution and Taboo.* London: Penguin.

Dragičević-Šešić, Milena
1985   Pokušaj definisanja dominantnih i produktivnih modela kulturnog života u Jugoslaviji. *Podkulture* 1:13-20.

Drakulić, Slavenka
1991   Krieg! In: Josip Furkes & Karl-Heinz Schlarp (hg.), *Jugoslawien. Ein Staat zerfällt.* Reinbek bei Hamburg: Rowohlt Taschenbuch Verlag. Pp. 9-19.
1993   *How We Survived Communism and Even Laughed.* New York: Harper Perennial Library.
1993   *Balkan-Expres.* Baarn: de Prom.

Dretar, Tomislav
1991   *Bol. Ciganska Rapsodija.* Novi Sad: Društvo Vojvodine za Jezik, Književnost i Kultura Roma.

Duerr, Hans Peter
1985   *Dreamtime. Concerning the Boundary between Wilderness and Civilization.* Oxford: Basil Blackwell.

Džepina, Mirjana
1982   *Društveni i Zabavni Život Starih Novosadjana.* Novi Sad: Prosveta.

Elias, Norbert
1983   On the Sociogenesis of Aristocratic Romanticism in the Process of Courtization. In: Idem, *The Court Society.* New York: Pantheon Books. Pp. 214-267.

Euripides
1973   *The Bacchae and Other Plays.* London: Penguin Classics.

Fabian, Johannes
1983   *Time and the Other.* New York: Columbia University Press.
1991   Culture, Time and the Object of Anthropology. In: Idem, *Time and the Work of Anthropology. Critical Essays 1971-1991.* Chur: Harwood Academic Publishers.

Fernandez, James
1986   *Persuasions and Performances. The Play of Tropes in Culture.* Bloomington: Indiana University Press.

Filipović, Milenko S.
1958   *Proučavanje Naseljavanja Vojvodine*. Novi Sad: Matica Srpska.
Forry, Mark
1990   *The Mediation of Tradition and Culture in the Tamburica Music of Vojvodina (Yugoslavia)*. Ph.D. Dissertation, Los Angeles: University of California.
Freud, Sigmund
1987   [1930] Civilization and its Discontents. In: James Strachey & Anna Freud (eds.), *The Standard Edition of the Complete Psychological Works of Sigmund Freud*, volume XXI: 59-145. London: The Hogarth Press & The Institute of Psycho-Analysis.
Furkes, Josip & Karl-Heinz Schlarp (eds.)
1991   *Jugoslawien. Ein Staat Zerfällt*. Reinbeck bei Hamburg: Rowohlt Verlag.

Gaćeša, Nikola L.
1984   *Agrarna Reforma i Kolonizacija U Jugoslaviji 1945-1948*. Novi Sad: Matice Srpske
Gal, Susan
1992   Bartók's funeral. Representations of Europe in Hungarian Political Rhetoric. *American Ethnologist* 18(3):440-459.
Geertz, Clifford
1973   *The Interpretation of Cultures*. New York: Basic Books.
1983   *Local Knowledge. Further Essays in Interpretive Anthropology*. New York: Basic Books.
1988   *Works and Lives: The Anthropologist as Author*. Stanford: Stanford University Press.
Gelhard, Susanne
1992   *Ab Heute ist Krieg. Der blutige Konflikt im ehemaligen Jugoslawien*. Frankfurt am Main: Fischer Verlag.
Glenny, Misha
1992   *The Fall of Yugoslavia. The Third Balkan War*. London: Penguin Books.
Glišić, Ivan
1990   *Idu Cigani*. Šabač: Biblioteka 'Ibis'.
Gmelch, Sharon Bohn
1986   Groups That Don't Want In. Gypsies and Other Artisan, Trader, and Entertainer Minorities. *Annual Review of Anthropology* 15:307-30.
Gojković, Andrijana
1964   Cigani i Muzika. *Narodna Stvaralaštvo Folklor* 9/10:722-728.
1977   Romi u Muzičkom Života Naših Naroda. *Zvuk* III:45-50.
1983   O Muzici Roma. *Zvuk* I: 75
1985   Muzika Jugoslovenskih Roma. *Etnološki Pregled* 20/21:47-52.
1989   Romska muzika u Jugoslaviji. In: Sait Balić, Milka Jauk-Pinhak, Čedo Kisić

e.a. (eds.), *Medjunarodni Naučni Skup Jezik i Kultura Roma.* Sarajevo, 9-11. VI 1986. Sarajevo: Institut za Proučavanje Nacionalnih Odnosa: 401-405.

Golubović, Vida & Irina Subotić

1991   Pogovor. In: Ljubomir Micić, *Zenitizam.* Beograd: DOV.

Good, Anthony

1989   Presentation. In: Tim Ingold (ed.), *Social Anthropology is a Generalizing Science or it is Nothing. A Debate held in the Muriel Stott Centre, John Rylands University Library of Manchester, on 29th October 1988.* Manchester: Group for Debates in Anthropological Theory.

Gouldner, Alvin

1973   *For Sociology. Renewal and Critique in Sociology Today.* London: Allen Lane.

Grabovac, Milica & Vladimir Knor

1991   *Bonton.* Sarajevo: Svjetlost.

Grašaković, Ivan

1985   Psovala Mi Mater Ciganska. *Studentski List* 885:8-9.

Grmek Mirko, Marc Gjidara & Neven Simac

1993   *Le Nettoyage Ethnique. Documents Historiques sur une Idéologie Serbe.* Fayard.

Goudsblom, Johan

1980   *Nihilism and Culture.* Oxford: Basil Blackwell.

Guy, Willy

1975   Ways of Looking at Roms. The Case of Czechoslovakia. In: Farnham Rehfisch (ed.), *Gypsies, Tinkers and Other Travellers.* London: Academic Press. Pp. 201-227.

Hadžić, Anton

1891   Die Serben in Südungarn. *Die össterreichisch-ungarische Monarchie im Wort und Bild. Ungarn, Band II.* Wien: Druck und Verlag der Kaiserlich-Königlichen Hof- und Staatsdruckerei.

Halpern, Joel M.

1967   *A Serbian Village. Social and Cultural Change in a Yugoslav Community.* New York: Harper & Row.

Hannerz, Ulf

1987   The World in Creolization. *Africa* 57(4):546-559.

Hedges, Inez

1983   *Languages of Revolt. Dada and Surrealist Literature and Film.* Durham, N.C.: Duke University Press.

Herzfeld, Michael

1985   *The Poetics of Manhood. Contest and Identity in a Cretan Mountain Village.* Princeton: Princeton University Press.

Hohmann, Joachim S.

1980   Zigeunermythos und -Vorurteil. Marginalien zu einer verleugneten

Minderheit. In: Joachim S. Hohmann & Roland Schopf (eds.), *Zigeunerleben. Beiträge zur Sozialgeschichte einer Verfolgung*. Darmstadt: MS Verlag. Pp. 47-83.

Huston, Nancy
1982 Tales of War and Tears of Women. *Women's Studies International Forum* 5(3/4):271-282.

Ilić, Mirjana
1964 'Klocalica, šerbulj ili čurka. Jedna maska u običajima Srba i Rumuna u Banatu', *Rad Vojvodanskih Museja* 12-13:45-68.

Ilić, V.
1953 Cigančе. In: Bogdan Popovic (1953), *Antologija Novije Srpske Lirike*. Beograd: 'Kultura'. P. 130.

Jelavich, Barbara
1991a *History of the Balkans. Eighteenth and Nineteenth Centuries*. Cambridge: Cambridge University Press.
1991b *History of the Balkans. Twentieth Century*. Cambridge: Cambridge University Press.

Jovanović, Jovan B.
1970 Leskovački Cigani. Prilog za Studiju Psihologije Leskovčana. *Leskovački Zbornik* 10:171-190

Jovanov, Jasna
1989 *Stevan Aleksić (1876-1923)*. Novi Sad: Galerija Matice Srpske.

Karahasan, Dževad
1994 *Sarajevo, Exodus of a city*. Kodansha.

Katsahnias, Iannis
1989 'Freaks, freaks...'. *Cahiers du Cinéma*, no.425 (November 1989):34-36.

Kaplan, Robert D.
1993 *Balkan Ghosts. A Journey through History*. London: Papermac.

Kaprow, Miriam Lee
1991 Celebrating Impermanence. Gypsies in a Spanish City. In: Philip R. de Vita (ed.), *The Naked Anthropologist. Tales from Around the World*. Belmont, Ca.: Wadsworth. Pp.: 218-230.

Katz, Fred E.
1993 *Ordinary People and Extraordinary Evil*. Albany: State University of New York Press.

Kennan, George F.
1993 *The Other Balkan Wars. A 1913 Carnegie Endwoment Inquiry in Retrospect with a New Introduction and Reflections on the Present Conflict*. Washington: The Carnegie Endowment for International Peace.

Kenrick, Donald & Grattan Puxon
1972   *The Destiny of Europe's Gypsies.* London: Heinemann.
Kić, Danilo
1990   [1972] *Hourglass.* London: Faber & Faber.
Kolarov, Miloš
1981   *Bećarci iz Šajkačke.* Kovilj: MO SSRN.
Kovać, Ante
1971   Razmišljana o Bećarcu i Bećarima. *Županjski Zbornik. Književnost, Povijest, Društvo* 3:81-87.
Kozarac, Ivo
1964   [1909] *Djuka Begović.* Zagreb: Matica Hrvatska Zora.
Kristeva, Julia
1991   *Strangers to Ourselves.* New York: Columbia University Press.
Krkeljić, Ljiljana
1977   *Predrasude prema Romima.* Beograd: Filozofski Fakultet, Odeljenje za Psihologiju, Diplomski Rad.
Krleža, Miroslav
1989   [1932] *The Return of Philip Latinowicz.* London: Quartet Encounters.
Kršić, Dejan
1989   Dejan Kršić za Novu Evropu. Slavic Soul. *Quorum* 4:604-607.
Kusturica, Emir
1989   Entre Ciel et Terre. *Cahiers du cinéma* no.425 (November 1989):37-38.
Kuzmanović, Bora
1992   Stereotipije o Romima i Etnička Distanca prema Romima. *Sociologija* 34(1):119-126.

Laermans, Rudi
n.d.   *Individueel Vlees. Over Lichaamsbeelden.* Amsterdam: de Balie.
Langer, Susanne K.
1979   [1942] *Philosophy in a New Key. A Study in the Symbolism of Reason, Rite and Art.* Cambridge, Mass.: Harvard University Press.
Lawrence, D.H.
1982   *The Complete Short Stories.* London: Penguin Books.
Leach, Edmund
1976   *Culture and Communication. The Logic by Which Symbols are Connected.* Cambridge: Cambridge University Press.
1982   *Social Anthropology.* Glasgow: Fontana.
Lepenies, Wolf
1986   Über den Krieg der Wissenschaften und der Literatur. Der Status der Soziologie seit der Aufklärung. *Merkur* 40(6):482-494.

Leskovac, Mladen
1979   *Bečarac. Antologija.* Novi Sad: Matica Srpska.
Libal, Wolfgang
1991   *Das Ende Jugoslawiens. Chronik einer Selbstzerstörung.* Wien: Europaverlag.
Lutovac, Momčilo S.
1987   *Romi u Crnoj Gori. Od Pojave do Danas.* Ivangrad: Društvo Prijatelja Knjige.

Macura, Vladimir
1992   Romska Enklava Orlovsko Naselje na Rubu Beograda. In: Miloš Macura (ed.), *Razvitak Roma U Jugoslaviji. Problemi i Tendencije.* Beograd: Srpska Akademija Nauka i Umetnosti. Pp. 131-147.
Magris, Claudio
1988   *Donau. Een ontdekkingsreis door de Beschaving van Midden-Europa en de Crisis van onze Tijd.* Amsterdam: Bert Bakker.
Mandić, Ljubinko
1971   *Bećarac.* Diplomski Rad, Universiteit van Pecs.
Maluckov, Mirjana (ed.)
1979   *Etnološka Gradja o Romima-Ciganima u Vojvodini.* Novi Sad: Vojvodjanski Muzej.
Marković, Živko
n.d.   Unpublished paper about the bohemian life in 19th-century Novi Sad.
Matasović, Josip
1928   Cigani u Doba Terezijanstva i Josefinizma. *Narodna Starina* 17(7):200-201.
Mayerhofer, Claudia
1987   *Dorfzigeuner. Kultur und Geschichte der Burgenland-Roma von der Ersten Republik bis zur Gegenwart.* Wien: Picus Verlag.
Mertus, Julie, Jasmina Tesanović, Habiba Metikos a.o.
1997   *The Suitcase. Refugee Voices from Bosnia and Croatia.* Berkeley: University of California Press.
Messick, Brinkley
1987   Subordinate Discourse. Women, Weaving and Gender Relations in North Africa. *American Ethnologist* 14(2):210-225.
Mihailćić, Rade
1989   *Boj na Kosovu. U Istoriji i Narodnom Sećanju.* Beograd: Beogradski Izdavački-Grafički Centar.
Mitrović, Aleksandra
1990   *Na Dnu. Romi na Granicama Siromaštva.* Beograd: Naučna Knjiga.
Mosse, George L.
1990   *Fallen Soldiers. Reshaping the Memory of the World Wars.* Oxford: Oxford University Press.

Nahoum-Grappé, Veronique (ed.)

1993   *Vukovar, Sarajevo...La Guerre en Ex-Yougoslavie.* Editions Esprit.

Nietzsche, Friedrich

1994   [1872] *The Birth of Tragedy: Out of the Spirit of Music.* London: Penguin Classics.

Obeyesekere, Gananath

1990   *The Work of Culture. Symbolic Transformation in Psychoanalysis and Anthropology.* Chicago: University of Chicago Press.

Okely, Judith

1983   *The Traveller-Gypsies.* Cambridge: Cambridge University Press.

1989   Presentation. In: Tim Ingold (ed.), *Social Anthropology is a Generalizing Science or it is Nothing. A Debate held in the Muriel Stott Centre, John Rylands University Library of Manchester, on 29th October 1988.* Manchester: Group for Debates in Anthropological Theory.

Okely, Judith & Helen Callaway (eds.)

1992   *Anthropology & Autobiography.* London: Routledge.

Ortner, Sherry B.

1984   Theory in Anthropology since the Sixties. *Comparative Studies in Society and History* 26 (1): 126-66.

Otto, Walter F.

1995   [1933] *Dionysos. Myth and Cult.* Indiana University Press.

Pantić, D.

1987   *Nacionalna svest mladih u SR Srbiji bez SAP.* Beograd: IIC SSO Srbije.

Pešić, Vesna

1977   Društveni slojevitost i stil Života. In: Mihailo Popović, Silvano Bolčić, Vesna Pešić e.a., *Društveni Slojevi i Društvena Svest.* Beograd: Centar za Sociološka Istraživanja. Pp. 121-196

Petrović, Dj.

1976   Društveni Položaj Cigana u nekim Jugoslovenskim Zemljama u XV i XVI Veku. *Jugoslovenski Istorijski Časopis* (1-2):45-66.

Petrović, Radmilla

1974   Narodna muzika Istocne Jugoslavije. Proces Akulturacije. Zvuk 2:155-160.

Petrović, Vasa J.

1894   Srpske Narodne Pripovijetke. *Bosanska Vila* 9(14/15):231.

Pitt-Rivers, Julian

1971   *The People of the Sierra.* Chicago: The University of Chicago Press.

Pool, Robert

1991   Postmodern Ethnography? *Critique of Anthropology* 11(4):309-331.

Popović, Dušan

1990a [1957] *Srbi u Vojvodini. Od najstarijih vremena do Karlovačkog mira 1699*. Novi Sad: Matica Srpska.

1990b [1957] *Srbi u Vojvodini. Od Karlovačkog Mira 1699 do Temišvarskog Sabora 1790*. Novi Sad: Matice Srpske.

1990c [1957] *Srbi u Vojvodini. Od Temišvarskog Sabora 1790 do Blagoveštenskog Sabora 1861*. Novi Sad: Matice Srpske.

Popović, Miodrag

1985a *Romantizam. Istorija Srpske Književnosti. Knjiga Prva*. Beograd: Zavod za Udjbenike i Nastavna Sredstva.

1985b *Romantizam. Istorija Srpske Književnosti. Knjiga Druga*. Beograd: Zavod za Udjbenike i Nastavna Sredstva.

Popović, Srdja, Dejan Janća & Tanja Petovar

1990 *Kosovski Čvor. Drešiti ili Seći? Izvestaj Nezavisne Komisije*. Beograd: Biblioteka Hrovob.

Port, Mattijs van de

1990 *Buitengewone Muzikanten. De Rol en Betekenis van Zigeunermuzikanten in Servië*. Ongepubliceerde Doktoraal Skriptie, Universiteit van Amsterdam.

1993 Zevenduizend Tranen. Oorlogservaringen, oorlogsgeschiedenissen en oorlogsherinneringen in Servië. *Etnofoor* 6(1):14-45.

1996 Coping with the Boob-Boom Dimension of War: Wartime Experiences and the Gypsy in Serbian Popular Culture. In: Waltraud Kokot & Dorle Dracklé (eds.), *Ethnologie Europas: Grenzen, Konflikte, Identitäten*. Berlin: Reimer.

1997 Outstanding Musicians & The Stranger Within. *Etnofoor* 10(1/2):7-27.

Povrzanović, Maja

1993 Culture and Fear. Everyday life in Wartime. In: Lada Čale Feldman, Ines Prica & Reana Senjković (eds.), *Fear, Death and Resistance. An Ethnography of War, Croatia 1991-1992*. Zagreb: Institute of Ethnology and Folklore Research.

1997 Identities in War. Embodiments of Violence and Places of Belonging. *Ethnologia Europaea* 27(2): 153-162.

Prćić, Ivo

1971 *Bunjevačke Narodne Pesme*. Subotica: Osvit.

Prica, Ines

1988 Mitsko Poimanje Naroda u Kritici Novakomponovane Narodne Muzike. *Kultura. Časopis za Teoriju i Sociologiju Kulture i Kulturne Politiku*: 80-93.

1991 *Omladinska Potkultura u Beogradu. Symbolička Praksa*. Beograd: Etnografski Institut SANU.

Price, Sally

1989 *Primitive Art in Civilized Places*. Chicago: University of Chicago Press.

Rakelmann, Georgia A.

1980a Das Phänomen Zigeuner. In: Joachim S. Hohmann & Roland Schopf (eds.), *Zigeunerleben. Beiträge zur Sozialgeschichte einer Verfolgung.* Darmstadt: MS Verlag. Pp. 25-44.

1980b Die Zigeuner und Wir. In: Joachim S. Hohmann & Roland Schopf (eds.), *Zigeunerleben. Beiträge zur Sozialgeschichte einer Verfolgung.* Darmstadt: MS Verlag. Pp. 149-171.

Ramet, Sabrina Petra [Pedro]

1988 The Serbian Orthodox Church. In: Idem (ed.), *Eastern Christianity and Politics in the Twentieth Century.* Durham: Duke University Press. Pp. 232-248.

1992 *Balkan Babel. Politics, Culture, and Religion in Yugoslavia.* Boulder: Westview Press.

Rihtman-Auguštin, Dunja

1988 *Etnologija Naše Svakodnevnice.* Zagreb: Školska Knjiga.

Rouget, Gilbert

1985 *Music and Trance. A Theory of the Relations between Music and Possession.* Chicago: University of Chicago Press.

Rushdie, Salman

1992 *Imaginary Homelands. Essays and Criticisms, 1981-1991.* London: Granta Books.

Savić, Svenka

1991 Obrazovanje dece Roma na SHJ u SR Srbiji. *Romologija* 1:31-39.

Schper-Hughs, Nancy

1993 *Death Without Weeping. The Violence of Everyday Life in Brazil.* Berkeley: University of California Press.

Schopf, Roland

1980 Bürgerfluch und Bürgersehnsucht. Zigeuner im Vorstellungsbild literarischer Intelligenz. In: Joachim S. Hohmann & Roland Schopf (eds.), *Zigeunerleben. Beiträge zur Sozialgeschichte einer Verfolgung.* Darmstadt: MS Verlag. Pp. 47-83.

Seigel, Jerrold

1986 *Bohemian Paris. Culture, Politics and the Boundaries of Bourgeois Life, 1830-1930.* Harmondsworth: Penguin.

Sheehan, Bernard

1980 *Savagism and Civilty. Indians and Englishmen in Colonial Virginia.* Cambridge: Cambridge University Press.

Simić, Andrei

1973 *The Peasant Urbanites. A Study of Urban-Rural Mobility in Serbia.* New York: Seminar Press.

1984 Urbanization and modernization in Yugoslavia. Adaptive and Maladaptive Aspects of Traditional Culture. In: Michael Kenny & David I. Kertzer (eds.), *Urban Life in Mediterranean Europe. Anthropological Perspectives*. Urbana: University of Illinois Press.

Simonović, Radivoj

1924 Etnografski Pregled. In: *Vojvodina. Izdaja Novosadska Sekcija Udruženja Jugoslovenskih Inženjera i Arhitekta*. Novi Sad: Štampa U.D.D. 'Natošević'. Pp. 84-118.

Sinclair, Andrew

1991 *The Naked Savage*. London: Sinclair Stevenson.

Šosberger, Pavle

1988 *Novosadski Jevreji*. Novi Sad: Kniževna Zajednica.

Spaendonck, Johannes A.S.

1977 *Belle-Époque en Anti-Kunst. De Geschiedenis van een Opstand tegen de Burgerlijke Cultuur*. Meppel en Amsterdam: Boom.

Spangler, Michael

1984 Urban Research in Yugoslavia. Regional Variation in Urbanization. In: Michael Kenny & David I. Kertzer (eds.), *Urban Life in Mediterranean Europe. anthropological Perspectives*. Urbana: University of Illinois Press. Pp. 203-224.

Steiner, George

1984 *George Steiner. A Reader*. New York: Oxford University Press.

Stevens, Anthony

1989 *The Roots of War. A Jungian Perspective*. New York: Paragon House.

Steward, Michael

1993 Gypsies, the Work Ethic, and Hungarian Socialism. In: C.M. Hann (ed.), *Socialism. Ideals, Ideologies, and Local Practice*. London: Routledge. Pp.187-204.

Sundhaußen, Holm

1973 *Der Einfluß der Herderschen Ideen auf die Nationsbildung bei den Völkern der Habsburger Monarchie*. München: R. Oldenbourg Verlag.

Swaan, Abram de

1994 Identificatie in Uitdijende Kring. Amsterdams Sociologisch Tijdschrift 20(3):6-24.

Szentklavan, Eugen

1891 Die Deutschen in Südungarn. *Die össterreichisch-ungarische Monarchie im Wort und Bild. Ungarn, Band II*. Wien: Druck und Verlag der Kaiserlich-Königlichen Hof und Staatsdruckerei.

Tatar, Maria

1992 *Off With Their Heads! Fairytales and the Culture of Childhood*. Princeton, New Jersey: Princeton University Press.

Taussig, Michael
1987   *Shamanism, Colonialism and the Wild Man. A Study in Terror and Healing.* Chicago: University of Chicago Press.
1993   *Mimesis and Alterity. A Particular History of the Senses.* New York: Routledge.
Thoden van Velzen, H.U.E.
1990   Social Fetishism among the Surinamese Maroons. *Etnofoor* 3(1):77-97.
1991   Antropologie en Droomtaal. *Etnofoor* 4(2):21-43.
Thoden van Velzen, H.U.E. & W. van Wetering
1988   *The Great Father and the Danger. Religious Cults, Material Forces, and Collective Fantasies in the World of the Surinamese Maroons.* Dordrecht: Foris Publications.
Thomas, Nicholas
1991   Against Ethnography. *Cultural Anthropology* 6(3):306-322.
Thompson, Mark
1992   *A Paper House. The Ending of Yugoslavia.* London: Vintage.
Tišma, Aleksandar
1987   *Vere i Zavere* [Croyance et Méfiance. Lausanne: Editions L'Age d'Hommes].
1990   *The Use of Man.* London: Faber & Faber.
1991   *Škola bezbožništva* [De School der Goddeloosheid. Amsterdam: Meulenhoff].
Tito, Josip Broz
1961   *Speech by President Josip Broz-Tito in Titovo Užice on July 4, 1961.* Beograd: Jugoslavija.
Todorova, Maria
1997   *Imagining the Balkans.* New York: Oxford University Press.
Tomandl, Mihovil
1953   *Srpsko Narodno Pozorište u Vojvodini I: 1736-1868.* Novi Sad: Matica Srpska
1954   *Srpsko Narodno Pozorište u Vojvodini II: 1768-1919.* Novi Sad: Matica Srpska.
Tomašević, Nebojša
1976   *Ivan Generalić. Leven en Werk.* Antwerpen: Mercator Fonds.
1978   *Naïve Maler Jugoslawiens.* Stuttgard: Parkland Verlag.
Tomašević, Nebojša Bato & Rajko Djurić
1988   *Cigani Sveta.* Beograd: Jugoslovenska Revija.
Torgovnick, Marianna
1990   *Gone Primitive. Savage Intellects, Modern Lives.* Chicago: University of Chicago Press.
Turnbull, Colin
1972   *The Mountain People.* New York: Simon and Schuster.

Turner, Victor
1988   *The Anthropology of Performance*. New York: PAJ Publications.
Tyler, Stephen A.
1978   *The Said and the Unsaid*. New York: Academic Press.
1986   Post-Modern Ethnography. From Document of the Occult to Occult Document. In: James Clifford & George E. Marcus (eds.) *Writing Culture. The Poetics and Politics of Ethnography*. Berkeley: The University of California Press. Pp. 98-122.

Ugrešić, Dubravka
1993   *Have a nice day: from the Balkan War to the American Dream*.

Verdery, Katherine
1991   *National Ideology under Socialism. Identity and Cultural Politics in Ceausescu's Romania*. Berkeley: University of California Press.
Verrips, Jojada
1989   Enige reflecties over de maan, de (weer)wolf en het weer. *Etnofoor* 2(1):34-56.
1991   'Ik kan je wel opvreten'. En(i)ge notities over het thema kannibalisme in westerse samenlevingen. *Etnofoor* 4(1):19-50.
1993   Op weg naar een Antropologie van het Wilde Westen. *Etnofoor* 6(2):5-21.
Veselinović, Rajko L.
1954   Ko su 'bećari' i šta su 'bećarske odaje' u putopisu E. Celebije. *Rad Vojvodjanskih Muzeja* 3, Novi Sad: 277.
Vujković, Sreten
1991   O postojanosti Romskog Življenja. In: Tomislav Dretar, *Bol. Ciganska Rapsodija*. Novi Sad: Društvo Vojvodine za Jezik, Književnost i Kultura Roma.
Vukajlović, Vera
1986   *Demografske karakteristike i crte ličnosti kao činioci etničkih stereotipija i socialne distance*. Dimplomski Rad, Filozofski fakultet – Odeljenje za psihologiju, Beograd.
Vukanović, Tatomir
1962   Musical Culture among the Gypsies of Yugoslavia. *Journal of the Gypsy Lore Society* 16: 41-62.
1983   *Romi (Cigani) u Jugoslaviji*. Vranje: Nova Jugoslavija.
Vulliamy, Ed
1994   *Seasons in Hell. Understanding Bosnia's War*. London: Simon & Schuster.
Vuyk, Kees
1987   Inleiding. In: Nietzsche, Friedrich, [1872] *De Geboorte van de Tragedie*. Amsterdam: International Theatre Bookshop. Pp. 5-17.

Washabaugh, William
1996   *Flamenco. Passion, Politics and Popular Culture.* Oxford: Berg.
Webster, Hutton
1948   *Magic. A Sociological Study.* Stanford: Stanford University Press.
West, Rebecca
1982   [1941] *Black Lamb and Grey Falcon. A Journey through Yugoslavia.* London: Penguin.
White, Hayden
1972   The Forms of Wildness. Archeology of an Idea. In: Edward Dudley & Maximilian E. Novak (eds.), *The Wild Man Within. An Image in Western Thought from the Renaissance to Romanticism.* Pittsburgh: University of Pittsburgh Press. Pp. 3-39.

Young, Dudley
1991   *Origins of the Sacred. The Ecstasies of Love and War.* London: Abacus.

Žarkov, Dubravka
1992   *Peasant Women Sexuality. The Question of Subjectivity.* Paper presented at the Women and Oral History Conference, 16-17 May, London.
Zirojević, Olga
1976   Cigani u Srbiji od Dolaska Turaka do Kraja XVI Veka. *Jugoslovenski Istorijski Časopis* 1-2 : 67-78.
Žižek, Slavoj
1995   *The Metastases of Enjoyment. Six Essays on Woman and Causality.* London: Verso.
Zulaika, Joseba
1988   *Basque Violence. Metaphor and Sacrament.* Reno: University of Reno Press.
1993   Further Encounters with the Wild Man. *Etnofoor* 6(2):21-41.

Index